CONTROLLING CURRENCY
m i s m a t c h e s
IN EMERGING MARKETS

CONTROLLING CURRENCY
mismatches
IN EMERGING MARKETS

Morris Goldstein and Philip Turner

INSTITUTE FOR INTERNATIONAL ECONOMICS
Washington, DC
April 2004

Morris Goldstein, Dennis Weatherstone Senior Fellow, joined the Institute for International Economics in 1994 and has held several senior staff positions at the International Monetary Fund (1970–94), including deputy director of its research department (1987–94). He has written extensively on international economic policy and on international capital markets. He is author of *Managed Floating Plus* (2002), *The Asian Financial Crisis: Causes, Cures, and Systemic Implications* (1998), *The Case for an International Banking Standard* (1997), *The Exchange Rate System and the IMF: A Modest Agenda* (1995), coeditor of *Private Capital Flows to Emerging Markets after the Mexican Crisis* (1996), coauthor of *Assessing Financial Vulnerability: An Early Warning System for Emerging Markets* with Graciela Kaminsky and Carmen Reinhart (2000), and project director of *Safeguarding Prosperity in a Global Financial System: The Future International Financial Architecture* (1999) for the Council on Foreign Relations Task Force on the International Financial Architecture.

Philip Turner has been at the Bank for International Settlements (BIS) since 1989, where he is the head of the secretariat group in the monetary and economics department, responsible for economics papers produced for central bank meetings at the BIS. His research interests include financial stability in emerging markets, banking systems, and bank restructuring in the developing world. He was a member of the Financial Stability Forum's Working Group on Capital Flows. Between 1976 and 1989, he held various positions, including head of division in the economics department of the Organization for Economic Cooperation and Development (OECD) in Paris. In 1985–86, he was a visiting scholar at the Bank of Japan's Institute for Monetary and Economic Studies.

INSTITUTE FOR INTERNATIONAL ECONOMICS
1750 Massachusetts Avenue, NW
Washington, DC 20036-1903
(202) 328-9000   FAX: (202) 659-3225
www.iie.com

Library of Congress Cataloging-in-Publication Data

Goldstein, Morris, 1994–
    Controlling currency mismatches in emerging markets / Morris Goldstein, Philip Turner.
        p. cm.
    Includes bibliographical references and index.
    ISBN 0-88132-360-8
    1. Foreign exchange rates—Developing countries. 2. Foreign exchange administration—Developing countries. 3. Monetary policy—Developing countries. I. Turner, Philip. II. Title.

HG3877.G65 2004
332.4´56´091724—dc22

2004048278

Contents

Preface   **ix**

Acknowledgments   **xv**

1 Introduction   **1**
Original Sin Hypothesis   5
Plan of the Book   8

2 Why Currency Mismatches Matter   **11**

3 Measuring Currency Mismatch: Beyond Original Sin   **21**
Original Sin: A Misleading Measure   21
Summary   34

4 Aggregate Effective Currency Mismatch   **37**
New Measure of Aggregate Effective Currency Mismatch   42
Modification of AECM   51

5 Coping with Potential Currency Mismatches   **57**

**6 Role of National Macroeconomic Policies and Currency
   Regimes**   **63**
Monetary Policy and Inflation   64
Currency Regime   67
Fiscal Policies   69
Debt and Reserve Management Policies   71

7 Role of Institutional Factors and Microeconomic Incentives   **77**
Bond Markets   79
Prudential Oversight of Financial Institutions   82
Regulation of Banks in Major Lending Centers   85
Regulation of Banks in Borrowing Countries   89

Aggregate Mismatches in the Banking System 97
Regulations of Other Financial Institutions 98
Rules for Nonfinancial Corporations? 102

8 International Solutions to Currency Mismatching? 105

9 Reducing Currency Mismatching: A Domestic Agenda 113
Summary 119

Appendix A Measuring Mismatches: Some Cautionary Notes 123

Appendix B Evolution of the Original Sin Hypothesis 135

References 145

Index 153

Tables

Table 2.1 Proxies for currency mismatches before the Asian crisis, 1995–99 12
Table 2.2 Borrowing by domestic banks from international banks, 1995–2002 13
Table 2.3 Domestic bank credit to the private sector 17
Table 3.1 Measures of original sin by country groupings, simple average 22
Table 3.2 Export openness, 1994–2002 23
Table 3.3 Bond market development, end-2001 26
Table 3.4 Foreign banks' consolidated claims, local and international, 1990–2003 28
Table 3.5 Emerging-market financing, all sectors, 1997–2001 31
Table 4.1 Australia: Foreign-currency exposure by financial sector, end-June 2001 39
Table 4.2 Thailand: Intersectoral asset and liability position, end-December 1996 40
Table 4.3 Net foreign-currency assets, 1994–2002 45
Table 4.4 Foreign-currency share of total debt, 1994–2002 47
Table 4.5 Original AECM estimates, 1994–2002 48
Table 4.6 Modified AECM estimates, 1994–2002 50
Table 4.7 Total debt as a percent of GDP, 1994–2002 52
Table 4.8 Original sin ratio in emerging economies 55
Table 5.1 Foreign exchange turnover 58
Table 5.2 Top 10 countries in bond trading volume, 2001 60
Table 5.3 Domestic debt securities outstanding, 1994–2002 61
Table 6.1 Type of domestic debt at issuance, end-2000 65
Table 6.2 Outstanding government debt by type, end-2001 73
Table 7.1 Guidelines or regulations for currency mismatches in banks 91

Table 7.2 Currency denomination of bank balance sheets 94
Table 7.3 Rules on fund managers' holdings of foreign-
currency assets 99
Table 7.4 Structure of pension fund assets in 2000 101
Table 9.1 Short-term external debt as a percent of foreign
exchange reserves 115
Table 9.2 Share of external debt denominated in local currency 118
Table A.1 Impact of an exchange rate change on borrowing costs 125
Table A.2 Survey on data published by major emerging-market
economies 130
Table A.3 Ratio of M2 to foreign exchange reserves, 1990–2002 132
Table A.4 Domestic debt securities outstanding, 1994–2002 133

Figures
Figure 2.1 The Mexican peso crisis, 1994–95 14
Figure 3.1 Market share of foreign-owned banks in emerging
markets 27
Figure 4.1 Foreign currency balance sheet of a partially dollarized
economy 38
Figure 7.1 Monetary authorities: Net foreign assets less currency
held outside banks, 1990–2003 81
Figure 7.2 Net foreign assets of monetary authorities in selected
emerging-market countries 82

Preface

The analysis of emerging-market financial crises, and of vulnerabilities linked in particular to exchange rate misalignments and to inappropriate currency regime choices, has been a key theme in the Institute's research agenda over the past decade. In *What Role for Currency Boards?* (1995), John Williamson analyzed the advantages and disadvantages of that particular form of monetary management. Lessons from the Mexican peso crisis were drawn by Guillermo Calvo, Morris Goldstein, and Eduard Hochreiter in *Private Capital Flows to Emerging Economies after the Mexican Crisis* (1996). In *The Crawling Band as an Exchange Rate Regime: Lessons from Chile, Colombia, and Israel* (1996), Williamson conducted an in-depth examination of one type of intermediate regime. The Asian financial crisis was then a motivation for several Institute publications, including Goldstein's *The Asian Currency Crisis: Causes, Cures, and Systemic Implications* (1998) and Marcus Noland et al.'s *Global Economic Effects of the Asian Currency Devaluations* (1998).

The scope and severity of the Asian crisis also ignited interest in reform of the international financial architecture. In *Toward a New Financial Architecture: A Practical Post-Asia Agenda* (1999), Barry Eichengreen put forward, among other proposals, the "bipolar" view of currency regimes in emerging economies. The Institute published later that year a Council on Foreign Relations (CFR) task force report on the future international architecture, *Safeguarding Prosperity in a Global Financial System* (1999). Representing the consensus views of distinguished experts and authored by Goldstein, the CFR report called for, among other recommendations, a cessation of IMF financial support for overvalued fixed exchange rates in emerging economies. The task force also rejected (albeit by a relatively narrow margin) a proposal (supported by myself, among others) for a target zone regime among the G-3 currencies.

In *Assessing Financial Vulnerability: An Early Warning System for Emerging Markets* (2000), Goldstein, Graciela Kaminsky, and Carmen Reinhart undertook a battery of empirical tests, aimed at identifying the best leading indicators of currency (and banking) crises in emerging economies. Returning to one of the Institute's long-standing analytical concerns, Simon Wren-Lewis and Rebecca Driver, in *Real Exchange Rates for the Year 2000* (1998), discussed how best to calculate equilibrium real exchange rates and presented their estimates for the major currencies. Williamson, in *Exchange Rate Regimes for Emerging Markets: Reviving the Intermediate Option* (2000), made the case for a BBC regime (basket, band, crawl).

More recently, Peter Kenen presented a comprehensive appraisal of efforts to reform the international financial architecture in *The International Financial Architecture: What's New? What's Missing?* (2001). In *Managed Floating Plus* (2002), Goldstein argued that the best currency regime choice for those emerging economies heavily involved with private capital markets would be managed floating plus, where "plus" is shorthand for a framework that includes inflation targeting and aggressive measures to reduce currency mismatching. And in *Dollar Overvaluation and the World Economy* (2003), John Williamson and I brought together a set of studies on what policy measures would be needed to correct the large overvaluation of the dollar, including changes in exchange rates in several of the large Asian emerging economies.

This new study by Dennis Weatherstone Senior Fellow Morris Goldstein and Philip Turner of the senior staff of the Bank for International Settlements addresses a vulnerability that has been present in virtually every major financial crisis in emerging economies over the past decade: currency mismatches. By "currency mismatch," the authors mean the sensitivity of an entity's net worth or net income to changes in the exchange rate. The implicit notion is that if an entity's balance sheet and net income statement were fully hedged against exchange rate changes, then those changes would have little impact.

In making the case for controlling currency mismatches, Goldstein and Turner note that the countries that have experienced the largest currency mismatches have typically been the ones that have suffered the largest output losses during crises. In addition, they explain how currency mismatches can adversely constrain the scope for cuts in interest rates during a crisis and can contribute to a "fear of floating" in the conduct of exchange rate policy.

In order to gauge the vulnerability of emerging economies to large output losses following a sharp depreciation of the local currency, it is necessary to have a comprehensive measure of aggregate currency mismatch as well as good indicators of sectoral currency mismatch. Goldstein and Turner maintain that it will generally *not* be possible to get a reliable picture of a country's aggregate currency mismatch by looking solely at the currency composition of cross-border bank loans and international bonds—the metrics that have been emphasized in the literature on "original sin" (where original sin is defined as the ability of a country to borrow abroad in its own currency). A good measure of aggregate currency mismatch has to consider the asset as well as the liability side of the balance sheet, along with the potential response of noninterest flows (like exports) to a change in the exchange rate. Derivative positions can also be important.

Going further, they argue that, in assessing the likely output effects of an exchange rate change, it is necessary to account for the ability of the country to borrow at home in the domestic currency. Domestic bond markets in developing countries tend to be denominated mainly in domestic currency, and they have become the single largest source of financing—larger (in flow terms) than domestic bank loans and much larger than international bonds.

Drawing these strands together, the authors construct a new measure of what they call "aggregate effective currency mismatch"—or AECM—and show how it has behaved for 22 emerging economies over the 1994–2002 period. One of the attractions of the AECM is that it can be compared across countries and over time. For example, the authors find that the largest aggregate currency mismatch in their sample was recorded by Argentina in 2001–02.

If the vast majority of developing countries displayed a roughly equal susceptibility to currency mismatches, then it would be harder to make the case that national policies and institutions matter a lot for controlling currency mismatches. The authors present evidence that there is a significant differentiation—or "tiering"—among emerging economies in their capacity to cope with potential currency mismatches, as revealed in the liquidity and maturity of their foreign exchange, bond, and derivative markets.

In contrast to some earlier studies that depicted the origins of currency mismatch as lying primarily in imperfections in international capital markets and network externalities, Goldstein and Turner highlight past and present weaknesses in economic policies and institutions in emerging markets themselves. Their action plan to control currency mismatches in emerging economies follows from this diagnosis and stresses inter alia (1) a managed floating currency regime (to produce an awareness of currency risk and an incentive to control it); (2) an inflation targeting regime for monetary policy (to produce the stability in long-term inflation expectations, so important in building a healthy domestic bond market); (3) regular publication of data on currency mismatches at the sectoral and economywide levels (to enhance market discipline); (4) stepped-up supervision and monitoring of currency mismatches in banks and in their loan customers, particularly when the latter have little foreign currency revenue (to limit losses to tolerable levels); (5) changes in official safety nets and in IMF policy conditionality (to produce greater incentives to limit bailout of losses stemming from currency mismatches and to reduce the size of mismatches); (6) implementation of more prudent debt and reserve management policies in emerging economies; and (7) a higher priority given in emerging economies to developing domestic bond markets, encouraging the availability of hedging instruments, and reducing barriers to entry of foreign-owned banks.

The Institute for International Economics is a private, nonprofit institution for the study and discussion of international economic policy. Its purpose is to analyze important issues in that area and to develop and communicate practical new approaches for dealing with them. The Institute is completely nonpartisan.

The Institute is funded largely by philanthropic foundations. Major institutional grants are now being received from the William M. Keck, Jr. Foundation and the Starr Foundation. A number of other foundations and private corporations contribute to the highly diversified financial resources of the Institute. About 18 percent of the Institute's resources in our latest fiscal year were provided by contributors outside the United States, including about 8 percent from Japan.

The Board of Directors bears overall responsibilities for the Institute and gives general guidance and approval to its research program, including the identification of topics that are likely to become important over the medium run (one to three years), and which should be addressed by the Institute. The director, working closely with the staff and outside Advisory Committee, is responsible for the development of particular projects and makes the final decision to publish an individual study.

The Institute hopes that its studies and other activities will contribute to building a stronger foundation for international economic policy around the world. We invite readers of these publications to let us know how they think we can best accomplish this objective.

C. FRED BERGSTEN
Director
March 2004

Acknowledgments

Work on this project began in November 2001, when Andrew Crockett, then general manager of the Bank for International Settlements (BIS), invited Morris Goldstein to spend a month at BIS to start, in collaboration with Philip Turner, a systematic study of currency mismatches in emerging economies. It was hoped that BIS banking and financial data might help to illuminate this issue. We are much indebted to Andrew and to Bill White for their encouragement and support throughout this project.

Here at the Institute for International Economics, C. Fred Bergsten once again provided his unique combination of helpful prodding and insightful comments, while Mike Mussa and Ted Truman were particularly generous in commenting on successive drafts of the entire manuscript.

Tim Geithner, then director of the Policy Development and Review (PDR) Department in the International Monetary Fund, is likewise deserving of our thanks for inviting Morris Goldstein to spend several weeks last year as a visiting scholar in PDR and for helping to sharpen the latter stages of the analysis.

Many others furnished useful comments on earlier drafts and/or supplied valuable research materials. In this connection, thanks go to Lewis Alexander, Mark Allen, Palle Andersen, Carlos Arteta, Martin Baily, Mario Blejer, William Cline, Karl Cordewener, Andrew Cornford, Kevin Cowan, Barry Eichengreen, Mohamed El-Erian, Andrew Feltenstein, David Folkerts-Landau, Gabriele Galati, Pablo Graf, Dale Gray, John Hawkins, Peter Hayward, Karen Johnson, Mohsin Khan, Peter Kenen, Nicholas Lardy, Leslie Lipschitz, Robert McCauley, Dubravko Mihaljek,

M. S. Mohanty, Ugo Panizza, Ramon Moreno, Christian Mulder, Yoshi Nakata, Carmen Reinhart, Nouriel Roubini, Miguel Savastano, John Taylor, Agustin Villar, Francis Warnock, John Williamson, and to seminar participants at the Bank of England, BIS, Board of Governors of the Federal Reserve System, Institute for International Economics, IMF, and US Treasury Department.

Rainer Widera and his team were most helpful in guiding us through the BIS's international banking statistics. Philippe Hainaut, Kenneth Merber, Gunilla Pettersson, and Pavel Trcala supplied excellent research assistance, and Marla Banov, Clare Batts, Madona Devasahayam, Lisa Ireland, and Katherine Sweetman prepared the manuscript for publication with both care and speed.

Last but not least, we have been stimulated by the many central bankers in emerging markets who have told us privately that currency mismatches remain an insidious threat in many countries.

Introduction

In financial markets today, sovereigns, banks, nonfinancial firms, and households make and receive payments not only in domestic but also in foreign currency. Similarly, the currency composition of their assets and liabilities may differ. When an entity's net worth or net income (or both) is sensitive to changes in the exchange rate, it is called a "currency mismatch."[1] The "stock" aspect of a currency mismatch is given by the sensitivity of the balance sheet (net worth) to changes in the exchange rate, and the "flow" aspect is given by the sensitivity of the income statement (net income) to changes in the exchange rate. The greater the degree of sensitivity (of net worth/net income) to exchange rate changes, the greater the extent of the currency mismatch.

Suppose an individual raises a mortgage to buy an apartment in London and then rents it out. Suppose also that he borrows in dollars instead of pounds. He then is faced with a currency mismatch. The stock aspect of the mismatch is that his asset (apartment) is denominated in pounds but his liability (mortgage) is in dollars. The flow aspect is that the rental income from the apartment is denominated in pounds but mortgage payments are in dollars. The consequence of this currency mismatch is that the owner of the apartment gains or loses as the dollar falls or rises against the pound even if the key parameters of his investment (i.e., apartment price and rent) do not change. In short, the net present value of his investment project has become sensitive to changes in the dollar-pound exchange rate.

---

1. This definition of currency mismatch is close to the one the Financial Stability Forum (2000) has proposed.

Borrowers in many emerging economies have at times faced currency mismatches on a massive scale. Foreign currency–denominated liabilities have frequently financed local-currency activities in emerging economies, and, too often, the stock of foreign currency–denominated assets has been comparatively limited. In such cases, a large depreciation of the domestic currency can destroy much of the net worth of firms and households and initiate a wave of insolvencies, a financial crisis, and a steep fall in economic growth. Indeed, research has shown that currency mismatches not only have been a major element in almost every major financial crisis in emerging economies during the past decade but also have made such crises very costly to resolve (Allen et al. 2002 and Cavallo et al. 2001). Moreover, large currency mismatches can severely handicap the conduct of monetary policy in a crisis and hinder the working of the exchange rate mechanism. No wonder then that Alan Greenspan (2001) characterized extensive currency and maturity mismatches of financial intermediaries in emerging economies as "tinder awaiting conflagration" and that the September 2003 Statement of G-7 Finance Ministers and Central Bank Governors in Dubai called on the International Monetary Fund (IMF) to identify currency mismatches in emerging economies as a key part of its efforts to improve the effectiveness and persuasiveness of Fund surveillance.

Currency mismatches pose a serious threat to financial stability and sustainable economic growth in emerging economies; as such, it has become important to understand how to measure currency mismatch, identify its causes, and decide how best to control it—the key issues examined in this book.

We argue that a good measure of the extent of currency mismatch has to consider the asset as well as the liability sides of balance sheets. It also ought to take account of the potential response of noninterest flows (like exports) to an exchange rate change. And it should pay attention to the ability of countries to not only borrow abroad in local currency but also borrow at home in the domestic currency. The latter is particularly relevant since domestic bond markets in developing countries (which are denominated mainly in domestic currency) now represent the single largest source of financing—larger than domestic bank loans and far larger than international bonds. We construct a new measure of aggregate effective currency mismatch (AECM) that has these attributes and improves upon earlier measures. We also analyze how the AECM measure has performed over the 1994–2002 period for a group of 22 emerging economies.

We see the origins of currency mismatch primarily in past and present weaknesses in economic policies and institutions in emerging markets themselves rather than in imperfections in international capital markets.[2]

---

2. De Nicolo, Honohan, and Ize (2003) share our view in their recent study on dollarization of domestic bank deposits. They conclude (p. 3) that "absolute pessimism with regard to the degree to which dollarization can be influenced by policy is not warranted: we show that

These national weaknesses include (1) inadequate incentives to hedge against currency risk, linked to fixed exchange rate regimes and poorly designed official safety nets; (2) shortcomings in national macroeconomic policies—especially monetary policies—and the legacy of poor inflation performance, which impedes the development of a local domestic currency–denominated bond market; (3) inadequate public information on the extent and sectoral composition of currency mismatches, which has undermined market discipline; (4) poor credit assessment by banks in the extension of foreign currency–denominated loans to corporate customers with little foreign-currency revenue; (5) problems with the design and/or enforcement of the regulatory regime operating on banks, especially as regards effective limits on banks' true exposure to exchange rate changes; (6) ill-advised debt management policies, especially excessive recourse to foreign currency–indexed debt when inflation-indexed debt would be a better transitional vehicle toward fixed-rate debt; and (7) according too low a priority to developing domestic bond markets, to encouraging the availability of hedging instruments, and to reducing barriers to the entry of foreign-owned banks.

Our action plan to reduce currency mismatches follows from this diagnosis of policy and institutional shortcomings and stresses the following eight recommendations:

- The 20 or so largest emerging economies that are heavily involved with private capital markets (and that are not already committed to joining the euro area) should opt for a managed floating exchange rate policy. Such a policy would produce an awareness of currency risk as well as the incentive to keep currency mismatches under control. Special care should also be taken to avoid policies that can contribute to overvalued exchange rates: experience suggests that crisis vulnerability is highest when large currency mismatches persist against the backdrop of a significantly overvalued exchange rate.

- A monetary policy framework of inflation targeting should be paired with a managed floating regime to provide a good nominal anchor against inflation. Such a framework should also contribute to stability in longer-term inflation expectations necessary to underpin healthy development of a domestic bond market.

- Banks in emerging economies should step up their monitoring of currency mismatches on the part of their loan customers and apply

---

policy does matter." Surveying the theoretical literature on explanations for currency mismatching, Jeanne (2001) places the explanations into the following categories: lack of monetary credibility by the sovereign; implicit or explicit government bailouts of mismatch borrowers; lack of domestic financial development; a commitment or signaling device for the government; and an insurance policy on the part of domestic firms in an emerging economy.

tighter credit limits on foreign currency–denominated loans to customers that do not generate foreign-currency revenues.

- Banking supervisors in emerging economies should strengthen the prudential oversight of currency mismatching by their banks, ensuring in particular that banks effectively monitor their clients' foreign exchange exposures. Even if ongoing innovations in capital markets mean that these regulations do not catch some open foreign exchange positions, determined efforts to limit exposures to a specified share of bank capital should help reduce losses to a tolerable level.

- To help harness the forces of market discipline, the IMF should regularly publish data on currency mismatches at the economywide and sectoral levels and should draw attention to those mismatches regarded as excessive. In this connection, we have constructed the AECM index, which includes foreign-currency assets as well as foreign-currency liabilities. The index takes account of the currency composition of domestic bonds and banks' loans (as well as those of their international counterparts) and normalizes net foreign-currency positions for cross-country and time-series variation in export openness.

- To reduce public-sector bailouts of losses stemming from currency mismatching by banks, more emerging economies should make "prompt corrective action" and "least-cost resolution" key elements of their bank supervisory and closure regimes, along the lines laid out in the Federal Deposit Insurance Corporation Improvement Act (FDICIA) of 1991 in the United States (Benston and Kaufman 1988). In addition, every request for an IMF loan should contain data on, or estimates of, currency mismatches at the economywide and sectoral levels, an IMF staff analysis of the sustainability of these mismatches, and explicit conditions for reducing the mismatch (if the existing or prospective mismatch is judged to be too large).

- Emerging economies should review their debt and reserve management policies to ensure that they are prudent enough to meet the realities of today's volatile global environment. More specifically, emerging economies with relatively high shares of public debt denominated in (or indexed to) foreign currency should adopt a medium-term objective of reducing that share; greater use of inflation-indexed bonds (as a transition device) should facilitate that objective. Emerging economies that do not have usable foreign exchange reserves sufficient to meet all repayments and interest on foreign debt falling due over the subsequent year should consider whether they should aim for higher reserve holdings.

- Emerging economies should accord higher priority to developing domestic bond markets, to encouraging the availability of hedging instruments, and to reducing barriers to entry of foreign-owned banks. Efforts to lengthen the maturity of government debt, develop benchmark securities that are highly liquid, broaden the investor base for government bonds (including fostering the development of pension funds), and remove outdated accounting rules that both inhibit active trading by institutional investors and bias decisions toward foreign currency–denominated borrowing would pay high dividends.

Original Sin Hypothesis

The principal challenge to our view of balance-sheet problems in emerging economies—that national policies matter most—has been put forward by Barry Eichengreen, Ricardo Hausmann, and Ugo Panizza in a series of papers (Eichengreen and Hausmann 1999, 2003a–c; Eichengreen, Hausmann, and Panizza 2002, 2003a–e; and Hausmann and Panizza 2002, 2003). They focus on the difficulties that emerging economies face when attempting to borrow abroad in their own currencies. They call this phenomenon "original sin"—a catchy metaphor meant to capture the idea of an innate weakness that is not due to past behavior but that limits what developing countries can achieve on their own merits. We refer to their line of argument as the original sin hypothesis (OSH). The OSH has attracted considerable attention.

Eichengreen, Hausmann, and Panizza measure the degree to which original sin affects a country by (one minus) the percentage of its international bonds and cross-border bank loans that are denominated in the domestic currency. They find that the vast majority of developing countries suffer from high levels of original sin and that original sin changes little over time. In their empirical work, they report that higher levels of original sin are associated, inter alia, with higher volatility of real output and international capital flows, with greater management of exchange rates, and with lower creditworthiness. Until very recently (September 2003), they seemed to suggest that measures of original sin were a good indicator of a country's aggregate currency mismatch,[3] that an effort to build deep and liquid domestic financial markets in emerging economies as a solution to the currency mismatch problem would take too long and would be increasingly difficult to achieve in a world of liberalized

---

3. In Eichengreen and Hausmann (1999) and Eichengreen, Hausmann, and Panizza (2002, 2003a, 2003b), the terms original sin and currency mismatch were frequently used interchangeably, relying on the proposition that "countries with original sin that have net foreign debt—as developing countries are expected to have—will have a currency mismatch on their national balance sheet" (Eichengreen, Hausmann, and Panizza 2002, 10). Also, in none of those earlier papers was there any statement that aggregate currency mismatch was not a necessary consequence of original sin for a net debtor developing country (see appendix B).

financial markets and floating exchange rates (Eichengreen, Hausmann, and Panizza 2002), and that domestic policies and institutions had little influence on original sin (and currency mismatch) relative to factors largely beyond the control of the individual country, such as network externalities, transactions costs, and imperfections in global capital markets.[4] Since original sin and currency mismatch were not viewed as primarily the fault of emerging economies, they rejected solutions based on national policy initiatives in favor of an "international" solution. Specifically, they contended that the best hope for solving the currency mismatch problem was to create a new basket index of emerging-market currencies, to encourage the international financial institutions (IFIs) and the G-10 countries to issue debt denominated in the index, and to arrange swaps between the IFIs and the G-10 countries on the one hand and the emerging economies on the other.

If the Eichengreen-Hausmann-Panizza diagnosis of original sin were applied to currency mismatch more generally, developing countries would find it hard to reduce their financial fragility. Efforts to strengthen their macroeconomic and exchange rate policies and to improve their institutional arrangements would either be ineffective or take too long to solve the currency mismatch problem. Furthermore, almost all developing countries would be in the same boat. If support for an international initiative to create and promote a new currency basket index were not forthcoming or if that initiative were not to deliver as promised, these countries would seem destined to suffer financial crises whenever their currencies depreciated significantly.

Fortunately, our analysis suggests that the original sin conclusions of Eichengreen, Hausmann, and Panizza were far too pessimistic. Moreover, in their most recent writings on original sin, currency mismatch, and debt intolerance—presumably written in part in response to criticisms of their earlier work by us (Goldstein and Turner 2003) and by Carmen Reinhart, Kenneth Rogoff, and Miguel Savastano (2003b)—Eichengreen, Hausmann, and Panizza (2003e) and Eichengreen and Hausmann (2003b) appear to have modified significantly their earlier views in at least three notable respects.[5] First, they now acknowledge explicitly that aggregate currency

---

4. Three quotes from the earlier papers are sufficient to convey their view: "Neither cross-country nor time-series evidence supports the view that efforts to strengthen policies and institutions at the national level will suffice to ameliorate the problem over the horizon relevant for practical policy decisions" (Eichengreen, Hausmann, and Panizza 2002, 42); "Yet evidence for the presumption that the incidence of original sin reflects the instability of policies and the weakness of market-supporting institutions is meagre. It is based more on presumption and anecdote than fact" (Eichengreen, Hausmann, and Panizza 2003a, 2); and "Even emerging markets that have made major investments in strengthening their policies and institutions have made relatively little headway in solving the mismatch problem" (Eichengreen, Hausmann, and Panizza 2003a, 24).

5. Eichengreen, Hausmann, and Panizza (2003e) contend that they have *not* changed their view from that expressed in their earlier papers on original sin; instead, they maintain that

mismatch is not a necessary consequence of original sin (since a net debtor country may respond to original sin with a large reserve accumulation), that original sin is not the only thing that matters for currency mismatches, and that authors concerned with currency mismatch versus original sin are attempting to measure different things. Second, they acknowledge that a growing number of emerging economies are showing an ability to surmount the difficulties of developing domestic bond markets and that no emerging economy has been able to escape from original sin without first developing a domestic currency–denominated bond market.[6] And third, they now acknowledge that domestic policies and institutions are important for the ability of countries not only to borrow domestically in their own currency but also to borrow abroad in their own currency. They still maintain that original sin is at the heart of financial vulnerability in emerging economies, that good domestic policies and institutions are not sufficient to overcome original sin, and that an international initiative for a new currency basket index provides the best chance of achieving redemption from original sin. They also emphasize that building up international reserves or limiting international capital flows to reduce or eliminate currency mismatch is also costly. A summary of the evolution of the OSH is presented in appendix B.

The revisionist view of the OSH, while moving it closer to the mainstream, is not without its own difficulties. If domestic financial markets and domestic policies and institutions are assumed to be "important" after all for escaping from original sin, then an international solution may not merit first priority; alternatively, since their empirical results find practically no relationship between policy/institutional variables and original sin, accepting those results at face value leaves unexplained a conclusion that good policies and institutions are "necessary" (if not sufficient) for escaping from original sin. Most of all, if there is no tight link between original sin and aggregate currency mismatches in emerging economies—as our empirical work indicates is indeed the case—then the large output losses stemming from currency mismatches during financial crises could not be attributed to original sin. As such, the "costs" of original sin would have to come from elsewhere. In this connection, Eichengreen, Hausmann, and Panizza (2003e) point out that the costs of original sin could take the form of excessive accumulation of foreign

---

others (including us) have misinterpreted their earlier writings and that the most recent papers simply set the critics straight. Obviously, we disagree (see appendix B).

6. In contrast, in their 1999 paper, Eichengreen and Hausmann describe the "original sin hypothesis" as follows: "This is a situation in which the domestic currency cannot be used to borrow abroad or to borrow long term, even domestically. In the presence of this incompleteness, financial fragility is unavoidable because all domestic investments will have either a currency mismatch (projects that generate pesos will be financed with dollars) or a maturity mismatch (long-term projects will be financed with short-term loans)."

exchange reserves or welfare-damaging restrictions on foreign borrowing. But they have yet to provide estimates to suggest that the costs of excess reserve holdings or of relying less on international capital flows are of the same order of magnitude as the widely documented large costs of currency mismatches. Moreover, if countries typically responded to high levels of original sin by limiting involvement with international capital markets or by holding more international reserves or both, then such a response would not sit easily with some of the OSH authors' empirical results. If countries with more original sin restrict their international borrowing, why do their results show that these countries also experience greater volatility in international capital flows? If they hold more reserves, why do their results show that they receive lower credit ratings? In short, if original sin is not highly correlated with aggregate currency mismatch, then the transmission mechanism by which it is alleged to impose such hardships on emerging economies becomes much more elusive.

It is ultimately for others to decide whether the latest (post-August 2003) interpretation of the OSH by its authors represents a significant modification of their much bolder earlier views (as we think) or instead is merely a clarification for critics who have misinterpreted the OSH (as they argue). In the end, we think what counts for policy-relevant analysis is to forge an agreement on what constitutes an operationally useful definition of currency mismatch, understanding why shorthand proxies— such as measures of original sin—are very poor approximations to the more comprehensive measure of currency mismatch. Policymakers need to understand how macroeconomic and other policies can help limit mismatches and how institutional factors (such as the legal framework, the domestic bond market, and prudential oversight of financial institutions) that condition microeconomic incentives are of central importance. In short, our objective is to explain *why*, in light of a large and growing body of empirical evidence, better policies and institutions in emerging economies are a sine qua non for any serious effort to control currency mismatches.

Plan of the Book

The rest of this book takes up these issues in greater depth. Chapter 2 outlines why currency mismatches matter so much for crisis prevention and crisis management. Chapter 3 discusses the measurement of currency mismatch and explains why measures of original sin do not provide a good metric for drawing inferences about aggregate currency mismatch either across countries or over time. Chapter 4 outlines a new measure of aggregate currency mismatch based on readily available statistics. Chapter 5 turns to differences among emerging economies in their ability to cope with potential currency mismatches, underlining why we reject the contention that almost all emerging economies are alike in the intractability of the currency mismatch problem. The roles of national macroeconomic policies (chapter 6) and of the microeconomic incentives created by institutional factors (chapter 7) in generating currency mismatches are then reviewed. Chapter 8 considers what role international solutions could play. The last chapter provides a summary of some key historical trends that reinforce the central argument that domestic policies can make a big difference in limiting currency mismatches. Two appendices elaborate on some themes contained in the main body of the book: appendix A discusses the definition and measurement of currency mismatch, and appendix B traces changes over time in the OSH.

2

Why Currency Mismatches Matter

Earlier financial crises provide ample evidence of the role currency mismatches have played in them. Consider the Asian financial crisis of 1997–98. As shown in table 2.1, widely used indicators of aggregate, short-term currency mismatch (particularly, the ratio of short-term external debt to international reserves and, less consistently, the ratio of broad monetary liabilities, M2, to international reserves) suggest that the Asian-crisis countries had a relatively high and/or rising currency mismatch in the run-up to the 1997–98 crisis. After the crisis broke, these mismatches were sharply reduced. More disaggregated measures of currency mismatch by sector also tell a story of increasing vulnerability. In each of the Asian-crisis countries, the net foreign exchange exposure of banks significantly increased (table 2.2). As detailed in Alba et al. (1998), in Korea, Thailand, and the Philippines, foreign liabilities of nonbank financial intermediaries (for example, merchant banks and finance companies) also mushroomed. In Indonesia, corporations saw their short-term foreign liabilities expand rapidly;[1] according to Dale Gray (1999), for Indonesian firms listed on the stock market, the share of foreign liabilities that were unhedged against currency risk in December 1997 ranged from 65 percent in the consumer goods sector to over 95 percent in the agricultural, mining, real estate and construction, and financial sectors. When the currencies of the countries in the Association of Southeast Asian Nations (ASEAN) plunged during 1998, it resulted in huge and unprecedented declines in their economic

---

1. Burnside, Eichenbaum, and Rebelo (1999) also document large currency mismatches (relative to GDP) for deposit money banks, other financial intermediaries, and nonfinancial firms in the run-up to the crises in Indonesia, Korea, Malaysia, the Philippines, and Thailand.

Table 2.1 Proxies for currency mismatches before the Asian crisis, 1995–99 (percent of foreign exchange reserves)

Country	Short-term external debt					M2				
	1995	1996	1997	1998	1999	1995	1996	1997	1998	1999
Indonesia	208	197	224	113	75	719	661	470	318	345
Korea	184	222	330	76	59	1,498	1,541	1,548	1,022	802
Malaysia	35	44	75	39	27	323	354	353	288	281
Thailand	124	125	152	88	45	371	391	358	457	383
Memorandum:										
Latin America	118	109	105	102	98	426	393	407	431	452

M2 = broad monetary liabilities

Sources: IMF's *International Financial Statistics*, national sources, and Bank for International Settlements.

growth rates. In contrast, a group of emerging economies in Latin America had smaller or less rapidly increasing currency mismatches or both on the eve of the Asian crisis;[2] some of these Latin American countries also suffered currency declines and growth slowdowns in 1998—but not nearly as pronounced as in East Asia. In analyzing the link between short-term, unhedged foreign currency–denominated debt and currency crises in 1997–98, Jason Furman and Joseph Stiglitz (1998) go so far as to conclude that "the ability of this variable, by itself, to predict the crises of 1997 is remarkable."

Consider next the Mexican peso crisis of 1994–95. In the run-up to that crisis, there was a large substitution of foreign currency–indexed tesobonos for domestic currency–denominated cetes. Indeed, between February and December 1994, the stock of tesobonos expanded tenfold (figure 2.1). By December 1994, the dollar value of Mexican public-sector debt exceeded the rapidly dwindling stock of international reserves by about $10 billion. Public-sector debt service relative to exports was also much higher in Mexico on the eve of the crisis than in almost all its neighbors (Brazil was the exception). Similarly, after rising rapidly over 1989–94, the dollar value of M2 had climbed to a level in December 1994 (just before the peso devaluation) that was almost five times higher than the maximum level of international reserves the country ever recorded (Calvo and Goldstein 1996). Between December 1993 and December 1994, the foreign currency–denominated liabilities of Mexican banks jumped from 89 billion pesos to 174 billion pesos. In addition, large and medium-sized Mexican com-

---

2. The Financial Stability Forum's report on capital flows (Financial Stability Forum 2000) notes that between end-1990 and end-1996, the ratio of short-term external debt to international reserves rose from 125 to over 150 percent in East Asian and Pacific emerging economies, whereas it fell from over 140 to 85 percent in a group of Latin American and Caribbean countries.

Table 2.2   Borrowing by domestic banks from international banks, 1995–2002 (percent of domestic bank lending to the private sector)

Region/country	1995	1996	1997	1998	1999	2000	2001	2002
Latin America[a]	21	25	21	18	18	18	17	25
Argentina	20	24	22	20	22	22	22	67
Brazil	15	22	23	17	24	27	26	32
Chile	13	12	10	8	5	5	5	8
Colombia	15	16	17	16	12	8	10	11
Mexico	28	35	22	23	16	12	10	9
Peru	23	26	27	26	18	15	11	8
Venezuela	44	28	18	16	10	9	9	14
Asia, large economies[a]	10	10	12	8	6	5	4	3
China	8	8	8	6	4	3	3	2
India	9	9	10	9	6	5	5	5
Korea	25	30	45	21	16	13	10	10
Taiwan	5	5	5	5	4	3	3	4
Other Asia[a]	27	26	34	27	35	36	30	20
Indonesia	19	18	30	29	52	58	43	25
Malaysia	n.a.	17	24	19	17	15	14	13
Philippines	17	21	27	27	26	27	30	28
Thailand	46	44	50	27	18	17	14	10
Central Europe[a]	18	18	20	23	22	19	17	17
Czech Republic	12	13	17	15	16	15	17	22
Hungary	58	55	54	70	58	40	32	27
Poland	7	7	9	11	13	14	12	11
Russia	113	115	73	146	90	37	25	22
Israel	2	1	3	3	4	2	3	3
Turkey	28	29	29	33	39	40	35	24
South Africa	9	10	9	8	6	6	12	8

n.a. = not available

a. Weighted average of countries shown, based on 1995 GDP and purchasing power parity (PPP) exchange rates.

Note: Cross-border foreign-currency lending by BIS reporting banks to domestic banks as a percent of loans outstanding of deposit money banks; outstanding year-end positions.

Sources: IMF's *International Financial Statistics*, national sources, and Bank for International Settlements.

panies were mismatched, as suggested by the comparison that roughly 10 percent of their sales revenues were denominated in foreign currency versus 60 percent of their financial liabilities (Goldstein and Turner 1996). In 1995, Mexico suffered a 7 percent fall in real GDP—its deepest recession in 50 years.

The Asian and Mexican crises do not appear to be outliers in the experience of emerging economies more generally. A large empirical literature now examines the relative performance of various macroeconomic variables as "leading indicators" of currency and banking crises in emerging

Figure 2.1 The Mexican peso crisis, 1994–95

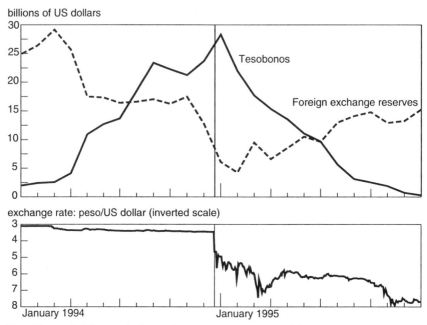

billions of US dollars

Tesobonos

Foreign exchange reserves

exchange rate: peso/US dollar (inverted scale)

January 1994   January 1995

Note: The vertical line marks December 22, 1994, the onset of the crisis.

Source: Banco de México.

economies over the past three decades.[3] While the out-of-sample performance of these models is still a matter of some contention and while
currency mismatch variables do not always win the horse race, some of
the mismatch variables (such as the ratio of short-term external debt to

---

3. See Berg et al. (1999), Edison (2000), Goldstein, Kaminsky, and Reinhart (2000), Hawkins
and Klau (2000), and Bell (2000) for a review of this literature. Wijnholds and Kapteyn (2001)
conclude from an examination of the experience of emerging economies in the 1990s that
"For most countries with a low level of R/STED (i.e., international reserves to adjusted
short-term external debt), a financial crisis ensued." Rodrik and Velasco (1999) find that
countries with a ratio of short-term external debt to reserves that was higher than unity
roughly tripled their probability of getting into a crisis. Mulder, Perrelli, and Rocha (2002,
15) conclude that the ratio of corporate and banking debt to exports is "especially significant" in predicting the probability of currency crises in emerging economies, suggesting that
"crises are more likely if banks and corporations are more exposed to foreign financing in
relation to exports, likely on account of currency mismatches and the balance-sheet effects
caused by currency movements." According to the Bank of England's *Financial Stability
Review* (June 2000), there were sizable currency mismatches (i.e., net foreign currency–
denominated liabilities) in both Turkey (public and banking sectors) and Argentina (public
and nonbank private sectors) in 1999; both these countries subsequently underwent financial crises in 2000 and 2001.

international reserves, the ratio of bank and corporate debt to exports, and the ratio of M2 money balances to international reserves) typically rank high, particularly for the more recent financial crises (Sachs, Tornell, and Velasco 1996; Furman and Stiglitz 1998; Kaminsky and Reinhart 1999; Berg et al. 1999; Bussiere and Mulder 1999; and Hawkins and Klau 2000). In addition, some evidence suggests that exchange rate volatility by itself—without regard to information on currency mismatches—is not a good contemporaneous or leading indicator of financial difficulties/crises (Worrell and Leon 2001). Analyzing balance sheet exposures during the emerging-market financial crises of the 1990s, Allen et al. (2002, 17) conclude that "almost all recent crisis episodes were marked by currency mismatch exposures."[4]

Currency mismatches not only increase the chance of getting into a financial crisis but also seem to increase the cost—especially the output cost—of getting out of one. A set of "third-generation" crisis models show how liability dollarization can interact with a large depreciation to produce a dramatic decline in the private sector's net worth and creditworthiness, a fall in spending and output, and a financial crisis.[5] If one seeks an explanation for the finding of Guillermo Calvo and Carmen Reinhart (2001) that devaluations in developing countries have been contractionary, it is difficult to find a more plausible candidate than currency mismatches. Focusing on currency crises of the 1990s, Cavallo et al. (2001) find that output contractions were larger in countries with both heavy foreign-currency debt burdens and large devaluations.[6]

---

4. Allen et al. (2002) note that currency mismatch risk on the part of the government was important in Mexico, Brazil, Turkey, Argentina, and Russia; that currency mismatches by the banking system were large in Korea, Thailand, Indonesia, Turkey, Russia, and Brazil; and that large currency mismatches in the nonfinancial private sector (corporations and households) were large in Korea, Thailand, Indonesia, Turkey, Argentina, and Brazil.

5. See, for example, Chang and Velasco (1999) and Krugman (1999). "First-generation" crises models highlighted the incompatibility between macroeconomic policies and international reserves needed to sustain a fixed exchange rate, while "second-generation" models emphasized how speculators could push the costs of holding on to a fixed exchange rate beyond the costs of reneging on the exchange rate commitment, generating a "self-fulfilling" attack.

6. Several recent empirical studies reinforce this conclusion. Disyatat (2001) shows that there was a much closer association between exchange rate depreciation and increases in banks' ratios of foreign liabilities to total assets in the Asian-crisis countries than in the exchange rate mechanism (ERM)–crisis countries; output declines in the former were much larger than in the latter. Using firm-level data from Thailand, Rodriguez (2002) reports that firms with larger fractions of their liabilities denominated in foreign currency were forced to cut investment more after a devaluation. Gupta, Mishra, and Sahay (2001), looking at currency crises among a large sample of developing countries over a long period (1970–98), report that output contractions are significantly related to some currency mismatch or debt variables (short-term debt to reserves) but not to others (change in the external long-term debt). Bleakley and Cowan (2002) show that when mainly exporting firms take on foreign

In cases when a large currency mismatch in the banking sector cum a large devaluation is not associated with a large output decline, it is usually because either the banking sector is small relative to the size of the economy or the mismatch has been "socialized" by moving it from the balance sheet of the private sector to that of the public sector (or both). John Hawkins and Philip Turner (1999) show that bank credit to the private sector relative to GDP tends to be much smaller in Latin America than in emerging Asia (table 2.3). Contrary to the Asian crisis, the private sector in Brazil was reasonably hedged before the huge decline in the real in 1999. This is because the Brazilian government, in an effort to demonstrate its commitment to the then pegged exchange rate and to meet the increasing demand for dollars, sold both foreign currency outright and a large amount of dollar-indexed bonds to the private sector. By so doing, the public sector suffered both large reserve losses and heavy fiscal costs (when the devaluation of the real came in January 1999), but economic growth (roughly 1 percent in 1999) was better shielded than in Asia where the private-sector currency mismatch was not addressed (before the crisis) and where it subsequently produced a wave of private-sector insolvencies.[7]

A second cause for concern is that sizable currency mismatches can undermine the effectiveness of monetary policy during a crisis. Consider the monetary-policy options of a country facing a decline in external demand resulting from an international recession. The orthodox prescription would be to lower interest rates, thus directly stimulating domestic demand, and to allow the exchange rate to fall, thus helping to insulate the local economy from the external recession. During the Asian crisis, Australia was able to follow just such an approach. Specifically, the Reserve Bank of Australia could lower interest rates and allow the Australian dollar to depreciate to cushion the effects of a slowdown in its two most important export markets (Japan and Korea). As a result, the Australian economy grew by over 5 percent in 1998.

But when a currency crisis hits an economy with substantial unhedged foreign currency–denominated debt and many highly leveraged firms, the road for monetary policy is not easy. If domestic interest rates are lowered (or even kept constant), there is a real threat that the currency could go into free fall, bringing with it widespread bank failures and cor-

---

currency–denominated debt, devaluation is expansionary (because the negative effect on net worth is more than compensated for by the positive effect on earnings and profits generated by improved competitiveness). Gupta, Mishra, and Sahay (2001) confirm that far from all currency crashes in developing countries are contractionary. They examine a sample of 195 crisis episodes in 91 developing countries over 1970–98 and find that about 40 percent of currency crises were expansionary; the corresponding figure for larger emerging economies was 30 percent.

7. Bevilaqua and Garcia (2000) report that the share of dollar-indexed bonds in Brazil's public debt increased from 7 percent in 1995–96 to 15 percent at end-1997 to 21 percent by end-1998.

Table 2.3 Domestic bank credit to the private sector
(percent of GDP)

Region/country	1990	1995	2002
Latin America[a]	**24.6**	**28.5**	**22.8**
Argentina	15.5	19.7	15.1
Brazil	31.1	30.8	29.3
Chile	46.1	48.1	65.7
Colombia	15.6	18.1	20.1
Mexico	22.3	36.6	10.4
Peru	8.1	15.8	22.6
Venezuela	16.6	8.7	10.2
Asia, large economies[a]	**70.6**	**73.0**	**107.5**
China	88.8	88.3	139.7
Hong Kong	129.4	141.8	144.9
India	25.2	22.8	32.6
Korea	48.5	50.7	92.3
Taiwan	100.4	146.8	125.5
Other Asia[a]	**53.0**	**70.0**	**57.3**
Indonesia	46.9	53.5	22.3
Malaysia	69.4	83.6	106.7
Philippines	20.5	39.3	38.8
Singapore	90.8	100.6	108.6
Thailand	68.5	103.9	95.5
Central Europe[a]	**42.1**	**31.8**	**32.2**
Czech Republic	76.1[b]	66.4	31.7
Hungary	46.6	22.6	34.0
Poland	23.9[c]	18.2	31.7
Russia	11.7[b]	8.5	17.7
Israel	57.9	68.2	97.8
Turkey	15.5	17.5	14.0
Saudi Arabia	16.7	22.7	29.2
South Africa	58.1	57.8	64.0
Memorandum:			
Australia	76.9	78.8	107.3
Sweden	136.5	105.1	122.3
Switzerland	167.9	168.4	158.9

a. Weighted average of countries shown, based on 1995 GDP and PPP exchange rates.
b. 1993 figure.
c. 1991 figure.

Sources: IMF's *International Financial Statistics* and national sources.

porate bankruptcies. If interest rates are increased sharply to support the domestic currency, the financing burdens of firms will be exacerbated, and aggregate demand will be reduced at a time when the economy is likely to be headed toward a recession. In such circumstances, neither monetary policy option—keeping interest rates low and letting the exchange rate fall or defending the exchange rate with very high interest rates—can avoid a fall in net worth so severe as to cause widespread bankruptcies.[8] Monetary policy becomes severely constrained, as several Asian countries with massive currency mismatches discovered during the Asian crisis.

Anne Krueger (2000), now the IMF's first deputy managing director, has argued that until a way is found to prevent the buildup of large currency mismatches in the financial systems of developing countries, the IMF will find its crisis management role difficult and complex. In addition, she apparently regarded the currency mismatch problem as sufficiently worrisome to propose two bold measures for discouraging such mismatches, namely, either making foreign-currency obligations incurred by domestic entities within emerging economies unenforceable in their domestic courts or passing and then enforcing legislation in G-7 countries that would require their financial institutions to accept liabilities abroad only if they were denominated in emerging-market currencies.

Yet a third concern about currency mismatches is that they will severely handicap the operation of floating rate currency regimes in developing countries. Calvo and Reinhart (2000) have shown in their empirical work that developing countries that declare they are following a floating rate regime do not "float" in the same way as industrial-country floaters. More specifically, emerging economies engage in more exchange market intervention and more interest rate action to manage their exchange rates (Calvo and Reinhart 2000). According to Hausmann, Panizza, and Stein (2000), this "fear of floating" appears to be related more to a heavy reliance on foreign currencies in their foreign borrowing than to high "pass-through" of exchange rate changes into domestic prices. The point is that once developing countries have allowed large currency mismatches to accumulate, they will be very reluctant to countenance a large depreciation—lest they drive many of their banks or firms into insolvency.

To the extent that developing-country floaters do not really float in practice, they give up the significant benefits of greater monetary policy independence and better cushioning against external real shocks. In addition, a strong fear of floating would also compromise the effectiveness of inflation targeting in emerging economies since such a targeting regime requires that low inflation (not the exchange rate) be the dominant nominal anchor. If no progress were made in reducing currency mismatches, the fear of floating could over time lead many emerging economies to conclude that they have little choice but to deal with mismatches by taking the radical step of "dollarizing" their economies. But as one of us has argued elsewhere (Goldstein 2002), dollarization does not offer a viable policy instrument to deal with domestic recession when monetary policy is made abroad, when external debt fragilities preclude countercyclical

8. See the model outlined in Jeanne and Zettelmeyer (2002).

pump priming, and when the domestic economy lacks the flexibility to correct a real exchange rate overvaluation on its own. In short, lack of attention to currency mismatching would continue to hamper the operation of floating rate regimes in emerging economies and could lead eventually to currency regime choices that would not be helpful for the overall economic performance of these economies.

3

Measuring Currency Mismatch: Beyond Original Sin

A currency mismatch refers to how a change in the exchange rate will affect the present discounted value of future income and expenditure flows. This will depend on two broad elements. One is the currency denomination of financial assets and liabilities: the more sensitive the net financial worth to changes in the exchange rate, the greater, ceteris paribus, the currency mismatch. The other is the currency denomination of future income and expenditure flows (other than returns to capital assets). Once such a broad perspective is adopted, significant differences in the degree of currency mismatch are revealed both across emerging economies and over time.

As an analytical counterpoint to our proposed definition of currency mismatch, suppose one attempted to gauge aggregate currency mismatch by looking only at the share of international bonds and bank loans denominated in the borrower's local currency—that is, suppose one used measures of original sin as a sufficient statistic for drawing inferences about aggregate currency mismatch. How might the original sin measures lead one astray? It turns out that the answer is helpful in understanding what should be included in a good measure of currency mismatch.

Original Sin: A Misleading Measure

Table 3.1, taken from Eichengreen, Hausmann, and Panizza (2002), gives three measures of original sin. These measures are defined as one minus the percentage of own currency–denominated securities in the relevant

Table 3.1 Measures of original sin by country groupings, simple average (billions of dollars)

Group	OSIN1 1993–98	OSIN1 1999–2001	OSIN2 1993–98	OSIN2 1999–2001	OSIN3 1993–98	OSIN3 1999–2001
Financial centers	0.58	0.53	0.34	0.37	0.07	0.08
Euroland	0.86	0.52	0.55	0.72	0.53	0.09[a]
Other developed	0.90	0.94	0.80	0.82	0.78	0.72
Offshore	0.98	0.97	0.95	0.98	0.96	0.87
Developing	1.00	0.99	0.98	0.99	0.96	0.93
Latin America and the Caribbean	1.00	1.00	1.00	1.00	0.98	1.00
Middle East and Africa	1.00	0.99	0.97	0.99	0.95	0.90
Asia Pacific	1.00	0.99	0.95	0.99	0.99	0.94
Eastern Europe	0.99	1.00	0.97	0.98	0.91	0.84

a. For 1999–2001, it was impossible to allocate the debt issued by nonresidents in euros to any of the individual member countries of the currency union. Hence, the number is not the simple average but is calculated taking Euroland as a whole.

$$OSIN1_i = 1 \frac{\textit{Securities issued by country i in currency i}}{\textit{Securities issued by country i}}$$

$$OSIN2_i = \max(INDEXA_i, OSIN3_i)$$

$$\text{where } INDEXA_i = \frac{\textit{Securities + loans issued by country i in major currencies}}{\textit{Securities + loans issued by country i}}$$

$$INDEXB_i = 1 \frac{\textit{Securities in currency i}}{\textit{Securities issued by country i}}$$

$$OSIN3_i = \max\left(1 - \frac{\textit{Securities in currency i}}{\textit{Securities issued by country i}}, 0\right)$$

Notice that $OSIN2 > OSIN3$ by construction and that, in most cases, $OSIN1 > OSIN2$.

Source: Eichengreen, Hausmann, and Panizza (2002).

total, so that the closer the ratio to one (zero), the greater (smaller) the original sin and implied currency mismatch. These original sin calculations suggest that currency mismatch is pervasive in all developing-country groups, and the mismatch has been persistent over 1993–2001. Another strong implication of table 3.1 is that developing countries face a much larger currency mismatch than not only issuers of the five major currencies but also small industrial countries.

Using original sin as a measure of aggregate currency mismatch would be misleading on at least five important counts. First, it ignores cross-country differences in export openness, reserve holdings, and the size of foreign assets more generally, which can be crucial for assessing currency risk. Consider two net debtor countries (A and B) that have identical shares of foreign currency–denominated debt in total external debt.

Table 3.2 Export openness, 1994–2002 (exports as a percent of GDP)

Region/country	1994	1995	1996	1997	1998	1999	2000	2001	2002
Latin America[a]	**14.4**	**16.9**	**17.7**	**16.9**	**16.3**	**18.0**	**19.5**	**19.2**	**22.5**
Argentina	7.5	9.7	10.4	10.6	10.4	9.8	12.5	11.5	27.7
Brazil	9.5	7.7	7.0	7.5	7.4	10.3	10.7	13.2	15.8
Chile	29.3	30.5	27.3	27.1	26.3	29.3	31.7	34.7	34.0
Colombia	15.0	14.5	15.2	14.8	15.0	18.3	21.5	20.8	19.7
Mexico	16.8	30.4	32.1	30.3	30.7	30.8	31.0	27.4	27.2
Peru	12.8	12.5	13.1	14.2	13.2	14.7	16.0	15.8	16.1
Venezuela	30.9	27.1	36.5	28.4	19.9	21.6	28.4	22.3	31.4
Asia, large economies[a]	**20.8**	**21.0**	**20.7**	**22.6**	**23.4**	**23.1**	**26.4**	**25.6**	**28.2**
China	22.0	21.0	20.9	22.9	21.7	22.1	25.9	25.1	29.3
India	10.0	11.0	10.6	10.9	11.2	11.8	13.8	14.2	15.2
Korea	27.8	30.2	29.5	34.7	49.7	42.3	44.8	42.8	40.0
Taiwan	43.9	48.5	48.4	49.0	48.4	48.0	54.0	50.2	53.7
Other Asia[a]	**37.9**	**39.6**	**39.1**	**44.0**	**60.4**	**53.5**	**60.4**	**57.5**	**54.4**
Indonesia	26.5	26.3	25.8	27.9	51.2	34.9	42.4	41.1	34.7
Malaysia	89.2	94.1	91.6	93.3	115.7	121.3	124.8	116.3	113.8
Philippines	33.8	36.4	40.5	49.0	52.2	51.5	56.2	49.0	51.7
Thailand	38.9	41.8	39.3	48.0	58.9	58.4	67.0	66.4	64.8
Central Europe[a]	**31.8**	**36.5**	**36.5**	**39.4**	**42.9**	**42.7**	**48.8**	**48.4**	**45.7**
Czech Republic	50.5	53.6	52.5	56.5	58.8	60.6	69.8	70.8	65.2
Hungary	28.9	44.4	48.5	55.1	62.6	65.2	74.9	74.4	64.5
Poland	23.8	25.4	24.4	25.6	28.2	26.1	29.4	28.4	29.6
Russia	27.8	26.9	24.2	23.9	30.6	43.8	44.1	36.2	34.4
Israel	32.6	30.6	29.8	30.4	31.6	36.0	40.6	35.5	36.9
Turkey	21.4	19.9	21.5	24.6	24.3	23.2	24.0	33.7	28.9
South Africa	22.2	23.0	24.6	24.6	25.7	25.7	28.6	30.6	34.0

a. Weighted average of countries shown, based on 1995 GDP and PPP exchange rates.

Note: Exports include goods and services per the national accounts definition, except China and Taiwan, for which the balance-of-payments definition is used.

Sources: IMF's *International Financial Statistics* and national sources.

Assume country A has twice as high a ratio of exports to income as country B. Should it then be concluded that the two countries face an identical currency mismatch? Of course not. Both sides of the net income statement and the balance sheet are relevant for gauging the extent of the currency mismatch. For most of the past decade, Argentina and Brazil, for example, have had ratios of exports to GDP that hovered in the 7 to 13 percent range—less than half that of Mexico and Chile and less than a fifth that of typical Asian emerging economies (table 3.2).[1] At identical original sin ratios, Argentina will, ceteris paribus, have a much larger currency mismatch than Mexico or Singapore. The same line of argument about

1. Argentina's ratio of exports to GDP mushroomed in 2002 because of the deep recession and the effects of the sharp fall in the peso exchange rate on both GDP measured in dollars and export earnings.

cross-country differences also applies to holdings of international reserves and foreign assets more broadly. Whereas monetary authorities of some emerging economies, such as Korea and Malaysia, have net foreign assets (in 2002) that are five to seven times larger than currency held outside banks, those in others, such as the Philippines, Brazil, and Poland, have much lower ratios (less than three). Likewise, data on net international investment positions taken from the IMF's *Balance of Payments Yearbook* reveal sharp differences among emerging economies. For example, foreign assets (in 2002) accounted for less than 10 percent of foreign liabilities in Ecuador but for 66 and 86 percent in Chile and the Czech Republic, respectively; in Hong Kong and Singapore, foreign assets exceed foreign liabilities (i.e., they are net creditors, not net debtors).[2] Since our preferred measures of currency mismatch consider both assets and liabilities, they are not subject to this pitfall.

Second, and in a similar vein, an original sin measure would ignore changes in foreign-currency receipts and assets over time. Consider a net debtor country where the share of foreign currency–denominated debt in total corporate debt increased from one-third in 1994 to one-half in 2000. According to the original sin measure, its currency mismatch would have increased. But suppose that over the same period its exports increased much more, so that the ratio of foreign-currency debt to exports fell from, say, almost four to one and a half. Clearly, the country's currency mismatch would have fallen, not risen. This is not a hypothetical case. It is in fact a summary of the evolution of (corporate) currency mismatch in Mexico (Martinez and Werner 2001). If one leaves out changes in the asset side of the aggregate currency balance sheet, one can miss much of the action in time-series variation of currency risk. When both sides of the balance sheet are considered, aggregate measures of currency mismatch are not nearly as persistent as original sin measures would suggest. In table 2.1, for example, the ratio of short-term external debt to international reserves in four Asian-crisis countries was roughly half as high in 1999 as it was in 1996. Another implication is that original sin ratios based on the liability side of the balance sheet are not likely to be good leading indicators of the timing of financial crises in emerging economies (since such ratios move very little over time).[3] In contrast, and as discussed earlier,

---

2. Figures on foreign assets and liabilities don't reveal the currency composition of these positions but are suggestive of nontrivial cross-country differences in currency risk.

3. Measures of dollarization in the *domestic* financial system show more variation across countries and over time than do original sin ratios (of external borrowing). Yet even empirical studies of domestic dollarization have produced quite mixed results. Arteta (2003), for example, finds no evidence that high liability dollarization in the banking system heightens the probability of banking crises or currency crashes in emerging economies or that such crises are more costly in countries where bank liability dollarization is high. Reinhart, Rogoff, and Savastano (2003a) find, inter alia, that dollarization has little impact on the

currency mismatch measures that capture both sides of the balance sheet (e.g., the ratio of short-term external debt to reserves and the ratios of bank and corporate foreign debt to exports) have done well in leading-indicator exercises of currency and banking crises in emerging economies, and the output costs of such crises have been shown to be higher when currency mismatch (so measured) was large than when it was small.

Third, the original sin measure—like all aggregate measures of currency mismatch—ignores the key question of who bears the currency risk within an emerging economy. This is particularly relevant when producers of nontradables that do not generate foreign revenue to service the debt undertake a significant share of external borrowing. Once again, consider (net debtor) countries A and B with identical original sin ratios. But assume that exporters exclusively undertake country A's dollar borrowing whereas real estate companies that operate exclusively in the domestic economy undertake country B's dollar borrowing. Do these two countries face identical currency mismatches? Certainly not. Country A's mismatch is likely to be much lower than country B's. One of the lessons of the Asian financial crisis of 1997–98 is that using short-term external foreign currency–denominated borrowing to fund long-term real estate investments is hazardous. Similarly, a country where the government does the bulk of external borrowing is apt to have a larger currency mismatch than one where exporters do the bulk of the borrowing because government taxes are typically denominated in domestic currency while most external borrowing is denominated in foreign currency. Going in the same direction, firm-level studies have shown that the investment effects of a currency depreciation are different when firms have export revenues and when they do not. Again, original sin ratios would not pick any of this up. To capture the incidence of foreign exchange risk in the economy, one needs disaggregated data on the allocation of credit and on the characteristics of the borrower. None of the aggregate measures of currency risk will capture this incidence of risk very well. But original sin measures of currency risk can be particularly misleading because they ignore differences across (net debtor) countries and over time in the asset side of the balance sheet; they are thus more likely to miss even gross differences in the tradable/nontradable distinction.

Yet a fourth problem with the original sin measure of mismatch is that it would restrict attention to international bonds and bank loans. It therefore ignores the currency composition and increasing importance of the domestic bond market, the participation of global investors in domestic bond markets, and bank lending by the domestic affiliates of foreign-

---

effectiveness of monetary policy, that output fluctuations are fairly similar in countries with different degrees and varieties of dollarization, and that exchange rate–linked government debt increases crisis vulnerability. De Nicolo, Honohan, and Ize (2003) find that financial intermediaries in dollarized financial systems are prone to higher risk.

Table 3.3 Bond market development, end-2001

Region	Bonds outstanding (percent of GDP)	Local currency–denominated (percent of total)	Dollar-denominated (percent of total)
Euro area	109	88	5
Japan	116	99	1
United Kingdom	92	74	15
Canada	92	71	23
Latin America	30	47	42
Emerging Asia	41	88	10
Other	59	75	13
Total non-US	85	87	7
United States	142	98	—

Sources: Burger and Warnock (2002). Data on dollar-denominated bonds and notes are from security-level data underlying table 14B (International Bonds and Notes by Country of Residence) in BIS, *International Banking and Financial Market Developments*. Local currency–denominated debt is the sum of the long-term debt component of BIS table 16A (Domestic Debt Securities) and the local-currency portion of table 14B. Domestic debt for countries not available in table 16A is from the IMF's *Government Finance Statistics Yearbook* and Merrill Lynch (2002). Total non-US includes only the 50 countries in Burger and Warnock's sample.

owned banks operating in emerging economies. It turns out that these exclusions are crucial for drawing conclusions about if and how emerging economies differ from industrial countries as well as about how significant financial activity in domestic currency vis-à-vis that in foreign currency is. What's more, one should guard against any suggestion that only external borrowing by emerging economies (because it involves a transfer of resources to relatively poor countries) should be considered in examining the path to lower financial fragility there; recent research indicates that domestic financial intermediation generates significant benefits and may well reduce some of the vulnerabilities associated with heavy reliance on external borrowing.

Until recently, it was not possible to get comprehensive data on the currency composition of domestic bond markets in emerging economies. In recent years, however, the scope of the Bank for International Settlements' banking and financial market statistics has been broadened to include domestic debt securities in emerging markets, complementing the data on international bond issuance. In a recent paper John Burger and Francis Warnock (2002) summarize and analyze these data (as of end-2001) for 50 countries (table 3.3). The key observation is that once the total bond market is considered, the share of the bond market denominated in local currency is not that different between emerging economies and industrial countries. In Asian emerging economies, the local-currency share of the bond market is 88 percent—higher than the local-currency

Figure 3.1   Market share of foreign-owned banks in emerging markets

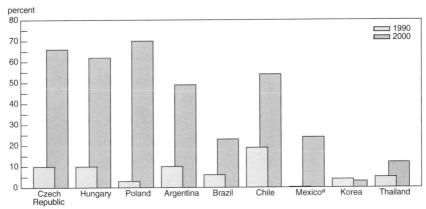

a. If the foreign-owned banks that have effective control without holding more than 50 percent of equity are included, the proportion would be over 40 percent in 2000.

Note: Data include banks where foreigners hold more than 50 percent of equity.

Source: Central banks.

share in Canada (71 percent) and the United Kingdom (74 percent) and identical to the local-currency share in the euro area (88 percent). It is in Latin America that the local-currency share of the bond market (47 percent) is significantly lower than elsewhere. Since global investors do participate in local bond markets and since local bond markets in all regions (including the industrial countries) represent the largest share of the total bond market, excluding them from the analysis of currency mismatch would be hard to defend.[4] As Burger and Warnock (2002) emphasize, the data in table 3.3 suggest that if there is a robust difference between industrial and emerging economies as regards bond markets, it is that the size of the total bond market (relative to GDP) is much smaller in emerging economies than it is in industrial countries—not a difference in the currency composition of the bond market, as the original sin hypothesis (OSH) suggests.

Similarly, a lot of the action in emerging-market finance is missed when one concentrates only on cross-border bank lending in domestic currency. A more comprehensive picture needs to include lending in local currency by foreign affiliates of industrial-country banks operating in emerging economies. Foreign presence in emerging-market banking systems has been increasing in the 1990s and now stands above 50 percent in Hungary, Chile, Poland, and the Czech Republic (figure 3.1). Also, lending

<hr />

4. Reinhart, Rogoff, and Savastano (2003b, 42) share this view when they argue that "the view that only external debt is a completely separate matter is clearly wrong. Foreigners often hold domestically-issued debt, and domestic residents often hold foreign-issued debt—indeed, the process of liberalization encourages active arbitrage across the two markets."

Table 3.4 Foreign banks' consolidated claims, local and international, 1990–2003 (billions of dollars)

Region	1990	1995	1996	1997	1998	1999	2000	2001	2002	2003 Q3
Developing countries										
Local	52	124	153	251	279	304	434	523	542	575
International	531	752	855	995	938	881	885	838	802	884
Africa and Middle East										
Local	6	14	12	14	16	22	24	27	34	36
International	110	115	111	122	136	140	137	130	134	144
Asia and Pacific										
Local	27	56	65	73	81	95	117	123	143	165
International	134	307	368	421	337	299	278	252	238	282
Europe										
Local	3	9	12	36	39	38	62	87	112	128
International	103	118	135	171	175	165	184	181	202	235
Latin America and Caribbean										
Local	15	44	64	128	144	149	231	287	253	245
International	184	212	242	280	290	277	285	275	228	223

Note: Local claims comprise those of BIS reporting banks' foreign offices denominated in local currency. International claims are the sum of cross-border claims in all currencies and local claims of BIS reporting banks' foreign offices denominated in foreign currency only.

Source: Bank for International Settlements.

by foreign affiliates of industrial-country banks has been on a steady upward trend (as cross-border bank lending to developing countries has declined). Indeed, as shown in table 3.4, such local claims (denominated in local currency) by foreign affiliates now amount to more than a third of total foreign-bank claims (in all currencies) in developing countries as a group; in Latin America and the Caribbean, the local-claims share is above half. Why might foreign banks prefer to do domestic-currency lending via their foreign affiliates within emerging economies rather than via cross-border flows? One plausible answer is that foreign-bank affiliates take in domestic-currency deposits; as such, the degree of currency risk (for the lending bank) is much lower for local lending than it is for cross-border lending (where there is no obvious offset). This distinction is also reflected in the regulatory capital structure facing international banks: whereas cross-border bank lending in local currency (of the borrower) faces a capital charge for foreign exchange risk, domestic-currency lending by affiliates with domestic-currency deposits is not subject to such a capital charge.[5]

---

5. On this shift, see Hawkins (2003); Wooldridge, Domanski, and Cobau (2003); and Lubin (2003).

Some might argue that expanding the sources of local currency–denominated finance beyond international bonds and cross-border bank lending to include bank lending by local affiliates of foreign banks and domestic bonds is inappropriate—either because foreign banks merely displace lending by locally owned banks or because domestic bond markets make little use of foreign saving (and hence do not involve the transfer of real resources associated with cross-border purchases of bonds). We disagree.

Considerable empirical literature now supports the view that lower entry restrictions on foreign-owned banks in emerging economies improve the efficiency of the banking system, are associated with significant upgrades in the quality of regulation and disclosure, and reduce vulnerability to a crisis.[6] Affiliates of foreign banks not only bring with them risk capital but also permit a diversification of risk and can serve as high-quality counterparties in hedging contracts. According to Gerard Caprio and Patrick Honohan (2001), there is no hard evidence that the local presence of foreign banks has destabilized the flow of credit or restricted access to small firms. Entry of foreign banks is thus by no means a zero-sum game for the host emerging economies—especially when it comes to reducing their financial fragility.

Likewise, as Richard Herring and N. Chatusripitak (2001) have convincingly argued, bond markets are central to the development of an efficient economic system, and further development of the domestic bond market in developing countries would offer significant benefits. Bond markets make financial markets more complete by generating market interest rates that reflect the opportunity cost of funds at each maturity; they avoid concentrating intermediation uniquely on banks; and they provide a useful market signal and disciplining device for macroeconomic policy. Having a well-functioning domestic bond market improves the supply of local currency–denominated finance and thus can help to reduce excessive reliance on (largely) foreign currency–denominated external finance. The existence of such a market also benefits those borrowers who rely on banks for finance: banks will be more able to offer long-term credit terms because they can use bond markets to hedge their maturity mismatches. Hence customers of banks, who never directly use bond markets, gain indirectly.

Summarizing a large body of cross-country empirical evidence, Caprio and Honohan (2001) report that there is a strong positive association between the level of financial development and economic growth and that both banking and market finance support economic growth.[7] They find

---

6. See Barth, Caprio, and Levine (2000). Caprio and Honohan (2001) also show that foreign bank ownership (i.e., the percent of total banking assets owned by foreign banks) has been lower in crisis countries than in noncrisis ones. For a recent review of foreign banks in emerging markets, see CGFS (2004).

7. For other studies analyzing the link between financial market development and growth, see King and Levine (1993a, 1993b) and Khan and Senhadji (2000).

that the deeper the financial system, the lower (ceteris paribus) the economic volatility. While legitimate questions remain as to whether it is preferable to first develop a local bond market before relying on the external bond market or vice versa, we are unaware of robust evidence from the empirical literature that indicates that external bond markets offer large benefits for economic growth and crisis prevention but domestic ones do not. It is true that domestic debt markets, especially new ones, tend to be thin and the pricing volatile. This often discourages local debt managers from using these markets. But it is all too often forgotten that the pricing of the sovereign debt of highly indebted borrowers in international markets is also very volatile—witness the sharp swings in Brazilian spreads from mid-2002 to mid-2003. There are reasons to believe—and some evidence—that pricing in local markets improves as debt markets deepen. Accepting volatility in the early stages of local-market development can be regarded as an investment in the future. Just running to international markets "because deals can be done faster" does not constitute such an investment.

Indeed, some analysts have even begun to suggest that the presumption may have begun to shift against unconditional or premature financial globalization (at least for those developing countries in the early phases of financial integration and with relatively poor quality of domestic institutions). In this connection, the conclusions of a recent IMF study (Prasad et al. 2003) that reviews and evaluates the empirical evidence on the effects of financial globalization on developing countries are worth noting. Financial integration or globalization is measured in the IMF study in a variety of ways, including by government restrictions on capital account transactions and by the observed size of capital flows crossing the border. The authors conclude: (1) "an objective reading of the vast research effort to date suggests that there is no strong, robust and uniform support for the theoretical argument that financial globalization per se delivers a higher rate of economic growth" (p. 5); (2) "procyclical access to international capital markets appears to have had a perverse effect on the relative volatility of consumption for financial integrated developing economies" (p. 9); and (3) "A number of researchers have now concluded that most of the differences in per capita income across countries stem not from differences in capital-labor ratios, but from differences in total factor productivity, which, in turn, could be explained by 'soft factors' or 'social infrastructure' like governance, rule of law, and respect for property rights" (p. 31). In short, no analysis of the path to reduced financial fragility and higher economic growth in emerging economies that concentrated exclusively on external sources of finance would be persuasive. Domestic financial markets in emerging economies should not be compared to some idealized version of cross-border capital flows but rather to their real-world counterparts—warts (sudden stops, cross-country contagions) and all.

An original sin measure of currency mismatch would leave out domestic bond markets. While much smaller relative to GDP than in

Table 3.5 Emerging-market financing, all sectors, 1997–2001
(billions of dollars)

	Domestic				International			
Region	Equities	Bonds	Bank loans	Total	Equities	Bonds	Bank loans	Total
Total emerging markets	158	2,367	907	3,432	80	303	214	598
Asia	112	342	883	1,337	63	113	96	272
Latin America	313	1,752	−1	1,784	12	172	103	288
Central Europe	13	273	25	311	6	18	15	38

Note: Emerging markets are Argentina, Brazil, Chile, China, Czech Republic, Hong Kong, Hungary, Korea, Malaysia, Mexico, Poland, Singapore, and Thailand.

Source: IMF (2003a, 78).

industrial countries, domestic bond markets in emerging markets are already anything but trivial. By end-2001, outstanding domestic debt securities in emerging markets amounted to over $2 trillion—up from $1 trillion in 1994. Likewise, the volume of emerging-market domestic debt that is tradable now exceeds by a wide margin that of tradable international debt—even though international bonds are still more liquid instruments. According to IMF (2003a) figures for the 1997–2001 period, public-sector domestic bond issuance by emerging economies was 13 times larger than international foreign-currency bond issues; international corporate bond issuance by emerging economies in 1997–2001 amounted to only about half of such bonds issued domestically; and the annual average value of international corporate bond issuance declined slightly between 1997–99 and 2000–01, whereas the corresponding average for domestic bond issuance rose tenfold. While emerging markets have traditionally been viewed as bank-dominated financial systems, local bond markets have now become the single largest source (in terms of flows) of domestic and international funding for emerging economies (table 3.5 covers both public- and private-sector financing). Clearly, by looking only at international bonds and cross-border bank loans, one would get a partial and misleading impression of both the key elements of emerging-market financing and of trends in these financing patterns.

While the maturity of financing in emerging economies remains much shorter than is available to industrial countries, the (original version of the) OSH went too far in claiming that emerging economies cannot borrow long-term (domestically) in their own currencies. Mihaljek, Scatigna, and Villar (2002) report that 37 percent of domestic-debt securities in Latin

America were short-term in 2000—down from 53 percent in 1995; the percentage of short-term debt for emerging economies in Asia and Central Europe is lower than in Latin America. Moreover, data collected by Salomon Smith Barney (2001) indicate that domestic currency–denominated bonds with maturities extending to 20 years currently exist in India, Malaysia, the Philippines, Poland, South Korea, and Thailand; if long maturity were defined as 10 years, then some domestic currency–denominated bonds in Argentina, Colombia, the Czech Republic, Hong Kong, Hungary, Mexico, and Singapore would also qualify. And in Chile—an emerging economy with original sin ratios close to one—the average maturity of inflation-indexed local currency–denominated corporate bonds now runs 15 to 20 years (up from 10 to 15 years in the first half of the 1990s), and the market for indexed local-currency bonds has tripled in size since 2000 (IMF 2003a). To be sure, some of these long-dated domestic-currency bonds in emerging economies are not as liquid as would be desirable, but this list belies the notion that it is simply impossible for emerging economies to borrow at long maturity from their own citizens unless they denominate this debt in one of the leading reserve currencies; equally important, as argued later, if emerging economies can improve their macroeconomic performance and institutions, they will be able to attract more longer-term finance.

In their latest papers (Eichengreen, Hausmann, and Panizza 2003e; Hausmann and Panizza 2003), Eichengreen, Hausmann, and Panizza construct a measure of "domestic" original sin to complement their external original sin measure; the earlier papers ignored almost completely the domestic bond markets. Domestic original sin is measured by the share of the domestic bond market accounted for by the sum of foreign currency–denominated instruments, short-term domestic currency–denominated fixed-rate debt, and domestic–currency debt indexed to the interest rate. The higher this measure of domestic original sin, the lower the share of long-term fixed-rate and long-term inflation-indexed debt denominated in domestic currency—and the assumed lower stage of "development" of the domestic debt market. Of the 22 emerging economies in their sample, 9 (Taiwan, India, South Africa, Slovak Republic, Thailand, Singapore, Hungary, Poland, and the Philippines) had domestic original sin ratios less than one-half. Perhaps more important, they find that there are *no* countries with poorly developed domestic bond markets that have been redeemed from external original sin—suggesting that domestic bond development is a necessary precondition for a country to borrow abroad in its own currency. Also of interest, seven emerging economies in their sample are free of domestic original sin but still suffer from external original sin—a result that Eichengreen, Hausmann, and Panizza interpret as suggesting that domestic bond market development is not a sufficient condition for a country's being able to borrow abroad in its own currency. But since their bond market figures refer to a single year (1999), another interpretation is that there is simply a time lag between domestic bond market development and the subsequent ability to borrow abroad in one's own currency.

Yet a fifth caveat about using original sin as a measure of aggregate currency mismatch is that the former concentrates on the "original" currency denomination of international bonds and cross-border bank loans; the original borrowers could use derivatives markets to limit their currency risk and/or transfer that risk to other parties (including foreigners). Consider a Polish nonfinancial corporation that issued an international bond denominated in US dollars but preferred to have its risk denominated in Polish zloties. It could use the swap, forward, or options market to switch or hedge its original exposure. In that case, the original currency composition of that corporate bond would not reveal much about the firm's currency mismatch. The IMF (2003a) reports, for example, that virtually all local companies in Brazil that have access to international financial markets raise funds denominated in US dollars but then use the local derivatives market to swap the international financial obligations into the local currency with an interest rate indexed to the overnight rate.

The early work on OSH did not take account of derivatives markets. In the later versions of the OSH, the authors (Eichengreen, Hausmann, and Panizza 2002) address the possibility that currency swaps could distort their measure of original sin. Their adjustment for this is to include all international bonds denominated in an emerging-market currency even if issued by countries other than the home country. They find that this makes little difference to their results since there are not enough local currency–denominated international bonds to sustain a large volume of currency swaps. But this procedure, while moving in the right direction, still suffers from several problems. Currency swaps are only one of many ways of hedging or transferring currency risk. In most of Latin America, for example, there is a greater reliance on forwards than on foreign exchange swaps, while the reverse holds for most of the Asian emerging economies; Eichengreen, Hausmann, and Panizza (2002) consider only currency swaps. Since foreigners also participate in local bond markets, domestic bonds denominated in local currency should also in principle be taken into account in gauging potential currency swap operations; and because (as argued earlier) the volume of domestic bonds outstanding far exceeds that of international bonds, there is no shortage of domestic-currency bonds for swap operations with foreigners.

What makes it difficult to assess the difference derivatives make for the correct measurement of currency risk is that still relatively little is known about who is on the other side of these transactions. Unlike Eichengreen and Hausmann (1999), we do not regard a redistribution of currency risk within an emerging economy as being of little significance, since a transfer of exposures from nontradable to tradable producers could (as argued earlier) generate a sizable reduction in currency mismatch. Still, it would be illuminating to know how prominent foreigners are in these transactions. A recent IMF study (2003a, 66) reports that foreign-investor participation in local derivative exchanges is usually "fairly limited" but has been considerable in Mexico, Hungary, Poland, and the Czech Republic; that in some emerging economies like Singapore, Hong Kong, and South Africa, foreign dealers account for the bulk of turnover in over-the-counter derivatives markets; that "real-money accounts" (both dedicated and cross-over investors) hedge relatively little of their risk exposures in emerging economies while speculative money accounts (hedge funds and proprietary trading desks of commercial and investment banks) use derivatives markets freely for either hedging or speculative position-taking; and that the main sellers of protection in credit derivatives markets are internationally active banks. In our own discussions with market participants, there was a view that internationally active banks and real-money funds were likely to be on the other side of derivatives transactions when locals wanted to short the local currency.

How far derivatives alter the currency exposure implied by the original currency composition of international bonds and bank loans will not be known until there is better information on the identity of counterparties in hedging transactions—both within and across countries. But the wide array of hedging instruments and markets makes it a leap too far to assume that the original currency composition of international bonds and bank loans provides a reliable picture of who is ultimately bearing the currency risk.

Summary

A useful way to sum up this discussion about the original sin measure of currency mismatch is to ask under what set of conditions it would produce a good estimate. Three such conditions are apparent.

Condition number one is that domestic bond and bank flows would either have to be very small relative to international flows or if large, would need to have the same currency composition as international flows. It is clear that condition one is grossly violated. As seen earlier, domestic financial flows are large relative to international flows, and the local currency share of domestic finance is much larger than for international flows.

Condition number two is that the asset side of balance sheets (and the income side of net income statements) would have to be similar across countries and relatively constant over time. If that were the case, then information on liabilities alone would track pretty well both cross-country differences and changes over time in currency mismatch. But, as shown earlier, this condition too is far divorced from what is observed in practice.

Condition number three is that neither the distribution of currency risk within an economy nor the redistribution of currency risk internationally (via the use of derivatives) would matter much. If that were the case, then data on aggregate currency mismatch and the original currency composition of bond and bank flows would be sufficient for gauging currency risk. But as argued earlier, it does matter which entities and sectors within an economy bear the currency risk, and some emerging economies do have enough access to decent derivative and hedging instruments to potentially alter significantly the allocation of currency risk implied by the original currency composition of financial instruments.

4

Aggregate Effective Currency Mismatch

Our preferred definition of currency mismatch—that is, the sensitivity of net worth or of the present discounted value of net income to changes in the exchange rate—is indeed much harder to measure than original sin. But it offers better guidance to what one should try to measure. Although no single measure captures all the relevant features of currency mismatches throughout the economy, we believe it is possible to get useful rough estimates of mismatch both across countries and for a given country over time by relying jointly on a number of available mismatch variables as well as by constructing a new measure of aggregate effective currency mismatch. Moreover, other potentially valuable indicators of currency mismatch could be obtained in the future—particularly for the corporate sector—if data collection for them were accorded higher priority.

As discussed earlier, empirical work suggests that the ratio of short-term external debt to international reserves has been a useful leading indicator of the probability of getting into a currency crisis. A recent IMF study (Aturupane et al. 2004) reports, inter alia, that virtually all emerging economies with access to international capital markets, which experienced a crisis during the January 2000–December 2002 period, had a ratio of short-term debt to reserves of greater than one. The ratio of broad money balances (M2) to reserves also appears to have value in signaling currency crises. These short-run liquidity measures are available for a large group of emerging economies.

Other indicators of currency mismatch—encompassing both sectoral and aggregate measures—are also worth monitoring because they can reveal sectoral mismatch vulnerabilities that may be submerged within the aggregate, or because they permit one to control for factors (like local

Figure 4.1 Foreign currency balance sheet of a partially dollarized economy

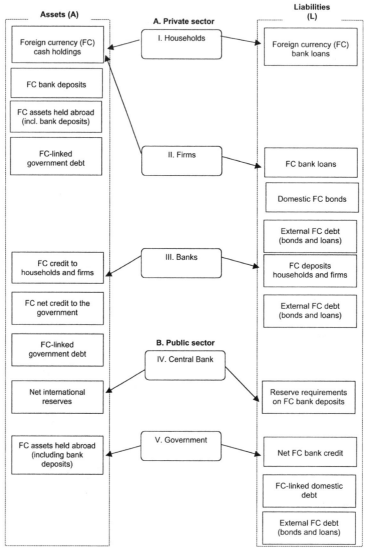

Source: Reinhart, Rogoff, and Savastano (2003a).

currency–denominated bonds and bank loans and the responsiveness of noninterest income flows to a change in the exchange rate) that ought to affect the severity of crises, or because they cover a wider range of foreign-currency assets and liabilities.

Figure 4.1, taken from Reinhart, Rogoff, and Savastano (2003a), shows components that would ideally make up sectoral foreign-currency bal-

Table 4.1 Australia: Foreign-currency exposure by financial sector, end-June 2001 (billions of Australian dollars)

Instrument	Banks	RBA and CBAs	Other financial corporations	General government	Other resident sectors	Total all sectors
Foreign currency–denominated financial debt assets	−69.8	−36.9	−33.6	−5.5	−10.6	−156.5
Foreign currency–denominated debt liabilities	186.5	8.8	61.4	4.1	60.1	321.0
equals						
Net debt position	116.7	−28.1	27.8	−1.4	49.5	164.5
Principal of foreign currency–derivative contracts in a bought position	−435.3	−11.3	−69.8	−0.4	−31.7	−548.4
Principal of foreign currency–derivative contracts in a sold position	325.8	32.1	61.8	8.9	34.9	463.4
equals						
Net debt position unhedged after derivatives	7.2	−7.4	19.8	7.2	52.6	79.5
Foreign-equity assets	−30.7	0.0	−84.0	0.0	−113.9	−228.5
equals						
Foreign-currency exposure	−23.4	−7.4	−64.1	7.2	−61.2	−149.0

RBA = Reserve Bank of Australia
CBAs = State and Territory Central Borrowing Authorities
Source: ABS (2001).

ance sheets. The rub is that, while data for some of these components (like international reserves, foreign-currency bank deposits held at home, and external foreign-currency debt) are now available for many emerging economies, data on other components (such as foreign-currency cash holdings, foreign-currency credit extended by banks to domestic households and firms, and foreign currency–linked domestic debt) are in much more limited supply.

Tables 4.1 and 4.2—the former for an industrial country (Australia) and the latter for an emerging economy (Thailand)—illustrate how sectoral balance sheets (usually taken from national sources) can be used to gauge currency mismatches and vulnerabilities.

Table 4.2 Thailand: Intersectoral asset and liability position, end-December 1996 (millions of dollars)

Issuer of the liability (debtor)	Holder of the liability (creditor)				
	General government and Bank of Thailand	Commercial banks	Nonbank sector	Rest of the world	Total
General government and central bank (Bank of Thailand)					
Domestic currency		2,394	11,885		14,279
Total other liabilities		5,555		5,152	10,707
Short term		3,616[a]		34	3,650
Medium and long term		1,939[a]		5,118	7,057
Commercial banks (including BIBFs)					
Total liabilities	10,327		139,299	48,790	198,417
Deposits and other short term:	9,366		131,866	28,858	170,090
In foreign currency			448	28,189	28,637
In domestic currency	9,366		131,417	669	141,453
Medium and long term:	961		7,434[a]	19,932	28,327
Equity (capital)					23,439
Nonbank sector					
Total liabilities		206,715		61,701	268,416
Short term:		555[a]		18,831[b]	18,831
Medium and long term		31,542[b]		42,870[b]	42,870
Equity (capital)				4,745	136,252
Rest of the world[b]					
Total liabilities	38,694	7,029			45,723
Currency and short term	38,694	2,580			41,274
Medium and long term		4,449			4,449
Equity			481		

BIBFs = Bangkok International Banking Facilities

a. In domestic currency.
b. In foreign currency.

Source: Allen et al. (2002).

Table 4.1 provides data on sectoral foreign-currency exposure for the Australian economy as of end-June 2001. The Australian Bureau of Statistics (ABS) collected the data, with the assistance of the Reserve Bank of Australia, as a supplement to the *Survey of International Investment.* According to the ABS (2001), the aim was to capture quantitative and qualitative data about Australian enterprises' foreign-currency exposure and the risk management practices associated with that exposure. More than 230 resident enterprises with significant foreign-currency exposure were approached (including general government entities), and the response rate was 77 percent. Information was requested about foreign-equity assets, foreign currency–denominated assets and liabilities, the notional value of derivative contracts with a foreign-currency component, the policies enterprises adopted on hedging foreign-currency exposure, and foreign currency–denominated receipts and payments expected from trade in goods and services in the following year (i.e., in the 12 months to end-June 2002).

Several results in table 4.1 are worth highlighting. The general government sector was the only one with a net foreign currency liability exposure, after accounting for hedging activities and foreign-equity positions; its net foreign currency liability position was A$7.2 billion. Although the "banks" subsector had considerably larger foreign currency–denominated financial debt liabilities (A$186.5 billion) than its foreign currency–denominated financial assets (A$69.8 billion), its hedging activities in the derivatives markets plus a sizable foreign-equity asset position turned its total foreign-currency exposure into an A$23.4 billion net asset position. Summing the sectoral exposures, Australian resident enterprises had an aggregate net foreign-currency asset position of A$149 billion.

The Australian sectoral balance sheet drives home the point that in countries where residents are widely using derivatives markets to hedge foreign exchange exposures, it is highly desirable to try and obtain information on those hedging activities to measure currency mismatch.[1] The Australian example likewise illustrates the valuable information that can be retrieved from surveys on foreign exchange exposure (including exposure in the nonbank and government sectors), if more governments were prepared to conduct them.

Table 4.2, taken from Allen et al. (2002), provides a picture of sectoral asset and liability positions in Thailand just before its 1997 crisis (end of December 1996). While short-term liabilities to the rest of the world were very small ($34 million) in the government sector, short-term liabilities in foreign currency were huge for commercial banks (almost $29 billion) and the nonbank sector (almost $19 billion). Thailand's aggregate short-term foreign-currency debt was therefore on the order of $48 billion. On the asset side, the monetary authorities—the Bank of Thailand (BOT)—held roughly $39 billion in foreign reserve assets, although the BOT already had some forward and swap obligations not shown in its balance sheet. Table 4.2 also shows that the banking system's foreign assets were just over $7 billion. Allen et al. (2002) estimate that of the $207 billion in claims of the commercial banking system on the domestic nonbank sector, about

---

1. The ABS (2001) study also includes a detailed breakdown of derivative contracts by type (i.e., forwards, interest rate swaps, futures, and currency options) and by sector, as well as a disaggregation of hedging activities by instrument (i.e., foreign-equity assets, debt liabilities, and fixed-income assets).

$32 billion was denominated in foreign currency. In the end, these sectoral balance sheets permit Allen et al. (2002) to draw the following conclusions about Thailand's currency mismatch: In December 1996, there was a roughly $10-billion financing gap between the government's foreign reserves and the country's total external foreign-currency liabilities falling due in the short term; the maturity and currency mismatches of commercial banks vis-à-vis nonresidents were enormous (on the order of $26 billion if none of the short-term liabilities was rolled over); and nonbank corporations and households had perhaps even larger mismatches than the commercial banks. The sectoral analysis also shows that currency risk was essentially being passed on from the commercial banks to the nonbank sector; since the latter had relatively little foreign currency–denominated revenue, the large devaluation that subsequently occurred was sure to generate large-scale insolvencies in the nonbank sector and ultimately sizable loan delinquencies and a systemic banking crisis.

New Measure of Aggregate Effective Currency Mismatch

At the aggregate level, a rough but nonetheless useful measure of aggregate effective currency mismatch (AECM) can be constructed using the international banking statistics of the Bank for International Settlements (BIS), the IMF's data on the international liquidity position of the monetary authorities and on the claims and liabilities of financial institutions, and some estimates of the currency composition of the total bond and banking markets. The main purpose of such a measure is to provide a shorthand stress test of the consequences for the domestic economy of an aggregate currency mismatch—*if* there were a large depreciation of the local currency. Our AECM measure has three components: net foreign-currency assets, exports (or imports) of goods and services, and the foreign-currency share of total debt.

Specifically, net foreign-currency assets (NFCA) are defined as follows:

$$NFCA = NFAMABK + NBKA\$ - NBKL\$ - IB\$ \tag{1}$$

where NFAMABK is net foreign assets of the monetary authorities and deposit money banks, from line 31 of the monetary survey in the IMF's *International Financial Statistics*; NBKA$ is foreign-currency assets of nonbanks (cross-border) held with BIS reporting banks; NBKL$ is foreign-currency liabilities of nonbanks (cross-border) to BIS reporting banks; and IB$ is international debt securities (bonds) outstanding, denominated in foreign currency.

Note that NFCA can be either negative (denoting a net liability position in foreign exchange) or positive (denoting a net asset position in foreign currency); a smaller negative figure for NFCA therefore denotes a smaller currency mismatch. When NFCA is negative (positive), a depreciation of the local currency will decrease (increase) net worth. In this book, we are mainly interested in crisis vulnerability, so we concentrate most of our attention on emerging economies with a negative foreign-currency mismatch.

Whereas data on nonbank exposures and international debt securities are collected by currency denomination, those on net foreign assets (as consolidated in the Fund's monetary survey) are not. As such, one has to assume that both foreign assets and liabilities are denominated exclusively in foreign currency; this will tend to overstate foreign-currency liabilities for those few emerging economies with relatively low shares of foreign currency in external liabilities (e.g., the Czech Republic, Poland, and South Africa). A second shortcoming of the data is the limited coverage of the foreign assets of corporations and households. The BIS statistics pick up some assets held with banks abroad, but there are reasons to expect that foreign-currency assets held abroad by corporations and households exceed those figures.

Next, the foreign-currency share of total debt (FC%TD) is written as follows:

$$FC\%TD = \frac{NBKL\$ + BKL\$ + DCP\$ + IB\$ + DB\$}{NBKL + BKL + DCP + IB + DB} \tag{2}$$

Here, the suffix "\$" refers to debt denominated in foreign currency, and NBKL is liabilities of nonbanks (cross-border) to BIS reporting banks, in all currencies; BKL is liabilities of banks (cross-border) to BIS reporting banks, in all currencies; DCP is domestic credit to the private sector, as reported in line 32 of the monetary survey in the IMF's *International Financial Statistics*; IB is international debt securities (bonds) outstanding, in all currencies; and DB is domestic debt securities (bonds) outstanding, in all currencies.

In the baseline calculations, all domestic bonds and domestic bank loans (domestic credit) are assumed to be denominated in domestic currency—that is, (DB\$/DB) and (DCP\$/DCP) = 0. FC%TD must fall between zero and plus one.

Finally, let us denote the country's exports and imports of goods and services as XGS and MGS, respectively. These trade variables are a proxy for the response of net-interest income flows to a change in the exchange rate and for the country's ability to service foreign-currency debts.

These elements can be combined to construct an overall currency mismatch variable. Since we have not proposed a formal model of mismatch, the choice of a specific functional form is to some extent arbitrary, in particular the weights attached to each element. One possibility is simply to multiply the elements (NFCA, FC%TD, XGS, and MGS). Accordingly, we define the AECM measure as follows:

$$AECM = (NFCA/XGS) (FC\%TD); AECM < 0 \qquad (3a)$$

Equation (3a) says that an emerging economy's (negative) AECM will be lower if its export receipts are higher and the share of foreign currency in total debt financing is lower. Observe also that equation (3a) is equivalent to expressing the effective mismatch as the product of the ratio of net foreign-currency assets to GDP, the ratio of GDP to exports, and the foreign-currency share of total debt, and is written as

$$AECM = (NFCA/GDP) (GDP/XGS) (FC\%TD) \qquad (4)$$

Equation (4) makes it clear that higher export openness (i.e., a low value for GDP/XGS) lowers the effective mismatch.

While equations (3a) and (4) are appropriate where the economy has a net liability position in foreign currency (AECM < 0), they need to be modified slightly when the economy has a net asset position (AECM > 0). When there is a net liability position, an exchange rate depreciation induces a negative "balance-sheet effect" (net worth falls) and a positive "competitive effect" (exports rise and imports fall); in other words, the competitive effect offsets the balance-sheet effect and makes the effective mismatch smaller. In contrast, when there is a net asset position in foreign currency, the balance-sheet effect (net worth rises) and the competitive effect (exports rise and imports fall) go in the same direction—that is, the competitive effect reinforces the balance-sheet effect and makes the mismatch larger. Replacing exports in equation (3a) with imports when AECM is positive recognizes the different implications of exports and imports for foreign exchange availability and allows an exchange rate–induced fall in imports to make the mismatch larger;[2] as such, when AECM is positive, the expression is written as

$$AECM = (NFCA/MGS) (FC\%TD); AECM > 0 \qquad (3b)$$

Tables 4.3 to 4.6 show for a group of emerging economies over the 1993–2002 period key components of the AECM, the effective mismatch indicator itself, and a modified version of the effective mismatch indicator that takes account both of the (estimated) share of foreign currency in domestic bank loans to the private sector and of the share of exchange rate–

---

2. This is in the same spirit of using the ratio of external debt to exports to track external debt sustainability, while using the ratio of international reserves to imports to track reserve adequacy.

Table 4.3 Net foreign-currency assets, 1994–2002
(billions of dollars)

Region/country	1994	1995	1996	1997	1998	1999	2000	2001	2002
Latin America[a]	−43.6	−51.1	−66.3	−85.5	−120.5	−131.7	−128.2	−169.8	−182.4
Argentina	−16.7	−24.6	−30.9	−41.2	−54.2	−62.6	−70.4	−103.9	−99.9
Brazil	4.0	6.6	−1.9	−25.4	−40.4	−47.1	−49.1	−64.2	−75.6
Chile	3.7	4.9	5.2	2.0	−0.3	1.3	0.5	−3.8	−6.6
Colombia	3.4	1.0	−1.4	−2.7	−4.4	−4.1	−3.0	−3.5	−4.4
Mexico	−54.2	−57.2	−63.9	−45.4	−46.3	−43.8	−34.6	−18.2	−19.4
Peru	7.0	6.6	8.4	6.8	6.1	6.2	7.9	8.1	8.3
Venezuela	9.2	11.6	18.3	20.4	18.8	18.3	20.4	15.6	15.3
Asia, large economies[a]	139.0	146.9	157.6	185.6	250.0	348.0	442.9	559.6	671.7
China	35.5	52.0	84.5	137.0	155.7	181.5	226.5	304.4	373.5
India	11.4	9.8	12.0	13.7	17.0	22.5	28.4	39.0	60.8
Korea	−3.2	−10.7	−36.8	−58.4	−23.9	16.4	45.0	52.8	46.7
Taiwan	95.3	95.9	97.9	93.3	101.3	127.6	143.0	163.3	190.7
Other Asia[a]	1.2	−13.1	−32.2	−78.0	−37.7	−5.3	5.3	20.1	28.4
Indonesia	−13.5	−14.0	−14.5	−27.8	−19.8	−11.5	−4.7	2.1	8.3
Malaysia	17.1	14.3	9.6	−4.5	8.9	16.1	13.3	12.9	7.9
Philippines	3.4	1.9	−3.8	−12.2	−9.1	−9.3	−11.6	−12.8	−14.6
Thailand	−5.8	−15.2	−23.5	−33.4	−17.8	−0.6	8.3	17.9	26.8
Central Europe[a]	0.7	16.8	18.6	18.2	25.4	28.4	31.4	39.5	39.4
Czech Republic	4.1	8.2	7.4	6.7	10.8	14.0	14.4	18.0	25.1
Hungary	−9.5	−6.2	−6.4	−6.8	−6.2	−4.9	−5.0	−2.3	−4.6
Poland	6.1	14.9	17.6	18.3	20.8	19.4	22.0	23.8	18.9
Russia	13.9	11.1	3.6	−15.0	−34.3	−21.4	1.4	11.0	16.4
Israel	6.0	6.4	9.3	13.6	16.4	15.4	15.9	14.3	14.1
Turkey	−12.3	−10.3	−11.5	−15.0	−19.0	−19.6	−37.2	−39.4	−46.2
South Africa	−10.6	−10.8	−13.4	−11.4	−12.4	−6.1	−5.8	−2.6	3.2

a. Sum of the countries shown.

Note: Net foreign-currency assets equal net foreign assets of the monetary authorities and deposit money banks, from line 31 of the monetary survey in the IMF's *International Financial Statistics* plus foreign-currency assets of nonbanks (cross-border) held with BIS reporting banks minus foreign-currency liabilities of nonbanks (cross-border) to BIS reporting banks plus international debt securities (bonds) outstanding, denominated in foreign currency; outstanding year-end positions shown.

Sources: IMF's *International Financial Statistics*, national sources, and Bank for International Settlements.

linked instruments in domestic public debt.[3] For purposes of comparison, table 4.8 provides Eichengreen, Hausmann, and Panizza's (2002) calculations of original sin ratios for the same countries.

A reassuring feature of the estimates of net foreign-currency assets, shown in table 4.3, is how large negative currency mismatches either lead

---

3. The time-series behavior of the export openness ratio is not shown, as it was presented earlier in table 3.2.

or are contemporaneous with currency and banking crises in this group of emerging economies. In this connection, we draw attention to the large negative net foreign-currency positions in Mexico in 1994–96, the Asian-crisis countries (Korea, Indonesia, Malaysia, the Philippines, and Thailand) in 1997–98, Russia in 1998, Argentina in 2001–02, Brazil in 2002, and Turkey in 2000–02. In terms of dollar values, the largest negative net foreign-currency position by far was Argentina's imbalance in 2001–02 (at around $100 billion); next in line were Brazil ($76 billion), Mexico ($64 billion), Korea ($58 billion), Turkey ($46 billion), Russia ($34 billion), Thailand ($33 billion), and Indonesia ($28 billion). It is also evident from table 4.3 that some emerging economies have had positive net foreign-currency positions consistently over the past decade and that some others—including all the Asian-crisis countries except for the Philippines—have turned negative net foreign-currency positions into positive ones. In 2002, China and Taiwan were the economies with the largest positive net foreign-currency positions (at $373 billion and $191 billion, respectively).

Table 4.4 gives our (baseline) estimates of the foreign-currency share of total debt, under the assumption that both domestic bank loans and domestic bonds are exclusively denominated in domestic currency. Several observations are in order. To begin with, the foreign-currency share of the total debt market is much lower virtually everywhere than the foreign-currency share of cross-border bank loans and international bonds (as represented, say, in original sin ratios). For the larger Asian emerging economies taken as a group (China, India, Korea, and Taiwan), the foreign-currency share of the total debt market is estimated to be less than 5 percent (in 2002). The second observation is that the foreign-currency share is much higher in Latin America than in the other emerging-market regions. Foreign-currency shares vary considerably within regional groups with, for example, Argentina's estimated foreign-currency share being higher than others in Latin America; the same could be said of Russia among European emerging economies and of the Philippines among the former Asian-crisis economies. As regards trends over time, table 4.4 suggests that the foreign-currency share has risen moderately (over the 1994–2002 period) in Latin America, fallen sharply in larger Asian emerging economies, and fallen less markedly in both the former Asian-crisis countries and Central Europe. Foreign-currency shares have increased notably in Argentina, Brazil, Chile, and the Philippines.

Table 4.5 presents the baseline AECM estimates. Since our estimates of the AECM "normalize" the nominal net foreign-currency asset positions for variations in both export openness and the foreign-currency share of total debt, they invite time-series and cross-country comparisons of currency mismatch. Going back again to the most prominent crisis episodes within our sample group, we observe that the size of the estimated currency mismatch is typically larger in the run-up to and espe-

Table 4.4   Foreign-currency share of total debt, 1994–2002
(percent)

Region/country	1994	1995	1996	1997	1998	1999	2000	2001	2002
Latin America[a]	**22.9**	**25.3**	**26.9**	**26.8**	**25.6**	**29.3**	**29.2**	**28.7**	**32.9**
Argentina	32.9	36.4	40.2	41.4	43.2	44.7	46.2	49.2	58.9
Brazil	15.1	15.8	16.6	17.1	14.3	18.4	19.6	19.0	23.7
Chile	17.8	17.3	18.7	22.8	23.3	23.7	22.7	24.4	26.8
Colombia	34.7	34.2	36.1	36.3	36.0	35.9	33.0	33.8	34.5
Mexico	26.8	39.4	46.3	40.5	44.4	40.1	37.0	33.9	33.8
Peru	38.6	40.5	44.0	38.7	34.5	29.2	26.3	23.1	24.6
Venezuela	44.6	38.7	44.5	47.4	48.3	48.4	41.6	38.4	47.9
Asia, large economies[a]	**10.2**	**10.6**	**11.4**	**12.1**	**9.0**	**7.3**	**6.2**	**5.5**	**4.8**
China	10.6	9.6	9.0	8.3	6.5	4.8	3.8	3.1	2.1
India	7.5	8.1	8.3	9.2	8.7	7.4	6.3	5.1	4.6
Korea	16.0	18.1	21.9	31.5	19.3	15.9	14.3	12.9	11.5
Taiwan	5.0	4.7	4.5	4.8	4.6	3.9	3.1	4.0	5.5
Other Asia[a]	**23.2**	**26.0**	**26.1**	**31.9**	**25.9**	**22.8**	**22.2**	**20.9**	**19.8**
Indonesia	33.0	32.6	32.9	46.7	42.9	33.1	32.0	28.9	22.5
Malaysia	13.9	13.8	14.6	19.8	17.7	16.9	15.8	15.9	18.2
Philippines	12.4	13.4	17.7	25.3	26.1	29.1	31.9	33.0	35.2
Thailand	26.4	32.8	32.5	35.2	23.3	18.8	17.9	15.7	12.7
Central Europe[a]	**19.2**	**19.6**	**18.0**	**19.5**	**19.2**	**20.1**	**19.8**	**18.0**	**16.9**
Czech Republic	11.5	13.7	14.2	16.8	14.2	13.5	13.5	15.1	13.0
Hungary	30.2	33.8	31.8	32.5	34.5	37.2	34.9	31.8	25.1
Poland	11.8	10.6	8.9	11.3	12.0	13.3	14.6	12.4	13.9
Russia	35.3	26.7	22.1	22.1	47.2	42.1	37.0	34.1	35.5
Israel	3.1	3.4	3.6	4.9	5.5	7.1	7.3	8.5	9.0
Turkey	40.6	35.6	33.0	33.5	31.2	31.2	31.4	24.6	22.9
South Africa	7.2	8.5	10.6	9.8	10.2	9.2	10.4	16.1	13.0

a. Calculated with aggregates of countries shown.

Note: See definition of foreign-currency share of total debt on page 43.

Sources: IMF's *International Financial Statistics*, national sources, and Bank for International Settlements.

cially during the crisis; again, see Mexico in 1994–96; Korea, Indonesia, Malaysia, the Philippines, and Thailand in 1996–98; Russia in 1997–99; Argentina in 1999–2002; Brazil in 2001–02; and Turkey in 2000–02. Comparing across crisis episodes, the effective mismatch in the recent Argentine crisis was by a factor of ten the largest one is our sample. Argentina's effective currency mismatch in 2001–02 was huge because the size of the net foreign-currency mismatch itself was so big relative to the size of the economy, because the foreign-currency share of total debt was significantly higher in Argentina than in other crisis episodes, and because its degree of export openness was low (particularly before 2002)

Table 4.5 Original AECM estimates, 1994–2002 (assuming zero foreign-currency share of domestic debt)

Region/country	1994	1995	1996	1997	1998	1999	2000	2001	2002	Foreign-currency share of total debt (2002)
Latin America										
Argentina	-28.40	-35.79	-43.80	-55.14	-75.09	-100.37	-104.42	-164.91	-207.88	58.90
Brazil	1.22	1.57	-0.60	-7.14	-9.87	-15.72	-14.99	-18.19	-25.14	23.70
Chile	4.56	4.52	4.45	1.86	-0.39	1.58	0.53	-3.99	-7.86	26.77
Colombia	7.07	1.76	-3.54	-6.20	-10.65	-9.37	-5.45	-6.96	-9.64	34.46
Mexico	-20.56	-25.90	-27.67	-15.14	-15.91	-11.90	-7.11	-3.60	-3.80	33.83
Peru	37.42	27.37	36.61	24.02	20.00	20.57	21.69	20.09	21.15	24.61
Venezuela	31.64	26.50	54.12	50.06	44.95	52.55	42.91	27.24	43.30	47.88
Asia, large economies										
China	3.37	3.70	4.95	6.95	6.16	4.59	3.48	3.48	2.42	2.10
India	2.56	1.77	2.21	2.49	2.71	2.69	2.61	2.93	3.84	4.56
Korea	-0.45	-1.31	-5.26	-11.09	-2.93	1.81	3.34	3.98	2.93	11.54
Taiwan	4.66	3.71	3.56	3.37	3.77	3.82	2.75	5.14	8.00	5.47
Other Asia										
Indonesia	-9.53	-8.61	-8.13	-21.57	-16.80	-7.65	-2.33	1.30	3.91	22.50
Malaysia	3.51	2.27	1.54	-0.96	2.34	3.57	2.23	2.39	1.56	18.18
Philippines	1.64	0.78	-1.98	-7.68	-6.95	-6.89	-8.80	-12.09	-13.42	35.15
Thailand	-2.71	-7.11	-10.68	-16.24	-6.29	-0.16	2.09	4.08	4.68	12.70
Central Europe										
Czech Republic	2.16	3.68	3.09	3.39	4.50	5.56	5.17	6.46	6.97	13.02
Hungary	-23.78	-10.65	-9.33	-8.75	-7.29	-5.87	-5.01	-1.90	-2.69	25.08
Poland	3.37	5.37	4.24	4.82	4.71	5.11	5.61	5.06	4.23	13.94
Russia	7.57	3.60	0.93	-3.23	-18.97	-10.58	0.80	5.16	7.07	35.46
Israel	0.51	0.54	0.77	1.59	2.24	2.40	2.22	2.51	2.66	8.98
Turkey	-17.91	-10.83	-9.68	-10.75	-12.17	-14.25	-24.37	-19.76	-20.17	22.87
South Africa	-2.55	-2.64	-4.00	-3.08	-3.70	-1.65	-1.65	-1.20	1.33	13.05

AECM = aggregate effective currency mismatch

Source: Authors' calculations.

relative to that in most other crises.[4] But the estimates in table 4.5 actually *understate* the size of the effective mismatch in Argentina in 2001–02 because the actual foreign-currency share of total debt is even higher than indicated by the estimates in the table. The next largest effective currency mismatches were those for the Mexican crisis, the Brazilian crisis (2002), and the Turkish crisis (2000)—all estimated to be roughly the same order of magnitude. Interestingly enough, effective currency mismatches during the Asian financial crisis are judged to have been significantly smaller (except in the case of Indonesia)—reflecting those countries' high export openness and relatively low foreign-currency share of total debt.[5] Korea's effective currency mismatch in 1997, for example, is estimated at less than half the size of those during the Mexican, Brazilian, and Turkish crises. In 2002, the largest effective currency mismatch was in Argentina, followed in descending order by Brazil, Turkey, and the Philippines.

In table 4.6, we revise our AECM estimates to reflect that domestic bank loans and domestic bonds are *not* exclusively denominated in domestic currency in all emerging economies. To get a fix on the share of foreign currency in domestic bank loans going to the private sector, we relied primarily on the estimates given in Reinhart, Rogoff, and Savastano (2003a); for those emerging economies not represented in that paper, we drew on the database in Arteta (2002, 2003). For China, Nicholas Lardy provided us with an estimate of the share of bank loans denominated in foreign currency which he put together from national sources. The five emerging economies in our sample with the highest share of foreign currency in domestic bank loans (1994–99 average) were Peru, Argentina, Turkey, Indonesia, and Hungary; among the economies with very low shares were Brazil, India, Taiwan, the Philippines, Venezuela, Malaysia, China, and Korea. To capture the share of foreign currency–linked instruments in domestic government debt, we again leaned on the estimates in Reinhart, Rogoff, and Savastano (2003a). Unfortunately, their estimates cover only 10 of the countries in our sample; still, the countries covered are generally considered to be the ones with the highest shares of linked

---

4. In some preliminary regression analysis, we found that, ceteris paribus, the *lower* the country's export openness, the higher the foreign-currency share of total debt. This is the opposite of what one would expect to find if there were good risk assessment in place. It is also opposite to what has been found in firm-level studies where firms that export tend to have a higher share of foreign-currency debt. This negative correlation between the foreign-currency share of debt and export openness is suggestive of economywide distortions (perhaps related to the currency regime and/or the official safety net) that create the wrong incentives for hedging currency risk.

5. In contrast, ratios of short-term external debt to reserves would suggest that the aggregate mismatch in some Asian-crisis countries (Korea) in 1997 was larger than recent mismatches in Latin America; this reflects, inter alia, the different nature of the two mismatch indicators, with short-term debt to reserves signaling near-term liquidity strains and the AECM signaling the severity of crises (contingent on a large change in the exchange rate).

Table 4.6　Modified AECM estimates, 1994–2002 (assuming nonzero foreign-currency share of domestic debt)

Region/country	1994	1995	1996	1997	1998	1999	2000	2001	2002	Foreign-currency share of total debt (2002)
Latin America										
Argentina	-69.74	-79.97	-89.64	-108.73	-143.77	-186.56	-189.33	-282.38	-309.58	87.71
Brazil	1.79	2.38	-0.90	-10.73	-15.72	-23.05	-21.44	-26.15	-32.84	30.95
Chile	7.05	7.08	6.74	2.61	-0.54	2.18	0.74	-5.45	-10.39	35.37
Colombia	8.65	2.16	-4.27	-7.44	-12.81	-11.20	-6.60	-8.36	-11.50	41.12
Mexico	-32.48	-34.32	-33.54	-18.91	-19.22	-14.56	-8.74	-4.50	-4.77	42.50
Peru	80.62	56.25	69.84	51.62	47.72	56.11	64.06	66.07	65.51	76.23
Venezuela	31.74	26.62	54.29	50.20	45.08	52.68	43.03	27.33	43.39	47.97
Asia, large economies										
China	4.88	5.52	7.55	10.87	10.61	9.03	7.65	8.71	8.08	7.01
India	2.56	1.77	2.21	2.49	2.71	2.69	2.61	2.93	3.84	4.56
Korea	-0.57	-1.59	-6.16	-12.36	-3.50	2.29	4.37	5.35	4.07	16.02
Taiwan	4.66	3.71	3.56	3.37	3.77	3.82	2.75	5.14	8.00	5.47
Other Asia										
Indonesia	-17.08	-15.49	-14.56	-30.92	-25.31	-13.61	-4.24	2.54	9.13	52.53
Malaysia	3.62	2.34	1.59	-0.98	2.39	3.65	2.29	2.45	1.60	18.59
Philippines	1.64	0.78	-1.98	-7.68	-6.95	-6.89	-8.80	-12.09	-13.42	35.15
Thailand	-3.73	-9.06	-13.65	-20.31	-8.95	-0.25	3.21	6.53	8.14	22.07
Central Europe										
Czech Republic	5.32	7.68	6.36	6.17	8.39	10.03	9.30	10.86	11.30	21.12
Hungary	-37.77	-15.86	-13.85	-12.81	-10.31	-7.82	-6.80	-2.68	-4.13	38.46
Poland	6.60	11.05	9.89	9.84	9.37	9.58	9.83	9.44	7.30	24.07
Russia	7.81	3.98	1.13	-4.06	-19.61	-11.07	0.84	5.38	7.38	37.04
Israel	2.28	2.23	3.13	5.03	6.52	6.15	5.74	6.00	6.01	20.30
Turkey	-26.52	-17.33	-16.21	-17.73	-21.05	-24.38	-41.70	-38.38	-41.32	46.84
South Africa	-3.01	-3.05	-4.53	-3.53	-4.25	-1.93	-1.89	-1.31	1.49	14.63

AECM = aggregate effective currency mismatch

Source: Authors' calculations.

50

debt. Where data on exchange rate–linked domestic public debt were missing, we assumed as a first approximation that the foreign-currency share was zero. The five emerging economies with the highest shares of exchange rate–linked domestic public debt were Argentina, Peru, Turkey, Brazil, and Russia; those with relatively low shares were China, Thailand, Venezuela, India, Korea, Malaysia, and South Africa.

As expected, the recognition of foreign-currency debt into both domestic credit and domestic bonds serves to increase our estimates of both the foreign-currency share of total debt and the size of the AECM—compare the entries in table 4.6 with those in tables 4.4 and 4.5. What is perhaps most interesting is the diversity of changes across countries from this modification in assumptions about the currency composition of domestic (bank and bond) debt. In three emerging economies (Argentina, Peru, and Indonesia), the new assumptions produce a new foreign-currency share of total debt that is equal to 50 percent or higher; indeed, in Argentina and Peru, that share rises to 88 and 76 percent, respectively, while in Indonesia it increases to 52 percent. With much higher foreign-currency shares, the AECM rises as well: in Argentina, the (peak) AECM climbs (in 2002) from 208 to 310 percent of exports, while in Indonesia, the (peak) AECM in 1998 advances from 17 to 25 percent of exports. The change in assumptions also has large consequences for Turkey: the foreign-currency share of total debt increases from 23 to 47 percent, and the (peak) AECM almost doubles in 2000 from 24 to 42 percent of exports. In sharp contrast, the change in assumptions produces very small changes in foreign-currency shares and AECMs in India, Korea, Malaysia, Taiwan, Venezuela, the Philippines, Russia, and South Africa. In the middle of the pack lie Brazil, Mexico, Chile, Hungary, and Thailand, where the rise in peak AECMs is moderate. And finally, in China, the Czech Republic, Poland, and Israel, the increases in foreign-currency shares and AECMs are large but start from a rather low level; these are also economies that have consistently run positive net foreign-currency positions over the 1994–2002 period.

Modification of AECM

The estimates in tables 4.5 and 4.6 represent in our view a significant improvement over what has been available heretofore on aggregate currency mismatch; nevertheless, our estimates of AECM should be regarded as only a "first pass" at what could be accomplished. They are based on data that are available for all larger countries, from IMF and BIS sources. National data sources will often be richer. In this connection, several alternative formulations of the AECM could be explored further, four of which are mentioned next.

First, we could attempt to incorporate cross-country and time-series variation in *leverage ratios* into our mismatch indicator. As discussed in

Table 4.7 Total debt as a percent of GDP, 1994–2002

Region/country	1994	1995	1996	1997	1998	1999	2000	2001	2002
Latin America[a]	**73.0**	**67.9**	**71.0**	**75.1**	**83.8**	**83.7**	**78.2**	**86.5**	**86.7**
Argentina	49.8	51.8	57.1	64.9	73.6	81.3	84.5	90.8	183.0
Brazil	84.3	75.7	84.2	91.7	110.4	118.3	107.6	136.2	118.2
Chile	124.3	115.3	115.3	124.9	130.6	139.4	142.1	155.1	162.4
Colombia	33.7	35.9	44.4	46.1	56.1	62.2	66.9	77.0	74.7
Mexico	81.6	78.2	64.5	61.9	56.5	56.7	50.3	50.6	51.6
Peru	17.4	19.1	21.0	29.4	33.6	41.2	40.1	41.5	39.3
Venezuela	58.3	44.4	38.4	35.8	36.7	36.9	35.4	40.3	50.5
Asia, large economies[a]	**114.0**	**110.8**	**117.3**	**112.6**	**146.3**	**150.9**	**150.4**	**159.1**	**181.7**
China	111.0	108.9	115.7	127.8	148.0	161.9	168.4	172.9	205.6
India	70.7	63.7	70.4	64.8	70.0	76.3	78.8	83.2	91.2
Korea	108.9	108.5	113.6	84.0	181.7	163.7	151.9	176.7	201.6
Taiwan	186.5	184.9	194.0	181.0	218.5	211.0	193.5	205.4	206.0
Other Asia[a]	**104.9**	**108.8**	**118.3**	**101.7**	**172.8**	**147.3**	**133.2**	**138.8**	**136.9**
Indonesia	66.6	67.7	71.7	55.7	119.8	92.8	78.0	76.2	75.5
Malaysia	168.6	176.3	199.8	172.2	238.3	225.0	220.9	238.4	236.7
Philippines	100.7	97.8	113.0	102.4	128.9	118.3	112.3	119.4	116.7
Thailand	120.7	127.3	133.6	120.4	201.3	177.7	150.7	153.7	158.4
Central Europe[a]	**90.0**	**81.6**	**77.5**	**75.8**	**83.5**	**81.9**	**81.9**	**86.4**	**98.5**
Czech Republic	94.0	96.2	91.5	91.8	109.9	107.3	108.2	104.3	114.9
Hungary	154.3	141.3	137.3	123.9	131.2	121.5	122.4	123.4	136.7
Poland	61.3	54.9	53.1	54.6	59.8	60.6	62.2	70.3	79.2
Russia	24.1	32.7	38.1	49.4	36.8	49.3	38.7	35.9	39.6
Israel	203.9	187.0	188.9	183.0	175.9	192.2	184.3	194.1	213.7
Turkey	50.9	50.1	56.2	60.3	69.9	84.5	98.7	150.3	134.1
South Africa	136.5	129.6	119.2	123.2	128.6	133.6	121.3	99.7	148.7

a. Calculated with aggregates of countries shown.

Note: Total debt is equal to liabilities of nonbanks (cross-border) to BIS reporting banks, in all currencies, plus international debt securities (bonds) outstanding, in all currencies, plus domestic debt securities (bonds) outstanding, in all currencies, plus domestic credit to the private sector, as reported in line 32 of the monetary survey in the IMF's *International Financial Statistics*. Outstanding year-end positions shown.

Sources: IMF's *International Financial Statistics*, national sources, and Bank for International Settlements.

appendix A, a more general equilibrium treatment of the sensitivity of net worth and net income to a change in the exchange rate would take on board the possibility that the shock causing the exchange rate to change (depreciate) might simultaneously affect (increase) the cost of borrowing. Similarly, the authorities might react to an exchange rate depreciation by increasing interest rates. In both cases, a high degree of leverage would alter the effects of a change in the exchange rate. One would also expect that, ceteris paribus, the larger the total debt relative to the size of the economy, the larger the effect of a currency mismatch in debt markets. Table 4.7 shows the ratio of total debt to GDP for our sample of emerging economies. It is evident that this debt ratio varies significantly across countries and within countries over time. In some initial experiments, we allowed the ratio of total debt to GDP to increase the mismatch indicator. The main results can be inferred from table 4.7. On a regional level, the relatively high leverage in Asian emerging economies tended to increase their AECMs vis-à-vis less-leveraged economies in Latin America, offsetting to some extent regional differences in mismatches attributable to differences in export openness. In Argentina, which has quite a low ratio of total debt to GDP, the leverage adjustment narrowed the gap between the peak mismatch and the rest of the field—for example, the leverage adjustment considerably raised Thailand's peak AECM (in 1997) and also those for Korea (in 1997) and Brazil (in 2000–02). In contrast, Russia's relatively low leverage ratio reduced its peak AECM. In Turkey, the increase in the total debt ratio over the 1994–2001 period contributed to the large aggregate currency mismatch in 2000–01. The pattern of aggregate effective mismatches increasing markedly remained in the run-up to and during financial crises.

Second, instead of using the *stocks* of bank loans and bonds as weights to derive the foreign-currency share of total debt, one could use financing *flows* to weight the various currency shares. This carries some attraction since the stocks of debt can sometimes produce a misleading impression of current financing opportunities—for example, when the domestic banking system is experiencing serious problems, new financing from banks may be close to zero or negative, even if the stock of bank loans outstanding is very large. Some simulations were done along these lines using the individual-country data on bond issues and new bank loans. More often than not (at least for the 1997–2002 period), the flow weights tended to produce somewhat lower foreign-currency shares of total debt and hence lower AECMs, but a disadvantage of the flow formulation was that the flows varied so much from year to year that they produced high (time-series) variability in the foreign-currency share of total debt—at least for those emerging economies where the foreign-currency share was quite different across the various financing components. Perhaps some combination of stock and flow weights may ultimately prove to be useful.

Yet a third scenario would employ a different weighting scheme (as between exports and GDP) to scale net foreign-currency assets. In this connection, it could be argued that for larger emerging economies, exports underestimate the share of tradables in GDP, and therefore a somewhat broader scaling variable would be appropriate to capture the sensitivity of noninterest flows to a change in the exchange rate. To cite one possibility, net foreign-currency assets could be scaled by giving exports a weight of two-thirds and GDP a weight of one-third.

Fourth, one could attempt to get a more comprehensive measure of foreign-currency assets and liabilities than is available from our definition of net foreign-currency assets in equation (1). For some emerging economies, debt owed to BIS reporting banks is significantly lower than total debt owed to foreigners; similarly, there are other foreign-currency debt flows, such as trade credit extended by nonfinancial corporations, that are not fully covered in our formulation of net foreign-currency assets. One could obtain a more comprehensive measure by deriving a currency-weighted transformation of a country's net international investment position (NIIP). The problem is that the NIIP data show only liabilities/assets vis-à-vis nonresidents—not assets and liabilities broken down by currency of denomination. Hence, assumptions about the currency composition of each broad component of the external balance sheet would have to be made in order to derive an estimate of the aggregate currency mismatch. Where available, data on the currency composition of external bond and banking flows and benchmarks from portfolio surveys could be used to inform such estimates. Once each major component of the NIIP is assigned a currency denomination, a weighted average estimate of the aggregate currency mismatch could be derived (where the weights are the value of each component in total foreign assets or total foreign liabilities). According to Allen et al. (2002), 78 countries now include their NIIPs in their submissions to the IMF's *International Financial Statistics*; from mid-2002 on, all countries that subscribe to the Fund's Special Data Dissemination Standard are expected to disseminate their NIIPs and publish quarterly external debt data. In summary, the use of NIIP data can provide a valuable cross-check on the mismatch variable defined here. One reason such a cross-check is important is that there are major conceptual and statistical discrepancies between debtor-based statistics (usually the international investment position statistics) and creditor-based statistics (e.g., from BIS banking statistics). Efforts to examine and document such discrepancies are important.[6]

For purposes of comparison, table 4.8 presents the original sin ratios (calculated by Eichengreen, Hausmann, and Panizza 2002) for the same 22 emerging economies listed in most of the earlier tables.[7] Recall that when the foreign-currency shares of cross-border bank loans and international bonds are both one, the original sin ratio is also one. The results in table 4.8 and those in tables 4.5 and 4.6 paint utterly different pictures. In

---

6. For an exploration of this, see BIS (2002). The origin of this study was that the statistical authorities in some emerging markets noted striking differences between their estimates of external debt and the joint BIS-IMF-OECD-World Bank statistics on external debt, which were heavily based on creditor data sources. For an overview, see von Kleist (2002). The volume contains a comparison of the data for Chile, China, the Czech Republic, India, Latvia, Mexico, the Philippines, Poland, and Thailand.

7. We chose OSIN2 ratios from Eichengreen, Hausmann, and Panizza (2002) for table 4.7.

Table 4.8 Original sin ratio in emerging economies

Region/country	1993–98	1999–2001
Latin America		
Argentina	0.98	0.97
Brazil	1	1
Colombia	1	1
Mexico	1	1
Peru	1	1
Venezuela	1	1
Asia, large economies		
China	1	1
India	1	1
Korea	1	1
Taiwan	1	0.62
Other Asia		
Indonesia	0.94	0.98
Malaysia	0.99	1
Philippines	0.98	0.99
Thailand	0.98	0.87
Central Europe		
Czech Republic	0.88	0.84
Hungary	1	0.98
Poland	0.95	0.89
Russia	1	0.98
Israel	1	1
Turkey	1	1
South Africa	0.91	0.76

Source: OSIN2 ratios from Eichengreen, Hausmann, and Panizza (2002).

the original sin calculations, there is little suggestion either of large differences in aggregate currency mismatch across emerging economies or of sharp variations in these mismatches over time. These original sin ratios certainly don't hint that aggregate currency mismatches are larger in the run-up or during financial crises, and there is no indication that mismatches diminish in the recovery from the crisis.

Another difference is that the original sin calculations imply that debtor countries must have negative net foreign-currency positions, whereas our approach (as seen in tables 4.5 and 4.6) is consistent both with some emerging-market debtors running consistently positive net foreign-currency positions and with emerging economies switching from negative to positive positions (or vice versa). Consider, for example, an emerging economy with a negative NIIP (i.e., a debtor). Assume that the bulk of foreign liabilities is direct foreign investment denominated in the domestic currency. In that case, a net debtor might easily have a positive net foreign-currency position, especially if it had recently undergone a sharp increase in its holdings of international reserves.[8]

To conclude on the measurement issue, it is possible to do a lot better (than relying on original sin ratios) in measuring currency mismatches at the aggregate level. Our proposed indicator of aggregate effective currency mismatch—shown in tables 4.5 and 4.6—is an attempt to buttress that claim with some illustrative calculations. These estimates could be improved further with a moderate increase in resource costs (at the international financial institutions) devoted to measurement and monitoring of mismatches.

At the sectoral level, the lack of data on the corporate sector is the biggest hole in the data needed to measure and assess currency mismatches. Better data on corporate balance sheets would permit a fuller and more systematic analysis of sectoral currency exposures and vulnerabilities. We therefore argue that the collection of such data ought to merit high priority in efforts by the official sector to monitor and provide early warnings of currency and banking crises. Some promising efforts to bring mismatches in the corporate sector into clearer focus are already under way. For example, Mulder et al. (2002) used the Worldscope database to construct a ratio of corporate foreign debt to exports for 19 emerging economies and found that this currency mismatch variable was helpful in explaining both the probability and severity of currency crises over the 1991–99 period. In another example, Gray (2002) applied contingent claims analysis already so popular in the pricing of corporate default risk in the largest industrial countries to a growing set of emerging economies. One attraction of contingent claims analysis is that because it relies heavily on forward-looking price information (i.e., information on the value and volatility of equity and junior claims), it is relatively parsimonious in its data requirements for corporate balance sheets yet it can still generate estimates of the vulnerability of various sectors (including the corporate sector) to changes in the exchange rate. While Gray's (2002) analysis is currently available for only a handful of the larger emerging economies, it could be extended to a wider sample.

---

8. In their latest paper on original sin, Eichengreen, Hausmann, and Panizza (2003e) now acknowledge that a net debtor will have an aggregate currency mismatch when there is a net debt to foreigners *denominated in foreign currency* (emphasis added); previously, they had asserted (incorrectly) that "countries with original sin that have net foreign debt as developing countries are expected to have will have a currency mismatch on their national balance sheet" (Eichengreen, Hausmann, and Panizza 2002, 10). See appendix B.

5

Coping with Potential Currency Mismatches

If the vast majority of developing countries displayed a roughly equal susceptibility to currency mismatches, then it would be harder, ceteris paribus, to make the case that national policies and institutions matter a lot in controlling currency mismatches. Chapter 4 has shown that more reliable measures of aggregate currency mismatch indicate that such mismatches differ substantially both across countries and over time. This chapter presents complementary evidence that there is significant differentiation—a "tiering" if you will—among emerging economies in their capacity to cope with potential currency mismatches, as revealed in the liquidity and maturity of their foreign exchange, bond, and derivatives markets.[1]

Table 5.1, taken from the 1998 and 2001 BIS triennial surveys of foreign exchange and derivatives market activity, shows foreign exchange turnover for emerging economies (where this turnover is the sum of spot transactions, forwards, and foreign exchange swaps). Trading in local currencies of emerging economies accounted for 4.5 percent of global foreign exchange activity in 2001, up from 3.1 percent in 1998. In 2001, the

---

1. In contrast, the original sin hypothesis (OSH) emphasizes the roughly equal susceptibility of the vast majority of developing countries to original sin (since their original sin ratios are very similar). Although Eichengreen, Hausmann, and Panizza (2002) find that about a half dozen emerging economies (the Czech Republic, Poland, South Africa, Hong Kong, Taiwan, and Singapore) have much lower degrees of original sin than the average, they point out that nonresidents, and especially international financial institutions, have been the dominant issuers of domestic-currency debt in these countries, and that this issuance pattern occurs because the markets value the ability to separate currency and credit risk.

Table 5.1 Foreign exchange turnover (daily averages in millions of dollars)

Currency	1998 (reported by residents of the country of issue[a])	2001 (reported by dealers in the country of issue[a])	2001 (reported by dealers outside the country of issue[a])	2001 (total)
Latin America				
Argentine peso	2,131	n.a.	n.a.	n.a.
Brazilian real	3,418	4,612	627	5,239
Chilean peso	1,212	2,282	n.a.	2,282
Colombian peso	n.a.	371	n.a.	371
Mexican peso	6,961	5,888	4,198	10,086
Peruvian sol	n.a.	203	n.a.	203
Asia				
Hong Kong dollar	14,833	19,016	8,365	27,381
Indian rupee	1,337	2,762	78	2,840
Korean won	2,288	7,916	1,841	9,757
Taiwan dollar	1,658	2,609	558	3,167
Indonesian rupiah	850	535	17	552
Malaysian ringgit	579	923	n.a.	923
Philippine peso	408	455	47	502
Singapore dollar	16,819	9,841	3,045	12,886
Thai baht	2,123	1,274	585	1,859
Central Europe				
Czech koruna	4,169	1,135	1,099	2,234
Hungarian forint	528	173	24	197
Polish zloty	910	3,376	2,949	6,325
Russian rouble	4,519	4,158	124	4,282
Israeli shekel	n.a.	506	n.a.	506
Turkish lira	n.a.	231	202	433
Saudi Arabian riyal	1,235	840	n.a.	840
South African rand	6,087	6,846	4,481	11,327
Memorandum:				
Australian dollar	19,638	20,076	29,577	49,653
Swedish krona	4,847	11,466	18,680	30,146
Swiss franc	21,748	17,767	53,286	71,053
Total[b]	1,429,284	634,650	538,416	1,173,066

n.a. = not available

a. Including local and cross-border transactions.

b. Since two currencies are involved in each transaction, the sum of transactions in all individual currencies would come to twice the total reported turnover.

Note: Figures are daily averages during April; the sum of spot, forwards, and foreign exchange swaps, adjusted for local and cross-border double counting.

Source: Bank for International Settlements, Triennial Central Bank Survey of Foreign Exchange and Derivatives Market Activity in 2001, March 2002.

Hong Kong dollar was the emerging-market currency with the largest turnover, followed by the Singapore dollar, the South African rand, the Mexican peso, the Korean won, and the Brazilian real. The ordinal ranking by the geographical location of market turnover (instead of turnover by currency) among emerging economies would be similar, although not identical (e.g., Singapore then replaces Hong Kong at the top of the list). Note from column 4 of table 5.1 that turnover in, say, the five most liquid emerging economies is 10 to 30 times greater than that in the least liquid markets (e.g., Colombia, Turkey, Peru, the Philippines, and Saudi Arabia).[2] If one concentrated only on currency derivatives, then a recent IMF (2003a) report indicates that Singapore (followed by Hong Kong) has the largest market among Asian emerging economies, that Mexico and Brazil lead the pack in Latin America, and that South Africa is preeminent among the other emerging economies (including Eastern Europe). Once again, cross-country differences within the emerging-market bloc are marked with, for example, the notional outstanding amounts of over-the-counter currency derivatives (at end-June 2001) being over 20 times greater in Singapore than in Malaysia. Observe also (as indicated in the bottom three rows of table 5.1) that even the most liquid of foreign exchange markets among emerging economies still fall short of what is available in the smaller industrial countries (e.g., Australia, Sweden, and Switzerland)—to say nothing about comparisons with the reserve-currency countries.

Two other qualitative conclusions also emerge from the BIS surveys: the more liquid the foreign exchange market, (i) the higher the share traded in the derivatives market relative to the spot market and (ii) the more sizable the share of trading activity undertaken outside the home market.

Again, bond markets also need to be taken into account because interest rate products can be used to hedge currency risk, because local currency–denominated bond markets create a natural demand for hedging currency risk, and because domestic local currency–denominated bond markets provide a source of local-currency finance that would otherwise be smaller if emerging-market borrowers had recourse only to external lenders. Here, too, there are large differences across emerging economies in liquidity and size as well as in the availability of (fixed-income) derivatives.

If the liquidity of local bond markets were to be measured by trading volume, then, as shown in column 4 of table 5.2, Mexico, South Africa, and Brazil would be the most liquid markets, followed by Poland, Hong

---

2. One can also look at other measures of foreign exchange market liquidity, such as bid-ask spreads, spot/turnover, and turnover/trade; likewise, these measures throw up large cross-country differences among emerging economies.

Table 5.2   Top 10 countries in bond trading volume, 2001
(billions of dollars)

Country	All issues	Rank in 2001	Country	Local instruments	Rank in 2000
Mexico	1,111	2	Mexico	868	1
Brazil	721	1	South Africa	99	6
Argentina	384	3	Brazil	82	2
Russia	299	4	Poland	73	8
South Africa	131	6	Hong Kong	70	3
Venezuela	92	8	Taiwan	50	—
Poland	90	10	Singapore	49	9
Hong Kong	87	7	Argentina	40	5
Turkey	67	5	Hungary	29	—
Singapore	64	—	Russia	28	7

— indicates the country was not in the top 10 in 2000.

Source: Emerging Market Trading Association, 2002, Annual 2001 Debt Trading Volume: Supplementary Analysis.

Kong, Taiwan, Singapore, and Argentina.[3] Trading volume in Korea's local bond market is five times greater than that in Thailand; it is over three times greater in Poland than in Hungary and more than 75 times greater in Mexico than in Chile. According to the IMF (2002c), the deepest and most liquid fixed-income derivatives markets among emerging economies are in Singapore, Brazil, and South Africa, with Hong Kong and Korea next in line; in Brazil and Hong Kong, the interest rate swap market is in fact more liquid than the underlying cash market and, as such, carries out functions normally provided by the cash market (e.g., supplying a benchmark for other bond yields).

Alternatively, if one asks which emerging economies have the largest domestic bond markets relative to the size of their economies (i.e., relative to GDP in 2001), then, as shown in table 5.3, Malaysia, Israel, Korea, Brazil, Singapore, Turkey, and Chile lead the way. Whereas the local bond market accounted for 50 to 94 percent of GDP in these countries in 2001, the corresponding figure was less than 35 percent of GDP in Mexico, Poland, Argentina, China, India, and Hong Kong, among others.

This impression (from central-bank surveys and bond-market statistics) of very significant cross-country differences among emerging economies in hedging facilities was reinforced by interviews with about a dozen large institutional players from industrial countries that were heavily involved in trading emerging-market currencies, or in managing emerging-market mutual funds, or in writing derivative contracts on

---

3. If one were to look at liquidity in the total bond market (local plus international), then the ranking would be: Mexico, Brazil, Argentina, Russia, South Africa, Venezuela, Poland, Hong Kong, Turkey, and Singapore; see column 2 of table 5.2.

Table 5.3 Domestic debt securities outstanding, 1994–2002
(percent of GDP)

Country/region	1994	1995	1996	1997	1998	1999	2000	2001	2002
Latin America[a]	**18.0**	**17.6**	**19.4**	**21.8**	**24.2**	**27.5**	**26.8**	**31.4**	**27.1**
Argentina	11.6	10.0	10.7	11.7	13.4	15.0	16.5	13.9	17.8
Brazil	31.7	32.8	38.3	42.6	49.6	54.8	49.6	61.2	46.8
Chile	48.5	43.8	42.6	44.1	42.6	45.2	46.2	50.9	52.1
Colombia	4.7	5.3	6.8	7.8	10.0	13.5	17.8	22.1	21.8
Mexico	8.8	7.6	7.2	9.6	8.9	11.8	12.7	14.3	13.8
Peru	1.8	1.9	2.4	3.1	3.6	5.8	6.7	7.6	7.0
Venezuela	n.a.	n.a.	6.6	4.8	4.2	5.2	8.2	10.9	12.5
China	12.2	13.3	14.5	17.9	23.9	29.3	32.9	35.1	38.8
India	19.7	19.3	21.0	17.9	20.3	22.8	24.3	26.7	30.7
Korea	46.0	46.4	45.9	27.3	75.7	65.4	58.3	68.5	79.9
Taiwan	28.0	28.6	35.8	34.9	46.5	43.7	39.7	44.2	50.1
Hong Kong	12.5	16.8	21.5	23.7	24.1	26.5	25.8	26.8	28.0
Singapore	28.3	27.3	26.7	24.9	35.9	44.5	47.2	60.4	63.4
Other Asia[a]	**24.3**	**23.1**	**23.2**	**17.2**	**29.3**	**29.5**	**28.9**	**33.2**	**33.2**
Malaysia	72.0	70.2	72.5	56.9	85.4	83.9	83.7	94.1	87.7
Philippines	40.5	35.4	33.6	22.4	32.2	29.4	27.1	30.0	28.0
Thailand	9.6	9.3	9.6	6.3	21.1	25.7	25.4	31.3	37.3
Central Europe[a]	**21.8**	**21.5**	**21.4**	**20.9**	**25.1**	**26.1**	**27.4**	**30.7**	**38.8**
Czech Republic	17.6	23.2	21.4	23.5	39.3	45.4	45.5	45.0	61.6
Hungary	29.0	26.5	33.5	30.6	33.6	34.5	35.4	38.0	47.5
Poland	21.0	19.5	17.9	17.4	18.3	17.6	19.5	24.1	29.2
Russia	1.1	5.3	10.9	15.9	2.9	4.7	3.0	1.7	2.0
Israel	114.6	103.7	103.8	99.9	95.7	97.9	89.8	90.0	102.2
Turkey	12.2	12.6	14.6	15.7	18.7	23.3	27.4	58.2	50.1
South Africa	71.3	64.8	55.3	53.5	51.5	52.3	45.2	34.0	51.3
Total[a]	**22.6**	**22.6**	**24.1**	**23.4**	**30.6**	**32.5**	**32.0**	**36.6**	**38.3**
Memorandum:									
Australia	28.7	26.9	30.0	23.1	18.4	22.0	15.4	12.7	15.4
Sweden	106.9	109.1	103.7	97.4	100.7	94.7	82.3	73.2	85.8

n.a. = not available

a. Weighted average of the countries shown, based on 2000 GDP and PPP exchange rates.

Note: Data are by country of issuer; outstanding year-end positions.

Sources: Central banks, IMF's *International Financial Statistics*, national sources, and Bank for International Settlements.

emerging-market securities or currencies. Here it is sufficient to note (1) that the availability, liquidity, and maturity of hedging facilities were regarded as much better (e.g., currency swaps running out to ten years) for the Hong Kong dollar and the Singapore dollar than for, say, the Thai baht, the Philippine peso, the Indonesian rupiah, or the Malaysian ringgit;[4] (2) that in Latin America, hedging facilities were seen as being best for the Mexican peso and the Brazilian real (albeit not as good as for the Hong Kong and Singapore dollars), with the Chilean peso next in line (and with much more meager opportunities available for other currencies in the region); (3) that the market for South African rand offered a full spectrum of hedging products—ranging from swaps (up to 10 years in maturity) to outright forwards and options on money-market instruments—and local companies were able to issue rand-denominated debt even in difficult conditions; and (4) that among the larger transition economies slated for EU membership (Poland, the Czech Republic, and Hungary), hedging facilities were benefiting from capital inflows based on "convergence plays"[5] and, with continued progress over the next 3 to 5 years, could resemble what is currently available in South Africa, whereas in Russia and Turkey a history of instability and recent financial crises have limited the appetite for all but short-term hedging instruments.

To sum up, while the ability to hedge against currency risk is considerably lower for emerging economies as a group than for industrial countries, emerging economies are not all alike in this regard. There is already a top tier of emerging economies with relatively good hedging facilities (in foreign exchange and bond markets). Without pretending to too much precision, this top tier would include Hong Kong, Singapore, South Africa, Mexico, Korea, and Poland. Brazil, the Czech Republic, Chile, and Taiwan might be regarded as making up a second tier, and so on. In most of the smaller emerging economies, current hedging offerings remain quite limited. It should be recognized that in most of the developing world, experience with de facto floating exchange rate regimes is still relatively new and limited; as such, the development of hedging instruments and markets should be expected to gain pace as that experience accumulates.[6]

---

4. Market participants noted that liquidity for some of the Asian currencies was hampered because of considerable segmentation between the onshore and offshore markets.

5. A convergence play is a market position taken in the expectation that interest rates on high-yield securities will "converge" to those on lower-yielding ones, thereby generating capital gains for the purchaser of the high-yield securities.

6. It is noteworthy that some emerging economies in our top tier (Mexico and Korea) are not on the list of outliers to original sin; indeed, under the OSH, Mexico faces the same external currency mismatch as Peru or Colombia, and Korea's original sin ratio is higher than those of both Thailand and Indonesia—even though liquidity measures and interviews with market participants paint quite a different picture.

6

Role of National Macroeconomic Policies and Currency Regimes

Weaknesses in national macroeconomic policies and institutions lie at the heart of the currency mismatch problem. Evidence suggests that countries can make significant progress (over periods no longer than a decade) in reducing the extent of the mismatch when they adopt appropriate policies, institutions, and financial-market structures and create the right pattern of incentives to discourage currency mismatches.

In contrast, the authors of the original sin hypothesis (OSH) have not been optimistic about the contribution that better national policies and institutions can make to solving the currency mismatch problem because (1) many emerging economies with good policies and institutions suffer from original sin; (2) it would be too costly for emerging economies to wait for the very slow impact of better policies on original sin; and (3) diversification with fixed costs implies that the optimal international portfolio will contain only a small group of currencies, and hence emerging-economy latecomers will find it harder to be included in the portfolio. In the OSH authors' view, currency mismatch is inherently an "international" problem that requires an international solution.

This chapter focuses on macroeconomic policies: (1) the role of monetary policy and inflation performance in generating currency mismatches and impeding local bond market development; (2) the role of the currency regime in creating incentives to hedge against currency risk; (3) the role of fiscal policies/debt burdens in generating and overcoming currency mismatches; and (4) the role of debt and reserve management policies. The next chapter takes a closer look at microeconomic policies, notably the role of an institutional infrastructure that creates the appropriate incentives.

Monetary Policy and Inflation

Most analysts regard poor inflation performance and weak credibility for monetary policy as leading suspects in the currency mismatch problem.[1] After all, why should foreign and domestic investors be willing to lend (long-term) in domestic currency if they expect that monetary authorities in emerging economies will sometimes engineer bouts of high inflation to lower their real debt obligations? If that expectation is widespread, then lenders will insist on lending either in foreign currency or in domestic currency at short maturity or on inflation-indexed terms. We agree with the mainstream view: a wide body of evidence and country experience supports the proposition that poor inflation performance contributes significantly to currency mismatching.[2]

A recent study by John Burger and Francis Warnock (2002) strongly indicates that high and variable inflation matters for currency mismatching and bond market development in emerging economies. We give considerable weight to their findings because it is the first study to employ data on the total bond market (in 50 countries), not just data on international bonds. Burger and Warnock (2002) find that countries that have had higher or more variable inflation tend to issue more foreign currency–denominated debt, and this result remains when high-inflation outliers are removed from the sample. Similarly, when the size of the local currency–denominated bond market relative to GDP is the dependent variable, they find that countries with lower or less volatile inflation (and thus likely more stable monetary and fiscal policies) have better-developed bond markets. Burger and Warnock (2002, 19) sum up their empirical results as follows: "[T]he results . . . indicate an important role for past policies in the current state of both the development and currency composition of countries' bond markets." Carmen Reinhart, Kenneth Rogoff, and Miguel Savastano (2003a) build a domestic dollarization index for developing countries that combines data on the ratio of foreign-currency deposits to GDP with those on the share of domestic debt denominated in a foreign currency. They obtain results similar to those of Burger and Warnock (2002); in particular, they find that domestic dollarization is higher, the higher the probability that annual inflation will be at or above

---

1. See, for example, Jeanne (2001).

2. In contrast, Eichengreen, Hausmann, and Panizza (2002) have been rather skeptical about the monetary credibility explanation for currency mismatching because their cross-country regressions of original sin on inflation find only a weak effect for inflation once high-inflation outliers are dropped from the sample because inflation-indexed debt in domestic currency is relatively rare in international securities and because the monetary-manipulation story does not explain why corporations in emerging economies (who, unlike governments, do not hold the monetary reins) also seem to have trouble borrowing abroad in their own currency.

Table 6.1   Type of domestic debt at issuance, end-2000
(percent of total)

Region	Floating-rate	Fixed-rate	Inflation-indexed	Exchange rate–linked
Latin America	34	16	28	22
Asia	35	63	0	2
Central Europe and others[a]	13	65	20	2
Total	27	48	16	9

a. Includes Israel and Saudi Arabia.
Source: Turner (2002).

40 percent. Reinhart, Rogoff, and Savastano (2003a, 49) conclude: "Considering that dollarization is a form of indexation, it is not surprising that inflation history is the most important variable in explaining domestic dollarization." Gianni De Nicolo, Patrick Honohan, and Alan Ize (2003), examining cross-country differences in the dollarization of bank deposits, likewise find an important role for inflation performance, with their estimates implying that a doubling of inflation increases the dollarization share by about five percentage points.

Mohsin Khan, Abdelhak Senhadji, and Bruce Smith (2001) also find a strong link between financial depth and inflation, using a large cross-country sample for the 1960–99 period. They look at several measures of financial-market activity, including bank lending to the private sector, stock market capitalization and trading volume, and measures that aggregate bank lending and stock market activity and bank lending and stock and bond markets. For all these measures, they find that there are significant threshold effects, such that *when inflation rises above the threshold of 3 to 6 percent per year, there is a strong negative effect on financial development.*

High and variable inflation is likewise cited as one of the key factors in the lower access of developing countries (vis-à-vis industrial countries) to long-term finance. While the literature shows that information asymmetries, poor collateral law, weak judicial efficiency, and various firm characteristics (e.g., firm size and the maturity of firm assets) contribute to this lower access, we can only echo the judgment of Gerard Caprio and Patrick Honohan (2001, 49) that "there is nothing like inflation for stifling a long-term debt market."

Once account is taken of domestic bonds, the use of inflation-indexed bonds is not as limited as some (e.g., Eichengreen, Hausmann, and Panizza 2002) have suggested. As shown in table 6.1, inflation-indexed bonds represent about 16 percent of domestic bonds (at issuance) for emerging economies as a group. Also, consistent with the view that inflation matters, in Latin America (where earlier inflation excesses have been most marked), the shares of inflation-indexed and exchange rate–linked debt are higher, and the share of fixed-rate debt is lower than in other regions (particularly in emerging Asia, where control of inflation has historically been most successful).

There is then little reason to doubt that better inflation performance in emerging economies would greatly aid in building deeper local bond markets and thus reduce the extent of currency mismatches. Moreover, better inflation performance and greater financial depth should be mutually reinforcing: lower inflation would promote financial depth, and greater financial depth would nurture a domestic political constituency to resist manipulated inflation surprises.

Consequently, our action program includes a proposal that emerging economies adopt inflation targeting as their monetary policy framework. We follow others (e.g., Bernanke et al. 1999, Mishkin 2000, and Truman 2003) in describing inflation targeting as a monetary policy framework that constrains discretion on four counts: there is an institutional commitment to low inflation as a primary objective of monetary policy; a numerical target or range for inflation is publicly announced, along with a time schedule for meeting that target; the central bank is given "instrument independence"; and there are transparency and accountability guidelines for monetary policy such that the public is informed about the reasons for monetary policy decisions and about how far monetary policy objectives have been attained. Though the implementation of inflation targeting in emerging economies faces more formidable challenges than in industrial countries, and its history is too recent for definitive conclusions, the track record of inflation targeting in emerging economies has been quite good on the whole. Specifically, studies find that countries adopting inflation targeting have been relatively successful in meeting their announced inflation targets, that the record in meeting inflation targets has been much better than in meeting announced monetary growth targets, that countries adopting inflation targeting still allow monetary policy to respond to falls in output, and that inflation targeting has rarely been associated with a subsequent loss of fiscal prudence.[3] And the better monetary policy credibility becomes in emerging economies, the better the medium-term prospects for reducing currency mismatches.

Pursuit of an inflation targeting framework for monetary policy does not mean that an emerging economy would have to follow a complete hands-off policy with respect to exchange rate movements that it considers excessive. It could still make episodic use of sterilized exchange market intervention, and the exchange rate could also influence the timing of

---

3. See IMF (2001); Corbo, Moreno, and Schmidt-Hebbel (2001); Mishkin and Schmidt-Hebbel (2001); and Schaechter, Stone, and Zelmer (2000). Truman (2003) arrives at a more mixed verdict.

interest rate movements decided on domestic grounds. But a publicly announced exchange rate target or band would be ruled out.

Currency Regime

The currency regime is another factor often put forward as generating currency mismatch. The traditional argument is that fixed exchange rates make market participants complacent about currency risk, with little incentive to hedge.[4] Supporters of the OSH reject this proposition as well as its policy implication that movement to a more flexible currency regime would reduce exposures to currency risk. They argue instead that the higher exchange rate volatility associated with floating rates means that hedging will be more expensive; hence, there will be less of it under floating rates than under fixed rates. In addition, Barry Eichengreen, Ricardo Hausmann, and Ugo Panizza (2002) report that 22 of the 25 developing countries (in their sample) with the most flexible exchange rate regimes had very high levels of original sin. Once again, we reject the original sin argument and stress three arguments in favor of the traditional view that greater (de facto) exchange rate flexibility would reduce currency mismatching.

First, almost all the emerging-market currency crises of the past seven or eight years have involved officially announced exchange rate targets and, usually, little precrisis de facto movement of exchange rates. For example, Indonesia, Korea, Malaysia, and the Philippines kept their exchange rates within narrow bands in the two-year run-up to the Asian financial crisis. As such, there is little to suggest that market participants are made as aware of currency risk by fixed exchange rate regimes as they would have been if regularly reminded by short-term movements in the nominal exchange rate. Nor is there persuasive econometric evidence that currency mismatches tend to be lower under fixed-rate regimes. While Carlos Arteta (2002) found that currency mismatches in emerging-market banking systems have been greater under floating exchange rates than under fixed rates, we do not regard his conclusion as reliable because he was not able to control for the share of bank loans going to producers of nontradables (which can lead to indirect exposure to currency risk), or for off–balance sheet exposure of banks, or for regulations that limit the net open position

---

4. Accounting rules can also compound this problem. Estimates of annual debt service charges on dollar debt may include the dollar interest payments due but not the capital losses due to currency depreciation. Hence a borrower with dollar debt appears to "pay" less debt service than an equally indebted borrower with local-currency debt. In many cases, borrowers—governments as much as corporations—are not required to report the impact of currency movements on the local-currency value of foreign-currency debt. Such misreporting of underlying exposures undermines market discipline.

of banks.[5] A recent IMF (2003) study on financial stability in dollarized economies concluded that the main source of currency risk for banks in highly dollarized economies was the exposed position of their borrowers; the same study also reported, for example, that the share of total dollar loans granted to borrowers in the nontradables sector reached, in mid-2002, over two-thirds in Bolivia, 50 percent in Costa Rica, 60 percent in Peru, and 80 percent in Paraguay. We likewise do not attach much weight to Eichengreen, Hausmann, and Panizza's (2002) finding that the vast majority of emerging economies with floating-rate regimes had high levels of original sin because, as argued earlier, original sin is not a good measure of currency mismatch. In the end, we agree with Max Corden (2002) who, after reviewing case studies of currency crises in Asia, Latin America, and Europe, concludes that the unhedged foreign currency–borrowing problem tends to be much worse under fixed but adjustable currency regimes than under floating rates.

Second, in cases where emerging economies have moved from fixed to floating exchange rate regimes, behavior toward currency risk seems to change for the better. A leading case in point is Mexico, which was forced off its peg in late 1994 and has since run a managed float. Using a large sample of firms listed on the Mexican stock exchange, Lorenza Martinez and Alejandro Werner (2001) report that while firm size was the main determinant of dollar debt during the fixed-rate period, exports became the key explanatory variable during the floating-rate period, as the composition of foreign-currency debt shifted toward borrowers better able to service that debt. They conclude that "Under a predetermined exchange rate regime, firms will not fully internalise their exchange rate risk, and they will be more likely to engage in balance-sheet mismatches than under a floating rate regime." Looking at 400 nonfinancial firms in five Latin American countries, Hoyt Bleakley and Kevin Cowan (2002) find similarly that, ceteris paribus, the share of foreign-currency debt is higher for firms producing tradables than for those producing nontradables, suggesting that there is a natural incentive to hedge so long as government intervention does not distort that incentive (either in the exchange market itself or in the implementation of the official safety net). Using the same database (as in Bleakley and Cowan 2002), Cowan (2003) reports in a recent paper that the share of dollar debt is higher in periods when the exchange rate is less volatile. Going in the same direction, growth in derivatives markets—be it in industrial countries or in emerg-

---

5. Banks face indirect currency exposure from the currency exposure of clients with large currency mismatches. A large depreciation can lead to widespread insolvencies of corporate clients with large currency mismatches, leading to large loan delinquencies to banks. Thus, even if the currency composition of bank deposits is equal to the currency composition of bank loans (i.e., no direct currency mismatch), there can be substantial *indirect* currency risk. We prefer to define currency risk in terms of sensitivity of net worth to changes in the exchange rate because it captures indirect as well as direct exposure to exchange rate changes.

ing economies—usually takes off when actual or prospective volatility in exchange rates or interest rates increases so much that market participants recognize that it is in their own interest to buy insurance against that volatility. With the exception of Hong Kong, all the emerging economies in our top tier of hedging facilities (Singapore, South Africa, Mexico, Korea, and Poland) now have floating—not fixed—exchange rate regimes.

Third, the "harder" the exchange rate peg, the more difficult it is likely to be for the authorities to introduce prudential measures against currency mismatching. For example, if the government pledges under its currency board arrangement that one peso is to be equal to one dollar for all time, then it may well find it awkward to argue simultaneously that its banks should be required to hold capital against a net open position in foreign exchange in case the peso depreciates against the dollar. An IMF (2003) report notes that two currency board countries (Argentina before its crisis and Bulgaria) formally excluded from their calculations of banks' open positions the positions in the currency to which the exchange rate was pegged.

To sum up, while we do not regard floating exchange rates as a sufficient precondition for controlling currency mismatching in emerging economies, it is surely pretty close to being a necessary condition; without it, efforts to limit currency mismatching will have to climb uphill. This is why our action program includes a currency regime of managed floating for those larger emerging economies that have significant involvement with private capital markets.

Fiscal Policies

The weaker a government's fiscal accounts, the greater will be its incentive to devalue or inflate in order to lower the real value of its obligations. We share the view that fiscal prudence and cautious levels of debt accumulation will aid efforts to reduce currency mismatching.[6] Indeed, experience with emerging-market debt problems suggests that neither national authorities nor international financial institutions have been conservative enough in gauging what constitutes a "sustainable" public debt ratio.[7]

---

6. The OSH rejects this view, finding little role for fiscal fundamentals in explaining cross-country differences in original sin. More specifically, Eichengreen, Hausmann, and Panizza (2002) report that neither the public debt to GDP ratio, nor the average fiscal deficit, nor the ratio of public debt to tax revenue, nor the principal components of these fiscal variables is associated with higher levels of original sin; in fact, if there is any relationship between the two, their empirical results suggest that countries with more original sin have less public indebtedness. They conclude: "Hence, we find no traction for fiscal interpretations of the causes of original sin" (2000, 21).

7. See Goldstein (2003) and Reinhart, Rogoff, and Savastano (2003b) for explanations of why the traditional framework for assessing public debt sustainability in emerging economies typically yields too optimistic an answer.

Reinhart, Rogoff, and Savastano (2003b) have recently undertaken a comprehensive empirical analysis of external and domestic borrowing, credit ratings, domestic dollarization, inflation, and debt restructuring in developing countries. Their results suggest a role for fiscal fundamentals, which is consistent with our view. They argue that the main reason behind the recurrent debt cycles in developing countries is not that they borrow too little but rather that they often borrow too much. They maintain that many developing countries suffer from "debt intolerance," which they define as a syndrome where weak institutional structures and a problematic political system make external borrowing a tempting device for developing-country governments to avoid hard decisions about spending and taxes. They measure debt intolerance as the ratio of the stock of external debt (scaled by GNP or exports) to an index of sovereign risk and find that there are large differences both between industrial and developing countries and between developing countries themselves in their measured debt intolerance. They show that debt repayment histories, debt levels, and the history of macroeconomic stability can explain cross-country differences in debt intolerance. While debt levels do not explain credit ratings for industrial countries, higher external debt ratios translate into lower credit ratings for developing countries.[8] They also find that higher debt levels and patchier credit histories are associated with higher levels of domestic dollarization in developing countries. They conclude (2003b, 4): "Debt intolerance can, of course, express itself in ways other than our core measure, including the maturity structure of a country's debt . . . as well as the currency composition of debt and degree of dollarization. . . . Indeed, both a short maturity structure and the degree of dollarization are factors that exacerbate a country's risk of a credit event. . . . Perhaps less well understood is that these risks are not due to 'original sin' but are in fact outcomes of a country's intolerance to repay its external and domestic debts."

In a historical study of how the United States, Canada, Australia, New Zealand, and South Africa overcame original sin, Michael Bordo, Christopher Meissner, and Angela Redish (2002) find that fiscal policies were anything but irrelevant. Their conclusion merits note: "[W]e consider the factors that may explain the evolution of the U.S. and the Dominions to a state free of original sin. The factors we emphasize for the

---

8. In their most recent paper, Eichengreen, Hausmann, and Panizza (2003d) dispute the empirical findings of Reinhart, Rogoff, and Savastano (2003b) on the link between credit ratings and debt burdens. They also argue that—contrary to the arguments made by Reinhart, Rogoff, and Savastano (2003b)—they never asserted that original sin was the only cause of debt intolerance. Much of the controversy here parallels that on original sin and currency mismatching, with the authors of the OSH claiming that the critics have misinterpreted their findings. Suffice it to say that we find the case made by Reinhart, Rogoff, and Savastano (2003b) more credible than the one made by Eichengreen, Hausmann, and Panizza (2003e).

common movements across the five countries include: sound fiscal institutions, credibility of monetary regimes, financial development, and big shocks such as the World Wars" (p. 4–5).

In summary, as the Asian financial crisis demonstrated, it is possible to get into serious currency mismatches even after following a path of fiscal rectitude. But this does not mean that sustained progress in controlling currency mismatches can be accomplished in an environment of irresponsible fiscal policies. The OSH dismisses the role of fiscal fundamentals because it looks at only one element (original sin) of currency mismatch. Once a broader view of currency mismatch is taken, including the degree of dollarization in the domestic financial system, sound fiscal policy becomes all the more important.

Debt and Reserve Management Policies

Prudent debt and reserve management policies are essential elements of a strategy to reduce currency mismatches. This section examines these two elements.

Debt Management

A government's decisions about the currency denomination of its own debt have a major impact on the degree of aggregate currency mismatch in an economy—especially in emerging markets where the government is often the largest borrower on capital markets. How should governments decide between issuing debt in domestic currency and issuing debt in foreign currency?

One approach is the balance-sheet perspective: the currency denomination of government liabilities depends on the currency denomination of government assets. New Zealand has attempted such an approach: government debt management is related to an overall government balance sheet, encompassing not just financial assets and debts but also physical assets (e.g., schools, roads, etc.) and future liabilities such as pensions (Anderson 1999). The logic of this approach is that borrowing aimed only at acquiring foreign-currency assets (e.g., official foreign exchange reserves and the exploitation of natural resources) should be denominated in foreign currency. Borrowing to finance local-currency assets (i.e., whose value is insensitive to exchange rate movements) should be in local currency. Since most public-sector investments are in the latter category, this argument would suggest that most government borrowing should be denominated in local currency. A related consideration is that the fact governments collect taxes in local currency (and often exempt exports from taxation) should further tilt the policy choice toward borrowing in local currency.

Another approach is to compare the macroeconomic consequences of different borrowing strategies. The main macroeconomic difference between domestic and foreign borrowing in the short term is that government borrowing locally pushes up domestic interest rates and so crowds out private-sector borrowing (perhaps forcing the private sector to borrow abroad). In the short term, foreign borrowing tends to avoid this crowding-out effect.[9] Over time, however, repayments rise, exerting a deflationary drag on the economy. Such a pattern of short-term benefits but long-term costs has tempted many governments to rely too heavily on foreign borrowing, and this has often made governments and their electorates too complacent about the size of fiscal deficits. Ensuring that the unpleasant consequences of heavy government borrowing are felt immediately (i.e., through higher domestic interest rates) may be more conducive to sober policymaking than resorting to devices such as foreign borrowing that postpone the pain.

A final point to remember is that, in a crisis, widening credit spreads and currency devaluation both tend to overshoot at the same time. In such circumstances, "cheap" foreign-currency debt can quickly become very expensive to service and refinance.

These considerations suggest that governments in many emerging-market countries should have, as a medium-term target, the objective of reducing reliance on foreign-currency debt. And, indeed, many did so in the late 1990s. Some comparative data shown in table 6.2 show that many governments in emerging markets do indeed rely mainly on domestic debt markets. A particularly notable example is that of India, which manages to finance a very large deficit entirely on domestic markets. In several other countries, however, there is still too much reliance on foreign-currency debt or on exchange rate–linked debt. Nevertheless, the *medium-term* objective of reducing foreign-currency debt does not necessarily determine *short-term* financing decisions, particularly when the exchange rate is very volatile. Very large exchange rate depreciation (often perceived as overshooting by the authorities) can create serious dilemmas for policymakers. Brazil's experience during 2001 when financial-market conditions were very difficult illustrates some of the issues involved. The Brazilian currency depreciated sharply during much of 2001 (about 40 percent from end-2000 to September 2001) and had the mechanical effect of increasing the share of outstanding foreign-currency debt in total debt. At the same time, the high yields on domestic paper made borrowing in domestic currency very expensive, and it seemed all the more expensive to those who believed the exchange rate had fallen too far and was likely to bounce back. A further consideration was that exchange rate volatility—and the prospect of further weaknesses—increased the private-sector demand for exchange rate

---

9. See Sokoler (2002) for an exposition of this argument.

Table 6.2 Outstanding government debt by type (original maturity), end-2001 (percent)

Country	Fixed-rate long-term[a]	Short-term[b]	Debt indexed to Inflation	Debt indexed to Exchange rate	Foreign-currency debt
Argentina	n.a.	n.a.	n.a.	n.a.	97.0
Brazil	3.9	42.0	7.9	20.4	25.5
Colombia	17.2	0.1	25.5	4.3	50.0
Mexico	28.2	40.5	2.2	0.0	29.0
Peru	2.0	2.0	11.0	n.a.	85.0
China	100.0	n.a.	n.a.	n.a.	n.a.
India	93.9	1.3	0.1	n.a.	4.7
Indonesia	12.1	17.2	15.8	2.7	52.2
Korea	74.7	0.4	n.a.	n.a.	24.9
Malaysia	80.0	3.0	n.a.	n.a.	16.7
Philippines	34.0	18.0	n.a.	n.a.	48.0
Singapore	24.1	66.0	n.a.	n.a.	n.a.
Thailand	57.5	7.1	n.a.	n.a.	35.5
Czech Republic	37.0	46.2	1.2	n.a.	n.a.
Hungary	36.4	33.3	1.6	n.a.	29.7
Poland	34.3	21.5	n.a.	n.a.	34.8
Russia	11.1	0.4	0.5	n.a.	88.0
Israel	22.2	4.3	47.0	3.0	23.5
South Africa	75.3	6.5	3.2	n.a.	15.0
Turkey	0.6	29.9	11.7	12.9	44.9

n.a. = not available

a. With a maturity longer than one year; maturity of one year or less classified as short-term.

b. Including debt indexed to short-term interest rates.

Source: Mohanty and Scatigna (2003).

hedges. In the event, the government decided to increase its issuance of dollar-linked notes, in effect allowing local companies to hedge. In this case, policymakers reacted to an exchange rate they believed to be significantly "wrong." If their judgment is vindicated, they can economize on financing costs.[10] But the inherent risks in such strategies, if the government's expectations prove wrong (e.g., the exchange rate falls further), argue for only sparing and limited use of foreign-currency borrowing.

---

10. The Brazilian real did indeed appreciate in the months that followed, appreciating by 17 percent against the dollar between October 2001 and March 2002. In retrospect, then, real-denominated borrowing during mid-2001 proved to be much more expensive than dollar-denominated borrowing. A similar story could be told for 2003—again the authorities were subsequently able to reduce reliance on foreign-currency borrowing (as of the time of writing in March 2004).

Increased Foreign Exchange Reserves?

Surveys of reserve managers suggest that one lesson drawn from the Asian crisis is that emerging-market countries need—in this new world of much greater capital mobility—to hold much larger reserves than previously thought. High levels of reserves can in effect reduce the risk of large or disruptive shifts in the exchange rate. The danger of course is that this can encourage borrowers to take on too much foreign-currency debt (see, e.g., Caballero and Krishnamurthy 2002). The main drift of this book, therefore, is that the first task of policymakers should be to ensure that the private sector manage and limit its own foreign-currency risk exposures. It was because such exposures were allowed to become excessive—partly because of implicit expectations of public-sector guarantees—that the Asian crisis was so severe.

Assuming that private-sector risk exposures are properly managed (and that government policies do not significantly distort such choices), governments will still have to decide how large their reserves should be. This depends on several factors. One key factor is the volatility of the real or financial economy—which is typically higher in emerging economies. Countries that operate a fixed-rate regime, or that are particularly vulnerable to exchange rate swings, may need even more liquidity. Countries with large current account deficits, undiversified exports, or that are vulnerable to contagion from weak neighbors may also need more conservative liquidity management policies. Some argue there is no objective way of calibrating the desired level of reserves: it may simply be necessary for developing countries to maintain reserves at a level that the market (and ratings agencies) perceives to be adequate in the circumstances. It is certainly clear that the level of reserves is a key element determining sovereign credit ratings.[11]

A simple rule of thumb (sometimes called the Guidotti Rule) is that usable foreign exchange reserves (including any available through contingent credit lines) should be sufficient to meet all repayments and interest on foreign debt falling due over the subsequent year.[12] This rule has the great advantage of simplicity but has two shortcomings. One is that it

---

11. A simple econometric test on the determinants of credit ratings reported in annex A of Hawkins and Turner (2000) found that the absolute value of the coefficient on foreign exchange reserves exceeded that of the coefficient on debt (suggesting that borrowing to build up reserves improved a country's credit rating), but that the difference is not statistically significant.

12. Pablo Guidotti proposed this rule in 1999. There are several versions of this rule, but the basic ideas are the same. An earlier measure used by Reddy (1997) combined two rules of thumb—he expressed India's reserves in terms of "months of payments for imports and debt service taken together" but also noted the need to supplement this statistic with other indicators.

does not take account of the current account deficit, but this fault can easily be remedied. The other is that it does not distinguish between different sorts of financial claims according to likely responses in a crisis. It could be argued that reserves should be related to some volatility-weighted aggregate of liabilities in order to quantify more precisely the exposure to sudden capital outflows. Liabilities that easily reverse might be thought to "require" higher reserves than more stable inflows—for example, foreign direct investment (FDI) and trade credit may be more stable than portfolio and bank flows. The complication with this approach, however, is that an investor who is "locked in" holding one asset (e.g., an FDI-type asset such as a factory) can easily take offsetting positions in other assets.

The benefits of building up larger foreign exchange reserves need to be balanced against the costs. It is important to analyze carefully the macroeconomic consequences of reserve accumulation. The opportunity cost of holding reserves is the alternative use of reserve assets. One possibility is that resources could have been invested in real domestic assets: in this light, the cost of reserves may be seen as the return on the domestic investment forgone. High rates of reserve accumulation in Asia since the Asian crisis can thus be viewed as the counterpart of a much-reduced rate of domestic investment. A second macroeconomic consideration is that a very large buildup of foreign exchange reserves is often associated with poor policies.

A different notion of the cost of reserves is the cost of policy mistakes that higher reserves either represent or make possible. High levels of reserves have often been the by-product of policies aimed at resisting currency appreciation—and this has sometimes impeded necessary adjustment or led to inflation. And it is not hard to point to cases where, at least in retrospect, larger reserves allowed flawed policies to be sustained longer and ultimately made them more costly.

Finally, there may be a certain "beggar-thy-neighbor" element lurking in the background. Foreign investors, lacking any firm basis to assess the adequacy of a country's reserves, may simply look at the level of reserves relative to that in comparable countries. If this is the case, it might become a significant problem for international economic policy: countries may be driven to "compete" with each other, and reserves might well rise to wasteful levels. This argues against any simple conclusion that "emerging markets need more foreign exchange reserves."

Nevertheless, it does seem clear that (1) countries with uncertain access to capital markets need higher levels of reserves than countries with a high credit standing, and (2) the "need" for reserves does need to take some account of the country's short-term foreign exchange liabilities even if simple, one-size-fits-all rules are not appropriate.

7

Role of Institutional Factors and Microeconomic Incentives

While institutional factors may not have the same proximate influence on currency mismatches as macroeconomic policies, dismissing their influence would be a mistake.[1] Institutional factors are important for three reasons. One, they govern the working of *microeconomic incentives*: mismatches often arise because government policies or the lack of effective market infrastructures distort private-sector decisions. Two, strong institutions increase the chances of *good macroeconomic and exchange rate policies* being adopted.[2] Three, strong institutions *nurture confidence.*[3] Confidence

---

1. Eichengreen, Hausmann, and Panizza (2002) consider the argument that investors might be reluctant to lend to governments and corporations where the institutions designed to enforce their claims are weak and where there is a significant danger of debt repudiation. But there too they find that original sin is not responsive to these national factors; specifically, they report that neither a measure of the rule of law nor an index of creditor rights is statistically significant in a regression explaining cross-country differences in original sin.

2. The IMF's (2003b) *World Economic Outlook* of April 2003 provides a very convincing survey showing there is by now a large body of empirical work that institutional factors such as the quality of governance (e.g., degree of corruption, political rights, and regulatory burdens), the legal protection and enforcement of property rights, and the limits placed on political leaders matter a good deal for the level of income per capita, economic growth, and the volatility of growth—especially among countries at a relatively early stage of economic development.

3. De Nicolo, Honohan, and Ize (2003), for example, report that cross-country differences in the degree of dollarization of bank deposits are significantly related to measures of institutional quality; as such, they argue that if emerging economies are to increase the attractiveness of financial contracting in the local currency, efforts to improve the institutional environment (e.g., enforcement of adequate legal rights for creditors, quality of accounting, political stability, and the overall quality of government) should be part of the reform agenda.

effects also influence the behavior of foreign investors in a crisis. For example, employing various indices of government and corporate transparency, Gelos and Wei (2002) find not only that emerging-market equity funds hold fewer assets in less transparent countries but also that "herding" among funds is less prevalent in more transparent economies. In addition, they conclude after controlling for other risk factors, that during the Asian and Russian crises, emerging-market funds withdrew more strongly from less transparent countries. La Porta, Lopez-de-Silanes, and Shleifer (1998) conclude that countries with less protection for minority shareholders have less developed equity markets and are more vulnerable to shocks.

One general conclusion should be emphasized at the outset. If governments "rescue" private institutions that have built up currency mismatches, then they must expect such imprudent behavior to recur. Of particular importance is the scope and generosity of the official safety net for financial institutions. When illiquidity in banks' foreign exchange exposure has been seen as posing systemic problems, the authorities (in both the industrial and the developing worlds) have frequently intervened. As noted in Hawkins and Turner (2000), generalized runs in the interbank market, as in Norway, Sweden, and Korea, led the monetary authorities to give access to their international reserves to banks to meet interbank liabilities denominated in foreign currency. In the 1980s, the Central Bank of Chile subsidized the rescheduling of banks' dollar-denominated liabilities after successive devaluations. During the Asian crisis, comprehensive government guarantees were also (eventually) offered to bank depositors and creditors in Thailand, Indonesia, and Korea. Alba et al. (1998) argue that the earlier generous public-sector bailouts in Thailand (1983–87), Malaysia (1985–88), and Indonesia (1994) probably encouraged risk taking in the financial sectors of the Asian-crisis countries in the 1990s. Reviewing the two decades leading up to the Asian financial crisis of 1997–98, Stephen Haggard (2000) details a long history of close relationships among governments, banks, and large corporations in the Asian-crisis countries, leading to a recurrent pattern of government bailouts of troubled financial (and sometimes nonfinancial) firms.

On the whole, official assistance to cushion widespread currency mismatching problems in the nonfinancial corporate sector has been less frequent but is hardly unknown. For example, in Mexico in the early 1980s (under the foreign exchange risk coverage trust fund known as FICORCA) and in Indonesia in the late 1990s (under the Indonesian Debt Restructuring Agency, INDRA), the government essentially assumed much of the foreign exchange risk (faced by corporations) to facilitate widespread restructuring of debt denominated in foreign currency (Hawkins and Turner 2000). More recently, there were selected episodes of government bailouts of nonfinancial corporations (with foreign exchange losses) in both Korea and Malaysia.

The presumption must be that currency mismatching would have been less frequent and less severe had private-sector borrowers believed that they would have to bear most of the consequences of poor currency risk management. The Financial Stability Forum (2000) came to a similar verdict when it concluded that implicit and explicit exchange rate guarantees provided by the authorities will tend to encourage excessive borrowing denominated in, or indexed to, foreign currencies. It is for these reasons that our action plan recommends that more emerging economies should make their official safety nets (for financial institutions) more "incentive compatible." This means ensuring that such safety nets include "prompt corrective action" and "least-cost resolution" features, and that activation of "too big to fail" measures requires explicit consent by a supermajority of the most senior economic officials—along the lines laid out in the Federal Deposit Insurance Corporation Improvement Act (FDICIA) of 1991 in the United States.

The following two sections explore two crucial elements of financial policy—development of bond markets and prudential oversight of financial institutions.

Bond Markets

The rapid development of bond markets in emerging economies in recent years was documented earlier in the book. Although developing bond markets has been an ostensible aim of policy in several countries for many years, certain shortcomings in implementation have meant that market liquidity has not developed as much as had been hoped. Part of the explanation is the lack of an adequate market infrastructure. This includes elements such as liquid money markets, a system of primary dealers obligated to provide two-way quotes, a repo market for government bonds, and the issuance of benchmark securities.[4] As these elements have been widely analyzed elsewhere, further elaboration here would be redundant.

There are, however, more fundamental impediments to liquid bond markets that deserve more attention than they have so far received. As Philip Turner (2003) has argued in greater detail, policies and practices (often seemingly unrelated) continue to stifle liquidity in bond markets:

Accounting rules that deter trading. In many countries, institutional investors are allowed to carry bonds on their balance sheets at historic cost irrespective of market price developments. This means that losses or gains are registered only on trading, so institutional investors tend to avoid trading because it makes the reported income and balance sheet

---

4. See, in particular, Haüsler, Matheison, and Roldos (2003); Mohanty (2002); Stebbing (1997); World Bank and IMF (2001).

more volatile. The absence of mark-to-market accounting therefore tends to inhibit trading in most markets.[5] Greater trading by pension or insurance funds in emerging markets should do much to develop better liquidity. Such long-term investors do not have the same need for liquidity as other participants in financial markets—banks, for example, have a constant need for liquidity—and therefore are especially well placed to trade by buying illiquid bonds that have become relatively cheap (thus earning the liquidity premium) and by selling highly liquid issues. Such activity could make bond markets as a whole much more liquid. The experience of several countries was that commercial banks became much more active traders in securities markets once they were required to mark at least parts of their portfolio to market. Institutional investors would respond in much the same way.

Fragmented issuance by official borrowers. One particular trap to avoid is that of issuing both government and central bank debt. If the government is issuing debt to finance a fiscal deficit, then the central bank should use government-issued paper. This would require careful coordination between the treasury and the central bank, which might have different interests. For instance, a central bank may want to issue bonds at a particular time or with particular characteristics, but the government might balk at this because such issuance competes with its own borrowing plans.[6] The failure to resolve differences between these two institutions often induces the central bank to issue its own paper—thus reducing the liquidity of the government-debt market.

As foreign exchange reserves rise sharply in Asia, and indeed the developing world more generally, the issue of the central banks' liabilities deserves more attention than it has so far received. The management of the central banks' balance sheet has far more significant consequences for financial markets now than when the public's holdings of bank notes were the single largest liability on the central banks' balance sheet. Aggregate foreign exchange reserves in emerging Asia (excluding the international financial centers Hong Kong and Singapore) now exceed aggregate domestic currency by more than $500 billion (figure 7.1). In some countries, reserves exceed domestic currency by several multiples (figure 7.2). In many countries, foreign exchange reserves have grown well above aggregate reserve money. Huge reserves on the asset side of a central bank's balance sheet mean that there is a large stock of liabilities on the other side. This in effect requires the creation of some form of domestic debt. Yet in many cases central banks actually create nonmarketable debt by simply absorbing the excess liquidity arising from foreign exchange inflows—that is, by taking (usually fixed-term) deposits from

---

5. For a summary of current mark-to-market practices, see Mohanty (2002, table 7).

6. For further development, see McCauley (2003).

Figure 7.1 Monetary authorities: Net foreign assets less currency held outside banks, 1990–2003

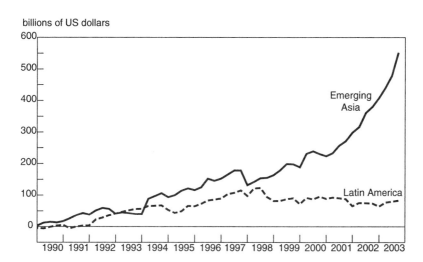

Source: IMF's *International Financial Statistics* and national sources.

the commercial banks. In some cases, commercial banks can be forced to make such deposits. A better alternative would be to issue marketable debt and thus deepen local debt markets.

Official attempts to stabilize bond markets. When faced with a sharp drop in bond prices, governments are often tempted to intervene. The justification usually given for this intervention is that "new" bond markets tend to be very unstable because market participants do not have a long history to guide their decisions. In such circumstances, expectations may be destabilizing: rather than increasing demand, a falling price may engender expectations of further falls. Preventing such extreme volatility by official intervention could reduce risk premiums and thus increase the underlying demand for bonds. These are strong arguments. But the danger with too much official intervention is that it impedes the development of the market for hedging instruments and reduces the incentive for financial firms to put in place proper risk management systems. It is important therefore that any such ad hoc intervention be subject to some form of constraint to ensure that the market determination of bond prices is preserved.[7]

A narrow investor base or captive market. Many see institutional investors such as insurance companies and pension funds as key to the development of debt markets because they need to hold long-term debt.

---

7. Reddy (2002) gives one example. Noting that the Reserve Bank of India deliberately moderates sharp movements in yields that could emerge in auctions, Reddy says that such policies are essentially an "intra-year smoothing process" and not an attempt to manipulate prices.

Figure 7.2 Net foreign assets of monetary authorities in selected emerging-market countries, 1995–2003 (percent of currency held outside banks)

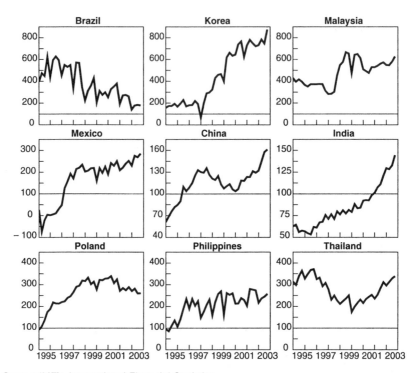

Source: IMF's *International Financial Statistics.*

Chile, which launched a funded pension system in 1981, is a classic example of pension fund development in emerging markets going hand in hand with bond market development.

However, governments should avoid forcing institutional investors to hold an excessive proportion of their assets in government bonds. In too many countries, these institutions under such compulsion just buy and hold until maturity virtually all the newly issued government bonds. This can undermine the creation of a true market in bonds and therefore deter other investors.

Prudential Oversight of Financial Institutions

Before considering the implications of currency mismatches for the prudential oversight of financial institutions, it is useful to consider first the underlying rationale for regulation. One rationale is that regulations are needed to counterbalance government policies that encourage market participants to run excessive foreign-currency risks. Such policies have been discussed throughout this book and are summarized below:

- *Overly managed exchange rate arrangements* make the private sector too complacent about exchange rate risk. The authorities often smooth short-term exchange rate movements even in countries with exchange rates that are "medium-term flexible" (i.e., where medium-term market trends are not resisted). Should the market turn against them, banks and other firms will often assume they will have time to cover their foreign exchange exposures because they know that the authorities will seek to limit how far the exchange rate can fall in any one day or any one week.

- *Bailouts of borrowers or lenders* who suffer huge losses after a substantial exchange rate depreciation—often motivated by a need to forestall a systemic threat to the banking system—almost inevitably distort incentives and create moral hazard risks.

- *Restrictions on hedging* of exchange rate risk by residents—often designed to buttress official management of the exchange rate—frequently lead to excessive private-sector exposures.

- *Taxation* of certain financial instruments inhibits the construction of efficient financial hedges.

- *Accounting rules* may allow borrowers to disguise the costs of foreign-currency borrowing. For instance, estimates of annual debt service charges on dollar debt may include the dollar interest payments due but not the capital losses due to currency depreciation. Hence a borrower with dollar debt appears to "pay" less debt service than an equally indebted borrower with local-currency debt. In many cases, borrowers—governments as much as corporations—are not required to report the impact of currency movements on the local-currency value of foreign-currency debt. Such misreporting of underlying exposures undermines market discipline.

The orthodox economic advice in such circumstances is of course that the first-best response is to correct such distortions. Such corrective measures would create the incentives for private players to limit their own currency mismatches. If all such distortions could be eliminated, and markets worked well, it could be argued that there would be no need for any specific prudential or regulatory response to currency mismatches. Only if such distortions cannot be eliminated is there a second-best case for direct regulation.

Most observers would accept this argument with respect to non-financial firms, at least in most industrial countries. But there are often greater distortions in emerging markets, some of which are hard to remove directly. In addition, emerging markets are much more exposed to large shocks. Hence there is probably a greater and wider need for regulation, at least initially.

With respect to banks, however, the case for regulatory intervention is altogether more compelling. Financial regulators have long recognized that currency mismatching by banks carries risks that could destabilize the financial system; that the "special role" of banks in the economy (e.g., as operators of the payment system, as major underwriters and purchasers of government bonds, and as suppliers of liquidity to fledgling securities markets) makes it harder to close a troubled bank; and that a regulatory "quid pro quo," which limits excessive risk taking, is necessary to balance lender-of-last-resort assistance. There is also a case—albeit admittedly weaker—for the regulation of financial institutions other than banks: the need to maintain confidence in local institutions and the strong interlinkages within the financial system normally dictate greater regulation of financial firms than of nonfinancial firms.

How extensive or intrusive such regulation should be is open to debate. In principle, the supervisory authorities could give banks a free hand in accepting foreign exchange exposures. Supervisory oversight could then be limited to ensuring that (1) regulatory capital requirements reflect the risks the bank is exposed to, (2) the banks have appropriate systems in place to monitor and control such exposures, and (3) transparent reporting exposes reckless risk-taking, subjecting it to market discipline. The system of regulatory oversight in most advanced economies is indeed moving in these directions, and supervisors in the developing world have much to learn from this experience.[8]

On the first point, a key reform would be to ensure that capital requirements more closely mirror underlying risks. In particular, borrowers with marked currency mismatches are worse credit risks than borrowers without such mismatches. This needs to be better reflected in regulatory capital than it is at present. On the second point, banks could be required to stress test their balance sheets for exchange rate changes—in particular allowing for the impact on off-balance sheet exposures in derivatives and other transactions. On the third point, it is clearly desirable that the quality of the corporate reports of financial institutions in emerging markets be improved. Of particular importance from the point of view of this study is the prompt, frequent, and accurate reporting of losses (and gains) from currency movements. Then the market can sanction reckless financial institutions and reward prudent ones.

In practice, however, financial-system regulation is usually more extensive than this model would suggest. The next part of this chapter reviews four main elements: regulations applying to lending institutions

---

8. For a further development of this argument, with particular reference to Basel II, see Neumann and Turner (2002).

in major financial centers, regulation of banks in borrowing countries, oversight of overall mismatches in the banking system, and regulation of other financial institutions. This review is not meant to be comprehensive but rather outlines the main issues that arise.

Regulation of Banks in Major Lending Centers

"There is no overborrowing without overlending." This catch-phrase has the virtue of focusing attention on the lender as well as the borrower.[9] Poor decisions by apparently sophisticated financial institutions in developed countries have often increased the vulnerability of developing countries to crisis. Large-scale, short-term, dollar-denominated lending has been one flagrant instance. This raises the question whether regulators in developed markets should do more to prevent or limit such activity by banks that are under their jurisdiction. The following paragraphs therefore review the regulation of banks in major lending centers.[10]

A few years ago Anne Krueger (2000) argued that regulators should indeed do more, and she put forward a simple but radical proposal.[11] She suggested that the G-7 countries pass and enforce legislation requiring their financial institutions to accept liabilities abroad only in the local currency of the borrower. The financial institution's resultant foreign exchange risk could then be hedged in international markets. Krueger (2000) believed that such a prudential measure would be effective because G-7 private financial institutions account for the bulk of external lending to emerging economies and because bank supervision in the G-7 countries should be up to the task at hand. The merit of this proposal is that strong, well-diversified private financial institutions in G-7 countries, along with their bank supervisors, are at present better placed to bear and oversee foreign exchange risk than are borrowers and bank supervisors in emerging economies.

However, we view this proposal as too draconian—to be adopted only if more market-oriented measures fail. A major drawback of a regulation that transferred currency risk to G-7 private lenders is that it would reduce the incentives for emerging economies to develop domestic bond

---

9. See Lamfalussy (2000) for a very lucid account of the major failures of international lending institutions, often the subject of high-level discussions at the BIS in which Lamfalussy participated for many years.

10. However, a word of warning is necessary about what is realistic to expect of supervisors in major international centers. An affiliate of a large international bank may be one of the biggest banks in a small country (i.e., it is very important for the host supervisor) but yet account for only a trivial percentage of the parent bank's balance sheet. Hence, the home supervisor of the international bank might regard its exposure in that country as immaterial and *therefore may not look too closely* at the risks involved.

11. She also put forward a proposal for local banks, which is discussed later.

markets and hedging instruments that would increase the domestic supply of local-currency finance. Such reforms within the emerging economies themselves are an essential part of the longer-term solution to the currency mismatch problem. In other words, the regulations in the G-7 countries would be a stopgap measure that would militate against an optimal medium-term solution.

Nevertheless, regulations in the major lending countries do merit a closer look because they may introduce distortions that bias lending decisions. In particular, they could in theory induce international banks to lend in the currency of the lending country (and thus avoid currency mismatches for the lending bank) instead of the currency of the borrowing country. How far specific regulations have such an effect is unclear because national practices vary widely. What follows next focuses on the broad outlines of the international regulatory framework—from the perspective of both the present Basel Accord and its proposed revision (Basel II).

The current international regulatory framework conditions lending by international banks to emerging markets by treating credit and market risks separately.[12] The existing credit risk framework does not distinguish between different corporate credit risks. In particular, it makes no distinction between lending in the borrower's own currency and lending in foreign currency (which can expose the borrower to a currency mismatch): both are regarded as being equivalent credit risks. Under the market risk framework, however, additional capital could be required for lending in the borrower's own currency because a capital charge of 8 percent would be levied on the overall net open foreign exchange position of the lending bank (Basel Committee 1996). If the bank is able to onlend local-currency borrowing (e.g., peso deposits as peso loans), or if it is able to lay off the foreign exchange exposure of new peso loans, then this loan would attract no additional capital charge for foreign exchange risk. In practice, an international bank would tend to book peso loans through local subsidiaries, which usually have some form of peso deposit base. As noted in chapter 3 (table 3.4), a major trend in recent years has indeed been the substitution of (usually dollar-denominated) cross-border lending of international banks with lending by subsidiaries. This allows for local-currency lending with no additional capital charge.

However, there will be many emerging-market currencies in which an international bank receives no "natural" deposits and against which it cannot find reasonably priced hedging instruments. Often all that is available locally to foreign banks is the local overnight interbank market—too risky a financing source for local lending. As most banks would not want a significant exposure in an emerging-market currency, they could in such circumstances refuse to lend in local currencies, insisting that bor-

---

12. This framework is based on the present Basel Accord, not on the proposed revision, which is currently under discussion.

rowers take only dollar loans. The regulatory capital charge for market risk reinforces this. Considering this capital charge in isolation, it could be argued then that emerging-market borrowers could be induced to accept currency mismatches when they borrow from international banks.

Credit Risk and Mismatches

Market risk cannot be considered in isolation because credit risk also enters the picture. Other things equal, a corporation with local-currency income but foreign-currency bank debt is a worse credit risk than a similar corporation with *both* income *and* bank debt denominated in the local currency.

The implication of all this is that a borrower that chooses dollar borrowing to cover local-currency business makes itself a worse credit risk. Borrowing in dollars may not be an important consideration for most industrial-country borrowers because the currency denomination of a loan would not normally be a key element of the borrower's credit risk profile. It might (or should?) send an adverse signal: a borrower that cannot afford to pay the interest on a local-currency loan could take a gamble on a dollar loan. For example, a US bank lending to a UK company would not *usually* perceive that the credit risk is any different between lending in US dollars or in pounds.[13] Credit risk would normally depend on other elements—the corporation's debt service ratio, the cyclicality of the industry, and so on. But the importance of the currency of denomination is far greater for emerging-market borrowers. One reason is that more borrowers have currency-mismatched debts. A second reason is that convertibility risk or transfer risk is significant. At the extreme, a country may simply prohibit its residents from paying their foreign-currency debts. A change in the exchange rate regime or any large devaluation can have virtually the same effect by making previously solvent borrowers insolvent. Such risks are not closely related to the health of the particular borrower but to more general country risk. Banks therefore incorporate country risk assessments in the decisions on lending to corporations in emerging markets. This may take the form of using a country's credit rating.

The importance of exchange rate–related credit risk means that a lending bank needs to know about the currency of denomination of the total portfolio of a customer. It is important to consider this currency dimension in countries that maintain a credit register that aggregates bank loans to each borrower.

However, just because a borrower with local-currency income but foreign-currency debt is a worse credit risk than one with an equivalent

---

13. The emphasis is on "usually": there have been cases when the currency of denomination was of relevant consideration.

amount of local-currency debt does not necessarily mean that lending risks differ at the margin (i.e., for new loans). Is the credit risk associated with a new foreign-currency loan to a given borrower greater than the credit risk associated with a local-currency loan? Views about this differ. One view is that the risk is identical because it depends only on the probability of default—in which case lenders in each currency lose equally.[14] The counterview is that the credit risk associated with a foreign-currency loan is greater. Major rating agencies appear to have begun taking such a view as they recently rated the local-currency debt of sovereigns above foreign-currency debt. The ability (and perhaps willingness) of countries to service debt in their own currencies is beyond doubt greater now, although quantification of this is difficult.[15] To the extent that banks' assessment of the convertibility risk of corporate loans depends on a country's credit rating, a similar currency-of-denomination differential might arise for corporate as well as sovereign borrowers.

Some international banks resolve the local/foreign-currency dilemma by, as a matter of policy, lending to all but the largest emerging-market borrowers only through their local subsidiary or branch. In many cases, they will offer loans only in local currency (to minimize both their customer's potential currency mismatch and their own exposure to transfer risk). Yet international banks report that customers often resist local-currency denomination of their loans because dollar loans are "cheaper" to service and permit greater leverage.

The proposed new Basel Accord should help stiffen banks' resolve by aligning capital requirements more closely to differences in credit risk. This means that a borrower that is highly leveraged with foreign-currency loans will be regarded as a worse credit risk and charged accordingly. The greater and more systematic use of default data should over time clarify the extent to which foreign-currency loans should be regarded as a worse credit risk than local-currency loans. The wider use of credit ratings in bank regulation will reinforce this. In short, then, regulators are likely to become more aware that the greater reliance on local-currency lending could reduce some of the risks facing international banks.[16]

---

14. It may not be so simple, however. It could be argued that the probability of default depends on the probability of devaluation. In a default after a massive currency devaluation, the dollar-denominated claims rise relative to local-currency claims. Hence, recovery values are higher for those who have lent dollars. See Aghion, Bacchetta, and Banerjee (2001).

15. Note, however, that this issue of the differential credit risk according to currency of denomination is controversial, and further theoretical clarification and empirical research are required. Packer (2003) shows that rating agencies differ sharply among themselves in the size of the rating differential across currency. Historical default data—which one uses to calculate an appropriate rating differential—are mainly from bank loans, and such data may not be a good guide.

16. Nevertheless, country or transfer risk will of course remain.

Regulation of Banks in Borrowing Countries

The regulation of foreign exchange exposures of banks in borrowing countries gradually became more comprehensive as internationalization proceeded. What form of regulation? Earlier, exchange controls drastically restricted access to foreign currency—usually only to those who needed foreign exchange for an approved purpose (usually trade). Virtually all local bank accounts were therefore denominated in the local currency. Loans were also denominated in local currency, so that there was no currency mismatch in the banking system. Over the years, however, exchange controls have become increasingly porous and have, in many cases, been dropped.

As exchange controls were eased, greater attention was given to prudential controls on banks. An early decision regulators needed to make was whether to allow residents to maintain accounts denominated in dollars (or other foreign currencies). Fearing that refusal would drive deposits offshore, many authorities allowed local banks to take dollar deposits from residents.[17] In some cases, governments (often via state banks) went even further and offered residents rates of interest on dollar deposits higher than obtainable on international markets. Such practices—subsidizing returns on dollar deposits—should be avoided in all but extreme circumstances.

Once the decision of taking local deposits is made banks and their regulators have to consider whether local- and foreign-currency deposits should be considered differently.[18] They also have to consider appropriate dollar-denominated assets to balance such dollar liabilities.[19] At the risk of some oversimplification, the supervisory authorities in various countries have used five types of regulatory rule/practice. The following sections outline such rules, pointing in particular to ways in which rules have been strengthened in recent years.

1. Limits on Net Foreign Exchange Positions

The most common rules limit the size of banks' net open positions. Banks' short or long positions in foreign exchange can be limited to a certain percentage of capital. Such exposures were traditionally defined in terms of

---

17. But some countries continued to prohibit banks from taking deposits from households.

18. The question of whether foreign- and local-currency loans represent different credit risks was discussed earlier. Broda and Levy Yeyati (2003) argue that peso and dollar claims are likely to be treated equally in the event of bank default. Where dollar deposits are the only source of default risks, it means that banks are induced to attract dollar deposits above the socially desirable level.

19. In some cases, it was a strong local demand for dollar-denominated bank loans that first induced banks to incur dollar-denominated liabilities (often interbank loans in international markets).

balance sheet ratios (usually supplemented by allowance for forward transactions) at a point in time. But underlying exposures can easily be hidden nowadays by the creative use of derivative instruments more complex than forward positions. Peter Garber (1998) shows how large-scale purchases by Mexican banks of tesobonos swaps and structured notes in 1994 permitted these banks to take leveraged long positions on the Mexican peso in the run-up to the crisis. According to accounting practices prevailing then (which did not cover off–balance sheet exposures), these derivative positions were booked as matched currency positions (involving both a dollar-denominated liability and a dollar-denominated asset); hence, they did not count against the prudential limit on banks' net open foreign exchange position (then, 15 percent of capital). When the peso plunged sharply at the end of 1994, however, these long positions on the peso saddled Mexican banks with huge losses and prompted a rush for cover—a process that drove the peso even lower. As the Mexican case study illustrates, when derivatives are involved, what one sees (about foreign exchange exposure) is not always what one gets.[20] In order to prevent such manipulation, *any* position in an asset or liability (whether cash or derivative) that increases its value measured in domestic currency when the currency depreciates should be considered as a long position in foreign exchange.[21] Provisions governing net open foreign exchange positions in emerging markets are summarized in table 7.1.

2. Limits on Foreign Exchange Liabilities

In addition to limits on net open positions, rules usually apply to the nature of gross assets. The first dimension is the proportion of dollar deposits to be invested in high-quality offshore and liquid markets (on which the bank can earn a retail/wholesale spread and possibly a yield curve spread) rather than onlent locally.[22] A safety-first policy would indicate that a high average proportion should be invested offshore, perhaps with specific liquidity requirements. Some form of marginal requirement could reinforce this—for example, sharp increases in dollar-denominated deposits, which often reflect increased nervousness about the exchange rate,

---

20. This example of Mexican banks purchasing tesobonos swaps and structured notes from international banks provides another case when nonresidents of emerging economies were willing to stand on the other side of hedging/speculative contracts.

21. O'Dogherty and Schwartz (2001) explain that the regulations in force in Mexico before the 1994–95 crisis took the form of static accounting valuations. Mexican banks were therefore able to circumvent regulatory limits on foreign exchange positions by holding structured notes denominated in pesos.

22. Rather different issues arise when banks invest in *low-quality* financial assets offshore; this is discussed below.

Table 7.1 Guidelines or regulations for currency mismatches in banks

Country	Nature of guidelines or regulations	Minimum for liquid foreign-currency assets[a]
Brazil	Consolidated net foreign capital cannot exceed 60 percent of total capital; capital requirement of 50 percent of total exposure for net positions exceeding 5 percent of capital	
Chile	Banks' foreign exchange mismatches cannot exceed 20 percent of core capital. Insurance companies and pension funds do not face any restrictions.	Demand: 19 percent; time: 14 percent
Colombia	Foreign exchange risk calculated by multiplying net positions by "highest possible variation of exchange rate."	No
Mexico	Open position is limited to 15 percent of Tier 1 capital. In addition, a rule limiting leverage in foreign currency: the difference between assets and liabilities denominated in foreign currency weighted by maturity cannot exceed 1.83 times Tier 1 capital.	Banks must keep liquid assets to cover the largest gap between liabilities and assets in four maturity bands: up to 1, 8, 30, and 60 days.
Peru	Banks must try to keep a balance between their foreign currency assets and liabilities. Banks' net currency foreign exchange positions are almost equivalent to their net worth.	20 percent
Venezuela		17 percent
China		Yes
Hong Kong	Aggregate net overnight open position (excluding HK$/US$) of domestic banks should normally not exceed 5 percent (some sophisticated banks are allowed up to 15 percent) of capital and any single currency should not exceed 10 percent against.	No; but need to state policy
India	Open position relative to capital is limited. Banks are required to adhere to the open position limit on a daily basis and allocate capital on the approved limit.	
Indonesia	Banks' overall position (defined as the sum of all long positions or the sum of all short positions, whichever is greater) should not exceed 20 percent of capital.	3 percent of foreign-currency cover
Korea	Banks' net open position should not exceed 20 percent of tier I capital.	

(table continues next page)

Table 7.1 Guidelines or regulations for currency mismatches in banks *(continued)*

Country	Nature of guidelines or regulations	Minimum for liquid foreign-currency assets[a]
Philippines	Banks must maintain 100 percent cover for their foreign exchange deposits, at least 70 percent of which must be in the same currency as the deposit. Long open foreign exchange position is limited to 5 percent of capital or $10 million, whichever is lower.	
Singapore	No limits on banks. For insurance companies, foreign-currency and overseas assets cannot exceed 30 percent of assets.	No
Thailand	Banks' net open position must not exceed 15 percent of Tier 1 capital.	No
Czech Republic	The net position in each currency not to exceed 15 percent (and total tonex position not to exceed 20 percent) of the bank's own funds	No
Hungary	Banks' net open position must not exceed 30 percent of capital.	
Poland	For banks, the limit on foreign exchange net open position is 15 percent of capital for an individual currency and 30 percent overall. For nonconvertible currencies these limits are 2.5 percent and 5 percent, respectively. There are no regulations on insurance funds. For insurance companies, the total value of assets in a single currency cannot exceed 5 percent (12 percent for euro).	No
Russia		No
Israel	Banks are subject to a directive consistent with Basel Committee recommendations.	Some reserve requirements
Saudi Arabia	No regulations, but banks run very tight open nondollar positions and higher net short positions against the dollar due to the fixed exchange rate regime and preference for dollar assets.	
South Africa		No

a. These data are usually expressed as a proportion of gross liabilities and are generally as reported in Hawkins and Turner (2000).

Note: This summary of guidelines was prepared in 2002 and is intended to be illustrative. The actual regulations are more complex and may have been revised since this table was prepared. In addition, some countries have complex rules that are difficult to summarize in a simple table.

Sources: Central banks.

could be subject to higher marginal requirements to redeposit offshore. Argentina's experience with such requirements is particularly instructive. A cornerstone of the currency board arrangement in that country was a high foreign liquidity requirement on the banks (20 percent of most banking liabilities). Only assets with a high credit quality were acceptable: they included highly rated foreign bonds and deposits with a major designated foreign bank in New York.[23] This provision helped the banks weather successive crises in the late 1990s. In early 2001, however, the Argentine government began to weaken this prudential requirement—by lowering the liquidity requirement and by replacing deposit accounts abroad with dollar accounts held with the central bank. These measures weakened the banking system.

A second dimension of such rules will often be specific guidelines about local-bank lending in foreign currency. Sometimes these are qualitative in nature—for instance, supervisory guidelines can allow foreign-currency lending only to those borrowers with foreign-currency earnings or assets. Or there could be a currency-denomination dimension to collateral requirements—for instance, foreign-currency loans could be secured only against foreign-currency assets such as export receivables.[24] Several central banks have recently required that the boards of directors at lending banks explicitly discuss foreign-currency exposures of corporate clients that exceed a certain size. Banks are required to ensure that their customers have effective hedging strategies. The Reserve Bank of India since November 2003 requires that "all foreign currency loans by banks above $10 million be extended only on the basis of a well laid out policy of the Board to ensure hedging."[25]

Sometimes such guidelines are quantitative. For instance, several authorities impose ceilings on liabilities a bank can hold in foreign currency in order to limit foreign currency–denominated lending to local borrowers. In Chile, banks are required to hold special reserves to cover lending to clients with large mismatches. Noting that crises in Mexico and Asia proved that "banks have a tendency to overestimate that ability of their

---

23. Allowing bank deposits rather than marketable instruments creates an additional monitoring need for the supervisors who will have to make sure that local banks do not conclude hidden arrangements allowing such deposits to be used as collateral for other business.

24. In practice, however, local-currency collateral is taken even for foreign-currency loans, which means that the collateralization needs to build in additional local-currency safeguards. One possibility is to apply a larger "haircut" to the collateral value of a local-currency asset. Another is to "remargin"—to require additional collateral as the exchange rate falls.

25. Except for trade finances, etc. See Reserve Bank of India (2003, 34–35) on unhedged foreign exchange exposures of corporates. This move was triggered as the combination of expectations of exchange rate appreciation and comparatively high rupee interest rates encouraged corporations to increase their dollar borrowing.

Table 7.2 Currency denomination of bank balance sheets
(percent denominated in foreign currency)

Region/country	Assets				Liabilities			
	1983	1993	2000	2002	1983	1993	2000	2002
East Asia								
Indonesia	n.a.	35.1	10.4	8.5	n.a.	36.4	9.4	4.9
Korea	5.1	4.1	5.9	4.5	12.6	3.9	4.3	6.9
Latin America								
Chile	41.6	19.7	24.1	25.8[a]	46.7	20.6	25.4	28.8[a]
Colombia	n.a.	13.0	6.5	n.a.	n.a.	11.1	7.5	n.a.
Mexico	41.7	26.7	18.1	15.0	47.2	28.2	17.8	14.5
Peru	35.0	76.3	82.0	78.9	44.0	69.0	70.0	65.3
Venezuela	7.0	12.2	4.5	6.4	9.3	3.5	0.1	0.1
Hungary	n.a.	28.8[b]	34.1	n.a.	n.a.	30.9[b]	34.2	n.a.
Israel	n.a.	36.1	30.4	33.1	n.a.	36.9	27.8	30.0
Russia	n.a.	29.0[c]	n.a.	n.a.	n.a.	25.1[c]	n.a.	n.a.
Saudi Arabia	12.3	25.6	22.3	18.8	21.5	29.1	14.2	8.5
Memorandum:								
United States	0.4	1.6	0.9	1.0	0.3	2.1	1.2	1.1
Japan	14.4	12.0	3.8	3.8	14.4	12.8	5.1	4.7
Germany	2.1	5.1	3.9	4.4	2.2	4.1	7.0	7.8
United Kingdom	90.6	69.7	53.3	52.6	93.2	70.7	48.0	49.0

n.a. = not available.

a. 2001 figure.
b. 1996 figure.
c. 1995 figure.

Sources: National sources and Bank for International Settlements statistics.

domestic borrowers to access foreign currency," O'Dogherty and Schwartz (2001) describe the regulations that the Bank of Mexico put in place after the Mexican crisis. One apparent consequence of this regulation (and of macroeconomic policies to lower inflation) has been a significant reduction in the degree of dollarization in banks' balance sheets in Mexico (table 7.2).

Balino, Bennett, and Borensztein (1999) report that a few developing countries set restrictions on foreign-currency loans to limit credit risk—by requiring that such loans only be extended either for trade-related purposes (e.g., Vietnam) or when the borrower can generate income in foreign currency. But in most cases foreign-currency loans are not restricted. This may suggest a need in several countries to tighten prudential oversight in this area.

3. Rules for Liquidity Risks

It cannot be emphasized too strongly that the management of liquidity risk is much more complex in a world of currency mismatches than it is in an environment where only the bank's local currency is used.[26] Even when a bank has its foreign-currency liabilities matched by foreign-currency assets, some of these assets (e.g., illiquid dollar-denominated bonds) may not be accessible "on short notice" to meet a depositor run or other unexpected shocks. Moreover, the consequences of mistakes in liquidity management can be much more dramatic because a bank in a developing country may not be able to borrow foreign currency in the event of a liquidity crisis. In addition, the strategy followed by commercial banks of combining short-term foreign-currency liabilities with long-term foreign-currency assets exposes them to an interest rate risk that must be managed.

The authorities need to oversee liquidity risk *both* in individual banks *and* in the banking system as a whole. Consider first liquidity risk in an individual bank. To address it, a bank needs to begin by constructing a "maturity ladder," so that it can calculate excesses or deficits at selected maturity dates—next day, next week, next month, next year. Such maturity ladders and other estimates of liquidity then need to be supplemented by various stress tests based on scenarios related to currency fluctuations. In particular, banks will need to allow for rapid changes in the liquidity profiles of assets and liabilities during a currency crisis. Increased expectations of currency depreciation—or just greater uncertainty—will induce borrowers to repay dollar loans and depositors to switch to dollar deposits—thus upsetting the bank's foreign-currency liquidity calculations. The key point to remember is that early action to maintain liquidity is essential because the closer a large liquidity gap gets, the more difficult it becomes to offset.

In principle, supervisors could be content with verifying that banks have proper liquidity management systems in place and ensuring that any official liquidity assistance (e.g., emergency central-bank financing) comes at a price. In practice, however, some form of direct regulation may need to support such measures. Supervisors in several emerging economies do require their banks to meet a menu of liquidity requirements across various maturities. Shorter-term liabilities typically incur higher liquid asset requirements.[27]

Consider next liquidity risk in the banking system as a whole. It would be very useful if bank supervisors or central banks were to aggregate the liquidity gap analysis of individual banks to construct maturity ladders for the whole economy. This analysis could then be stress tested for various exchange rate scenarios, which could give early warning of liquidity shortfalls at particular maturities and perhaps allow rules on individual banks to be tightened.

---

26. Further details of liquidity risk management are given in two short documents issued by the Basel Committee (see Basel Committee 1992, the updated Basel Committee 2000, and table 7.1).

27. Liquidity coefficients applied in major emerging-market countries are shown in Hawkins and Turner (1999).

4. Reserve Requirements

In principle, reserve requirements for foreign-currency deposits should be higher for dollar than for local-currency deposits—because the central bank cannot supply foreign currency as readily as domestic currency in times of stress. In practice, however, some countries set very low reserve requirements for foreign-currency deposits because they do not want to risk driving deposits to centers where reserve requirements are lower. In some countries (e.g., India), reserve requirements on foreign-currency deposits have been modified over time in line with the policy stance on capital flows.

The review by Balino, Bennett, and Borensztein (1999) of actual practices in 36 developing countries (as of end-1996) found that in only about 20 percent of the countries were reserve requirements higher for foreign-currency deposits; in two-thirds of the countries, they were usually set at the same rate as domestic-currency deposits, and in roughly one-seventh of the sample, they were actually lower than for domestic-currency deposits.

5. Limits on Banks' Holdings of Foreign Currency–Denominated Securities

In addition to earning a maturity spread, banks can choose to accept some credit risk by investing in paper issued by lower-rated borrowers. Banks in emerging markets are often particularly attracted to the high yields of international foreign-currency bonds issued by their governments. When sovereign debt spreads widen sharply, such debt becomes more attractive to local banks, which are already exposed to country risk through their holdings of local-currency bonds. As these banks tend to regard international and local bonds as equivalent credit risks, even though some would argue that greater risks normally attach to foreign-currency bonds, they tend to sell local-currency bonds to buy foreign-currency bonds. This means that a widening of spreads in international markets can in effect induce banks to increase the dollarization of their balance sheets, encouraging them to take dollar deposits from residents. Increased dollarization could make them more vulnerable in a crisis. For these reasons, limits are sometimes placed on local banks' holdings of foreign currency–denominated debt of their own government or other less-than-investment-grade issuers.

Will Prudential Rules Suffice?

The preceding discussion suggests that supervisors in emerging markets have many tools at their disposal to keep in check currency mismatches in their banking systems. Before leaving this topic, however, mention must be made of the view that the authorities in emerging markets go further and virtually prohibit foreign currency–denominated intermediation within the financial system. Some have argued in favor of such a step. Before becoming first deputy managing director of the IMF, Anne Krueger (2000) suggested that emerging economies consider making foreign-currency obligations incurred by domestic entities (residents and businesses) within their boundaries unenforceable in domestic courts. This would presumably transfer abroad more of the currency risk and would remove any implicit government guarantees to offshore borrowing. This proposal amounts to placing an implicit "tax" (i.e., nonenforceability of contracts) on foreign-currency obligations incurred by domestic entities. We would not support such a tax. The concern should not be with foreign-currency liabilities per se but rather with foreign-currency mismatches. If domestic entities in emerging economies balance their liability positions with foreign-currency assets, then the former should not lead to adverse consequences after an exchange rate change. Indeed, as noted elsewhere in this book, empirical research suggests that firms with foreign-currency revenues are more likely to incur foreign-currency liabilities than firms without such revenues. Policy measures should seek to encourage and spread the use of such "matching" measures. By taxing foreign-currency liabilities rather than the currency mismatch, the Krueger proposal could inhibit natural risk-reducing strategies at the level of individual firms and banks in emerging economies.

Aggregate Mismatches in the Banking System

In addition, supervisors may need to monitor aggregate mismatches in the banking system (the so-called "macroprudential" dimension). There are several reasons why this is necessary in addition to overseeing mismatches in individual institutions. The first is that those responsible for the detailed supervision of individual institutions cannot check everything but need to be given guidance as to what is important in quantitative terms. Large or rising currency mismatches (even if crudely measured) for the system as a whole give such a signal. The second reason is that individual institutions acting in isolation may overestimate their ability to hedge foreign exchange risk over a short period of time during a crisis. Banks will typically not hedge for very large exchange rate changes. Instead, they will often cover themselves against a near-term movement of up to, say, 5 percent in the exchange rate and then roll over such hedges. They will often implicitly count on the existence of markets to put on new hedges, should the rate move sharply against them. Individual banks may be quite aware that aggregate exposures mean that other banks will try to hedge at the same time, putting hedging markets under strain. This is likely to be a major risk in thin, comparatively underdeveloped foreign exchange markets.

An aggregate measure for the economy as a whole such as that outlined in chapter 4 could be of some use. So could the aggregations of the standard measures based on reported balance sheet positions that were outlined earlier—notably net open positions and gross foreign-currency lending to domestic firms. But such indicators tell only part of the story. Other questions that need to be asked: Is foreign-currency lending concentrated in firms with foreign-currency earnings? Do firms with foreign-currency bank loans also have foreign-currency assets? Do banks take such assets as collateral? How can off–balance sheet exposures be aggregated? And so on. Designing a reporting framework to answer these questions in order to support effective "macro" oversight of currency mismatches would be complex but nevertheless an important endeavor. To our knowledge, relatively little progress has been made on this to date.

Regulations of Other Financial Institutions

Banks are not the only financial institutions in emerging economies (or industrial ones) to face prudential measures on the currency composition of their operations. Mutual funds/unit trusts and pension funds too face guidelines or limits. When such limits are imposed, it is usually on the share (or absolute amount) of assets that can be invested abroad. Table 7.3 provides a summary of rules for fund managers in most of the major emerging economies (as of 2001).

In industrial countries, concerns of prudence originally motivated such limits on foreign assets—that is, investments in emerging markets were treated like other high-risk assets. There was a concern that fund managers who purchased assets in emerging economies would be taking on excessive risk, would be jeopardizing the fund's performance, and would not be respecting their conservative investment mandates. Gradually, however, this view gave way to a more liberal regime that was more in tune with the lessons of modern portfolio theory. Specifically, the argument was that since stock market returns in the OECD areas were weakly correlated with those in emerging economies, greater diversification would allow OECD investors to obtain higher risk-adjusted returns. In addition, by almost any metric, studies showed that investment portfolios in all the G-7 countries were subject to a large "home bias" that left the share of emerging-market assets well below what would be regarded as optimal; indeed, to justify the existing portfolio allocation, G-7 investors would have to be expecting unrealistically optimistic returns on their home investments.[28] More recently, the expected effects of population aging on expected OECD pension returns have boosted the case for

---

28. See Obstfeld (1993), Mussa and Goldstein (1993), and Reisen (2000).

Table 7.3 Rules on fund managers' holdings of foreign-currency assets

Country	Mutual funds/unit trusts	Pension/superannuation funds
Argentina	<25 percent	<17 percent
Brazil	Allowed, with limits depending on the type of fund	<10 percent
Chile	No limit	<16 percent (gradually raised from <2 percent in 1992)
Colombia	No limit	<10 percent foreign investments <50 percent sovereign external debt
Mexico	Allowed	<10 percent in investment grade securities registered in Mexico
Peru	No limit	No limit
Venezuela	No limit	No limit
China	Not allowed to invest abroad	
Hong Kong	No restrictions	No restrictions, except for funds under Mandatory Provident Fund scheme; Capital Preservation Fund (CPF): 0 percent; non-CPF: <70 percent
India	<$50 million in ADRs/GDRs of Indian companies and related foreign companies	
Indonesia	Only if issued by local company	Only if issued by local company
Korea	No restrictions	No restrictions
Singapore	No restrictions	<30 percent
Thailand	Permission required from the central bank	Permission allowed for the holding of foreign currency–denominated securities issued by public enterprises and Thai commercial banks only
Czech Republic	Only deposit money or OECD marketable securities	Only deposit money or OECD government bonds
Hungary	Limited	Limited
Poland	<5 percent	<5 percent
Israel	No limit	No limit for January 1, 2003
South Africa	<15 percent (and under asset "swap mechanism" can only accumulate foreign assets while they can find foreign parties investing an equal amount in the domestic market)	<15 percent (and under asset "swap mechanism" can only accumulate foreign assets while they can find foreign parties investing an equal amount in the domestic market)

ADR = American depository receipts
GDR = Global depository receipts
OECD = Organization for Economic Cooperation and Development

Note: This summary of guidelines was prepared in 2002 and is intended to be illustrative. The actual regulations are more complex and may have been revised since this table was prepared.

Source: Central banks.

greater diversification into emerging-market assets. Once the baby boomers start retiring, the rise in the capital-labor ratio will reduce the return on capital relative to wages; also, as the baby boomers draw on their pension assets to fund their retirement, prior asset accumulation will give way to a long period of asset decumulation. But as Helmut Reisen (2000) argues, both these effects can be mitigated if OECD pension funds increase their asset allocation toward emerging markets. In a global capital market, a declining labor force or asset decumulation will not lower the returns to capital because the younger population of emerging economies will be entering the labor force, making a net contribution to their pension funds, and increasing their demand for capital.

In emerging economies, guidelines or regulations limiting the share of mutual- or pension-fund assets that can be invested abroad had a different rationale. As argued by Hawkins and Turner (2000), the most likely explanation is that authorities wanted to retain more scarce capital at home for domestic development. Moreover, since average stock market returns are normally expected to be higher in emerging economies in the period ahead than in industrial countries, such limits on foreign assets would not entail a sacrifice in terms of expected average returns. But this self-reliance argument ignores risk and diversification. Small economies and small financial systems have a higher concentration of risks than larger ones. Consistent with this proposition, empirical work by Caprio and Honohan (2001) shows that small financial systems in emerging economies have had over the past three decades a much higher incidence of financial crises than larger ones. Again, because of the low correlation of returns between industrial and emerging economies, the latter could reduce their risk by investing a higher share of pension and mutual funds in OECD countries; as in industrial countries, investment portfolios in emerging economies also show a pronounced home bias that leaves actual diversification far short of what would be optimal. Reisen (2000) argues that a lower-risk portfolio would be consistent with the needs of pension beneficiaries in emerging economies, many of whom are poor and cannot tolerate high risk. He also maintains that the existing home bias in emerging-market pension funds is more than sufficient to generate a demand for domestic financial assets (e.g., domestic bonds), as these countries seek to deepen their domestic financial markets and strengthen their institutional infrastructure. Williamson (2000) also (implicitly) backs greater international diversification of emerging-market portfolios by arguing that concerns about large foreign investments affecting the exchange rate and domestic bond markets are misplaced: since the diversification of pension assets would encourage international equity market integration rather than interest rate linkages, it would do little to limit monetary-policy sovereignty in emerging economies. If there is a case for initial and temporary localization requirements for pension-fund

Table 7.4 Structure of pension fund assets in 2000 (percent)

| Country | Foreign securities | Domestic securities | | |
		Public-sector bonds	Other bonds	Other securities
Chile	11	36	6	45
Colombia	23	35	18	24
Peru	7	9	36	48
Korea	n.a.	2	43	55
Indonesia	n.a.	n.a.	42	58
Hungary	2	66	12	18
Poland	0	92	0	8
Israel[a]	1	71	5	23
Saudi Arabia	10	90	n.a.	n.a.

n.a. = not applicable

a. Average of pension funds.

Sources: National sources. Summarized in Mihaljek, Scatigna, and Villar (2002). Table 17 in that paper shows estimates for 1995.

investments, Reisen (2000) concludes that it is in easing the fiscal costs of moving from unfunded to fully funded pension systems in emerging economies.

As revealed in table 7.3, limits on foreign-asset holdings tend to be somewhat more restrictive for pension funds in emerging economies than for their mutual funds. Worthy of note also is the substantial increase in the foreign-asset limit of Chilean pension funds, going from less than 2 percent in 1992 to 16 percent in 2000. As explained in Marshall (2000), the allocation of resources in Chile is highly specialized, with exports still highly dependent on copper. By allowing greater international diversification of pension- and mutual-fund assets, the Chilean authorities have sought to reduce the concentration of risk in domestic assets and thereby improve the resilience of the economy to shocks. With the exception of Chile, Colombia, and Saudi Arabia (and of course, Hong Kong and Singapore), the pension funds in most emerging markets invest little in foreign securities (table 7.4).

Because pension and mutual funds in emerging economies have liabilities denominated exclusively in local currency, because their liabilities are not redeemable at par, and because their foreign assets are likely to be weighted heavily toward equities, their net open position in foreign currency is of quite a different character (less subject to a liquidity crisis) than that of banks in emerging economies. For such institutional investors (pension and mutual funds), measures that lead to a larger currency mismatch typically are associated with a *creditor* net open position and reduce risk—not increase it. The nature of the mismatch (long on foreign currency) goes in the opposite direction to the mismatches that have plagued emerging markets.

Rules for Nonfinancial Corporations?

The official sector in industrial countries has been considerably more cautious and less intrusive in subjecting nonfinancial corporations to guidance or regulations on currency mismatching. This presumably reflects a view that a failure of a large corporation would have less adverse spillovers for the economy (ceteris paribus) than would failure of a large bank, that it is the business of commercial banks—not the official sector— to monitor credit and market risk in its more important clients, and that their market discipline over excessive risk-taking in the corporate sector can be effective if there is good public disclosure of foreign exchange exposure. For example, the Financial Stability Forum's Working Group on Capital Flows (2000, 3) concluded that "the primary mechanism for risk control in this area [nonbank private sector] should be improved transparency." Current public disclosure of currency mismatches in the corporate sector is meager.

In emerging economies, those countries that still maintain some controls/restrictions on capital flows often put conditions on foreign borrowing by corporations. For example, India regulates foreign borrowing (other than trade credit) by companies, insisting on a minimum maturity of five years for loans over $20 million and outlawing put options to subvert this constraint (Hawkins and Turner 2000). Malaysia has long required that firms taking on foreign-currency obligations be able to point to a tangible source of foreign-currency earnings to service the debt.

Interestingly enough, the private international capital markets themselves have sometimes made sharp distinctions between producers of tradables and nontradables in granting access to foreign currency–denominated credit. In this connection, Anne Krueger and Aaron Tornell (1999) report that Mexican export firms and their affiliates have been able to obtain financing in international capital markets since the early 1990s: the 1995–97 credit crunch mainly hurt small and medium-sized firms in the nontradables sector. The 142 nonfinancial firms listed on the Mexican stock exchange are composed mainly of tradable-sector firms. In 1997, this set of firms had an export-to-sales ratio of 40 percent and over half (53 percent) of their liabilities denominated in foreign currency. Even more notable is the fact that these firms with the highest share of liabilities denominated in foreign currency had a higher-than-average export-to-sales ratio. Their explanation for this tradable/nontradable distinction is that firms exporting a substantial portion of their sales are more likely to be able to provide collateral in the form of receivables denominated in dollars.[29]

---

29. Caballero and Krishnamurthy (1998) present a theoretical model where insufficient domestic collateral in emerging economies drives financial crises.

To the extent that the tradable/nontradable nature of a firm's output affects its access to foreign currency–denominated financing, two implications would seem to follow. First, a currency mismatch of a given size is apt to be more a cause for concern (i.e., have higher crisis vulnerability) when it occurs in the nontradable than in the tradable sector; as such, one can reduce crisis vulnerability by redistributing currency risk within an emerging economy from producers of nontradables to those of tradables. In other words, hedging of currency risk is not exclusively about getting nonresidents to assume more of it; there are things that can be done domestically as well. The second implication is that vulnerability and sustainability of an emerging economy's external debt burden should take some account of the size of its export sector. In this regard, perhaps one reason Argentina and Brazil had such difficulty in recent years in convincing private creditors that their external debt position was sustainable related to the fact that their debt-to-export ratios were so high. Pointing out to investors that these external debt ratios expressed in terms of GDP are much more moderate may not cut much ice.

The Asian crisis may have caused regulators in both industrial and emerging economies to reassess their views on the merits of a relatively "hands-off" approach to currency mismatching for corporations. In that crisis, banks did not exercise careful credit assessment over foreign exchange risks in their corporate customers (indeed, neither banks nor the official sector may have fully appreciated the size of the external debt of the corporate sector) nor was the market careful in constraining the foreign-currency borrowing of nontradable firms (including property developers).[30] And in the end, the need for substantial corporate restructuring in several of the crisis countries greatly complicated the task of restructuring the banking system and contributed to the depth of the recession. This has led to a renewed interest in, inter alia, (real-time) credit registries for companies, incorporating foreign exchange hedging as one of the conditions to qualify for bank loans, and making the currency and maturity composition of assets and liabilities a more prominent feature of companies' audited reports and accounts.[31]

---

30. Goldstein (1998) and BIS (1998) emphasize the lending boom and the concentration of credit going to real estate and equities as an important factor in the Asian crisis. BIS (1997) provided a precrisis analysis of financial fragility in Asia.

31. See Financial Stability Forum (2000) and the discussion in chapter 5.

8

International Solutions to Currency Mismatching?

The previous two chapters laid out in detail the emerging-market policies that can help reduce currency mismatches. Is there also a role for the international community and, if so, what is it?

First of all, we are not persuaded by Eichengreen, Hausmann, and Panizza (2002) that creating an emerging-market currency basket and encouraging the international financial institutions (IFIs) and G-10 governments to issue debt in that composite currency is the approach most likely to succeed in mitigating the currency mismatch problem. Very small economies are, of course, more vulnerable than large ones. And it is certainly true that liquidity factors and network externalities lie behind the emergence of "vehicle" and reserve currencies. Nevertheless, such elements do not justify a new currency basket index. The track record of such indices—even those including the major currencies—has not been impressive. There are simpler and more straightforward ways both of unbundling currency and credit risk for emerging-market borrowers and of making debt obligations more contingent on the borrower's ability to pay.

A central empirical result of Eichengreen, Hausmann, and Panizza (2002, 2003e) is that the only variable that is robust in explaining cross-country differences in original sin is economic size—measured by a country's total GDP, or its total domestic credit, or its total trade, or the principal component of the first three measures. In cases where countries have less original sin than predicted from their economic size, the explanation offered is either that they are financial centers (the United Kingdom and Switzerland) or that nonresidents (especially IFIs) have issued the bulk of the international debt denominated in local currencies (as in Poland, South Africa, and the Czech Republic). Nonresidents are said to have denominated debt in local currencies because emerging-market borrowers were willing to pay them a premium to swap out of the latter's dollar liabilities. The authors of the original sin hypothesis (OSH) also argue that in a world with transactions costs, the optimal portfolio will have a finite number of currencies, and that with each additional currency added to that portfolio, the benefits of diversification will fall faster than the costs.

All this leads Eichengreen, Hausmann, and Panizza (2002) and Eichengreen and Hausmann (2003a, 2003c) to offer an "international" solution to the original sin problem. They propose that an emerging-market (EM) index be created, composed of an inflation-indexed basket of the currencies of roughly the 20 or so largest emerging economies, with the weights in the basket corresponding to each country's GDP (at purchasing power parity). The World Bank and other multilateral institutions would issue debt denominated in this index, undoing any currency mismatch on their own balance sheets by converting a portion of their existing loans into claims denominated in the inflation-adjusted currencies of each of the countries included in the index. G-10 sovereigns would also be asked to issue debt in the EM index and would swap their currency exposure with countries whose currencies were included in the EM index. By so doing, emerging-market borrowers would get rid of their dollar-denominated liabilities (i.e., their original sin). Institutional investors and mutual funds would be encouraged to create products that added credit risk to the index as a way of further encouraging the development of the market. Once the market for the new currency basket index was sufficiently developed, the role of the IFIs and the G-10 governments could be scaled back. The OSH authors maintain that their new basket index and plan have several desirable characteristics, including a better separation of credit and currency risk, the creation of an attractive form of diversification for institutional and retail investors, and a better matching of emerging-market debt obligations with the debtor's ability to pay.

Since measures of original sin are highly correlated with country size, it is hard to know if emerging economies with relatively high degrees of output and capital-account volatility and relatively low credit ratings (the so-called "pain" of original sin) are at a disadvantage because they have high levels of original sin or because their economies are small. There are many indications that emerging economies with very small financial systems are more vulnerable to economic instability and financial crises— and not just because of original sin or currency mismatch more broadly defined. Caprio and Honohan (2001) note that more than 150 countries have banking systems with total assets of $10 billion or less. They go on to argue that small financial systems underperform because they suffer from a concentration of risks (i.e., from low diversification), because they provide few services at higher unit costs (reflecting low competition and less ability to exploit economies of scale), and because regulation and supervision of small systems are disproportionately costly. McCauley and Remolona (2000) suggest that government bond markets that are smaller than $100 billion to $200 billion are apt to be less liquid than would be desirable.[1] Many of the best companies in emerging economies choose to list their shares on the larger stock exchanges in the major industrial countries to reap the advantages of greater liquidity and a wider investor base. Goldstein (2002) observes that most countries that have adopted either currency boards or formal dollarization tend to be very small economies, and many analysts (e.g., see Mussa et al. 2000) conclude that very small economies are better off adopting fixed exchange rate regimes.

To compensate for their size, small countries typically respond with measures to increase diversification or with "outsourcing" of services to larger countries with better liquidity and scale advantages, so that residents of small countries still get access to good financial services even if they do not produce such services.

We go some way in this direction by recommending that emerging economies reduce barriers to entry for foreign-owned banks, and that mutual and pension funds in emerging economies relax restrictions on investment in foreign assets. Our point is that small economic and financial size does indeed create challenges for many developing countries, but there is no presumption that creating a currency basket index for denominating debt is the only or best way to compensate for it—or for currency mismatch per se.

A similar argument can be made for the implications of networking externalities and transactions costs. Frankel (1995, 9) captures the notion of network externalities when he defines an international currency as "one that people use (internationally) because everyone else is doing it." The theory of "vehicle" currencies also gives a prominent role to transactions costs when it suggests that vehicle currencies will emerge whenever indirect exchange costs between the vehicle are lower than direct exchange costs between the two nonvehicle currencies (Chrystal 1984). Although Eichengreen, Hausmann, and Panizza (2002) concentrate on the currency denomination of debt contracts, the "international" dimension of currency use is much broader, encompassing, inter alia, the currency composition of international reserves and of exchange rate pegs, currency invoicing in international trade, and the private holding of currency abroad. In addition, the literature on the emergence of international currencies indicates that many factors are involved, including control of inflation; behavior of

---

1. Flandreau and Sussman (2002), reviewing emerging-market borrowing in the 19th century, also argue that market liquidity was the key factor in explaining the currency composition of initial public offerings of governments in foreign markets and secondary-market trading of bonds.

the nominal exchange rate; net creditor/debtor position; economic size; open, deep, and broad financial markets; official attitudes toward international currency use; and advantages of incumbency (Frenkel and Goldstein 1999). Moreover, the most successful "international" currencies are those that carry out simultaneously all the functions of money (medium of exchange, unit of account, and store of value). It is one thing to argue that these characteristics of international currencies (particularly economic size, anti-inflation credibility, and synergies among the various functions of money) portend well for the future international role of the euro. It is another to argue that an emerging-market currency basket that contains the currencies of many small economies and that is to be used mainly as a unit of account to denominate debt contracts can also grab substantial market share from incumbent reserve currencies. Our point here is that the role of network externalities and transactions costs in the evolution of international currencies does not inexorably lead to an international solution to the currency mismatch problem of emerging economies.

Nor have the last three decades of experience with currency baskets (created outside monetary unions) been kind to the case for the proposed new index. We point to two examples. The first is the IMF's special drawing right (SDR), created in the late 1960s by full international agreement and aimed at becoming "the principal reserve asset in the international monetary system." Indeed, at the time of its creation, the SDR's diversification properties were thought to confer on it such an advantage over each of the incumbent reserve currencies that it was regarded as desirable to put some restrictions on the SDR's use to prevent an excessively rapid switch out of the existing reserve currencies. Suffice it to say it has not worked out this way, with the SDR's share of foreign exchange reserves falling from 6 percent at its peak in 1981 to about 1 percent in 2002, and this despite substantial official support, including using the SDR as the unit of account for all IMF operations. It is relevant to also recall that whereas the SDR was originally constructed as a weighted average of the 16 major currencies, the number of currencies in the basket was later reduced to just the five major currencies. If the advantages of diversification fall as rapidly with each additional currency, as Eichengreen, Hausmann, and Panizza (2002) suggest, why should the basket contain so many currencies (20 or more)? In addition, as a recent IMF (2003a, 85) report notes, stronger emerging-market players may not find it advantageous to participate in the index because of concerns that others may engage in strategic devaluation (days before their coupons are fixed) to lower their debt obligations.

The second example is the Emerging Local Markets Index (ELMI) that JP Morgan created in 1996 and updated to the ELMI+ the following year, 1997. The ELMI+ tracks total returns for local currency–denominated market instruments in 24 emerging economies—the vast majority of which also appear in the index proposed by Eichengreen, Hausmann, and Panizza

(2002). Admittedly, the ELMI+ and the index proposed by Eichengreen, Hausmann, and Panizza (2002) have some nontrivial differences—including that the ELMI+ is not inflation-indexed and that it tracks money-market returns, not currencies exclusively. But the bottom line is that despite the alleged strong diversification benefits of the ELMI+ index, it has so far attracted very little interest from the Belgian dentist and other global investors.

We too regard an unbundling of credit and currency risk as helpful to emerging economies since it permits a reallocation of currency risk to those most willing and best placed to bear it. But this unbundling can be achieved without any new emerging-market currency basket. As noted earlier, the global credit derivatives market is fast growing; its main instruments (credit default swaps, credit-linked notes, and collateralized debt obligations) provide protection against credit events; it covers an expanding group of emerging economies; and international banks participate actively in it. An IMF (2003) study reports that the most actively traded contracts reference the external bonds issued by Brazil, Russia, Mexico, Turkey, and Venezuela, and that while activity in Asia has been more limited than elsewhere, credit default swaps are rapidly gaining popularity there too. As outlined earlier, derivatives facilities for hedging currency risk are also available in a top tier of emerging economies, and others are moving up the ladder. Even in cases where capital-account restrictions and other impediments prevent physical delivery of the currency, a nondeliverable forwards market has developed to provide hedging opportunities (see chapter 3). Also, as emphasized by Burger and Warnock (2002), deeper and longer-maturity local bond markets in emerging economies will lead to the creation of a yield curve and derivative instruments that enable decoupling of the bond and currency investment. In short, a new currency basket index is not likely to be the best way to separate credit and currency risk.

We share (with Eichengreen, Hausmann, and Panizza 2002) the view that financial resilience and economic performance in emerging economies would be aided by reforms that would make debt payments more contingent on the debtor's ability to pay. How could debt contracts be designed to achieve this objective and yet maintain the simplicity that is essential if such debt securities are to be easily traded in liquid markets? This is not an easy balance to strike. One proposal worth exploring further would be to encourage both emerging-market debtors and private creditors to issue and accept GDP-indexed dollar-denominated bonds (as a transitional device toward greater reliance on local currency–denominated bonds). Eduardo Borensztein and Paolo Mauro (2002) show that such bonds have several attractive features: they restrict the range of variation of the debt/GDP ratio and hence reduce the likelihood of debt crises; they reduce the need for emerging-market governments to engage in procyclical fiscal policy; they should carry a low insurance premium (reflecting the very low cross-country comovement of GDP growth rates and hence the largely diversifiable nature of cross-country GDP growth risk for an investor holding a portfolio of GDP-indexed bonds); they would cover a much higher share of output fluctuations for a typical emerging economy than bonds indexed to commodity prices; and they contain certain protections against manipulation and cheating aimed at lowering debt obligations (e.g., it is high, not low, growth that is typically considered a success and gets politicians reelected).

These GDP-indexed bonds might operate as follows.[2] Instead of an emerging economy with a trend growth rate of 3 percent issuing a plain vanilla bond with, say, an 8 percent coupon rate, this country would issue a GDP-indexed bond where annual coupon payments would be reduced, say, by half a percentage point for every percentage point by which GDP growth falls short of trend (3 percent). If growth turns out to be 1 percent, the coupon would be 7 percent (plus a small insurance premium); in years when growth comes in at 5 percent, the coupon would be 9 percent (plus the same insurance premium).[3] Assuming (like Eichengreen, Hausmann, and Panizza 2002) that the nominal exchange rate in emerging economies depreciates in years when growth outcomes (shocks) are poor (worse than trend) and appreciates when they are good, dollar-denominated GDP-indexed bonds would reduce the adverse consequences of currency mismatches. As Borensztein and Mauro (2002) note, global investors are already highly exposed to risk under standard debt contracts. With a standard dollar-denominated bond, bad growth and/or currency developments can render a country's debt unsustainable. Would global investors be better off receiving lower debt repayments through indexation (agreed in advance by the contract) than facing uncertain recovery values through a chaotic default process? Similarly, while standard local currency–denominated debt contracts reduce currency risk for the borrower, the lender must then assume the currency risk and may well be repaid in a depreciated currency if the borrower faces an adverse shock. GDP-indexed bonds could therefore serve as a helpful transition device during the period in which emerging economies are enacting those national policy reforms that would boost sufficiently the confidence of global and local investors to increase the share of local currency–denominated, fixed-rate bonds. Admittedly, GDP-indexed bonds would face the same hurdles of product uncertainty and of coordination problems that typically beset any financial innovation, but (following Borensztein and Mauro 2002) these hurdles could be reduced by some temporary assistance from the official sector (e.g., to set statistical standards and verify

---

2. The example is taken from Borensztein and Mauro (2002).

3. If a greater degree of cushioning is desired, one could increase the sensitivity of coupon payments to the deviation of GDP growth from trend.

the reliability of national accounts and to foster a dialogue among potential participants in the market for these instruments). On the latter count, it is noteworthy that the official sector has been helpful in promoting the inclusion of collective action clauses in sovereign bond contracts issued under New York law, as several emerging economies have now followed Mexico's recent lead.

9

Reducing Currency Mismatching: A Domestic Agenda

The central message of this book is that simultaneous and deliberate policy action, taken on a number of fronts mostly at the national level, can nurture real and financial development in emerging-market economies and reduce currency mismatching. Hence, we expect that the currency mismatch problem is likely to become less severe as countries develop. On this score, we are more optimistic than the authors of the original sin hypothesis (OSH).[1] In support of our optimism, we stress five points.

First, most studies find a positive relationship between financial-market depth and the level of economic development. Burger and Warnock (2002), for example, find that *the size of a nation's local currency–denominated bond market (expressed as a ratio to GDP) is significantly related to GDP per capita but not to country size.* This reinforces the point made earlier (from Burger and Warnock 2002) that what distinguishes emerging economies from industrial countries is overall bond market development, not the currency denomination of outstanding debt. Caprio and Honohan (2001) show that stock market turnover, liquid liabilities of banks and nonbanks, and both government and private bond capitalization (each expressed as a share of GDP) all increase with the level of per capita income. Since financial-market development helps

---

1. One of the main reasons the original sin school opts for an international solution to the currency mismatch problem is that their empirical work reveals no significant association between original sin and the level of economic development (per capita GDP). Therefore, they argue that emerging economies cannot expect the currency mismatch problem to become less severe as they develop.

increase the supply of local currency–denominated finance, we see little reason to be pessimistic about longer-term prospects.

Second, as demonstrated earlier, available measures of aggregate currency mismatch—be they short-run liquidity measures (like the ratio of short-term external debt to reserves) or broader indicators of "effective" mismatch (like our aggregate effective currency mismatch index, AECM)—indicate that many emerging economies have been able to reduce significantly their aggregate currency mismatch over medium-term periods (tables 9.1 and 4.6). Note, for example, the large reductions in the ratio of short-term debt to reserves and in estimated AECMs achieved by the former Asian-crisis economies (since 1997), South Africa (since 1996), and Russia (since 1997–98). At the same time, the entries in tables 9.1 and 4.6 serve notice that there is nothing automatic about reducing currency mismatches. With the exception of Mexico, most of the larger economies in Latin America saw aggregate currency mismatches rise appreciably between 1995–96 and 2001, and Turkey experienced a significant exacerbation of its mismatch in the same period as well.[2]

Third, a more intensive examination of individual country cases provides encouragement that if the right measures are implemented, progress on currency mismatching can be substantial over periods no longer than a decade. Mexico's experience since its 1994–95 crisis speaks to this point: as outlined by Cuevas and Werner (2002) and the IMF (2002b), (1) the inflation rate decreased from over 50 percent in 1995 to less than 5 percent in 2002; (2) the move to a floating exchange rate resulted in a reallocation of currency risk from those (nontradable producers) who were least capable of bearing it to those (exporters) better able to do so; (3) in 1995, the government started issuing inflation-indexed debt and by July 2002 was able to issue a 10-year bond with a fixed yield in Mexican pesos; (4) the average maturity of domestic government debt has increased from 8 months in 1995 to 25 months in 2001, and the share of fixed-rate debt in the total rose to 15 percent by end-2001; (5) the corporate sector followed the pattern of the government fixed-income market;[3] (6) market-makers were introduced in the domestic fixed-income market in 2000 and have contributed to an increase in both liquidity and maturity; (7) the role of

---

2. In some cases, the ratio of short-term debt to reserves and the estimated AECM point in different directions; for example, Hungary's aggregate currency mismatch (as measured by its AECM in table 4.6) improved significantly since 1995, whereas its ratio of short-term debt to reserves deteriorated (table 9.1). This is not altogether surprising since the ratio of short-term debt to reserves emphasizes short-run liquidity conditions, while the AECM covers a broader range of assets and liabilities and incorporates longer-term structural factors that are relevant for assessing the output costs of a currency mismatch during a currency crisis.

3. According to IMF (2003c) figures, local bond markets in Mexico increased from less than 8 percent of GDP in 1995 (just after the crisis) to over 14 percent in 2001. See also Sidaoui (2002).

Table 9.1 Short-term external debt as a percent of foreign exchange reserves

Region/country	1990	1995	1996	1997	1998	1999	2000	2001	2002
Latin America[a]	**197**	**117**	**108**	**106**	**104**	**99**	**113**	**104**	**84**
Argentina	165	181	167	178	160	159	238	242	215
Brazil	299	75	90	108	109	115	124	111	77
Chile	67	55	53	63	59	48	67	60	73
Colombia	51	77	70	79	96	71	59	56	47
Mexico	191	207	167	116	103	91	89	75	58
Peru	191	52	60	62	78	73	109	82	63
Venezuela	57	69	32	39	45	40	37	47	62
Asia, large economies[a]	**120**	**51**	**49**	**58**	**31**	**22**	**19**	**15**	**11**
China	31	34	27	25	23	13	13	10	7
India	339	46	38	33	33	28	26	16	10
Korea	141	184	222	330	76	59	44	40	37
Taiwan	13	22	22	26	19	16	12	10	8
Other Asia[a]	**164**	**144**	**141**	**181**	**97**	**60**	**58**	**53**	**39**
Indonesia	183	208	197	224	113	75	74	63	44
Malaysia	22	35	44	75	39	27	28	31	26
Philippines	369	73	82	179	108	64	62	65	56
Thailand	66	124	125	152	88	45	40	36	26
Central Europe[a]	**n.a.**	**23**	**29**	**37**	**45**	**37**	**38**	**44**	**46**
Czech Republic	n.a.	30	38	56	62	44	44	41	23
Hungary	240	40	59	67	87	62	61	63	91
Poland	70	13	14	17	22	25	28	39	41
Russia	n.a.	150	235	255	230	139	50	46	37
Israel	34	28	18	14	13	16	14	18	19
Turkey	129	88	80	105	116	101	140	129	81
Saudi Arabia	n.a.	n.a.	46	50	69	65	57	66	58
South Africa	684	384	1234	298	325	232	200	177	162

n.a. = not available

a. Weighted average of countries shown, based on 1995 GDP and PPP exchange rates.

Note: Short-term liabilities (with a maturity of less than one year) to BIS reporting banks, as a percentage of foreign exchange reserves; short-term debt defined as consolidated cross-border claims to all BIS reporting banks on countries outside the reporting area with a maturity up to and including one year plus international debt securities outstanding with a maturity up to one year; outstanding year-end positions.

Sources: IMF's International Financial Statistics and Bank for International Settlements statistics.

local institutional investors, particularly Mexican pension funds, increased markedly over the past decade and supported the development of the derivatives market; and (8) by 2000, spreads on seven-year interest swaps and three-year exchange rate forwards had dropped to 20 and 10 basis points, respectively. A recent *Wall Street Journal* article ("Mexico Turns to a New Lender: Mexico—Economic Stability Sets Up Thriving Peso-Debt Market Tapped by Companies, State," November 13, 2003) reports that these favorable trends continued in 2003, with the Mexican federal government having issued a 20-year fixed-rate peso bond in October and with Mexican companies and state and local governments having issued about $10 billion of peso debt in the first 10 months of 2003 (four times the amount issued just five years ago). Although currency mismatches still exist for the government and corporate sectors in Mexico, Werner (2002) concludes that the scale of the problem has diminished.[4] Our own measures of aggregate effective currency mismatch for Mexico (recall table 4.6) support this conclusion, with large declines in the AECM from its peak in the crisis and the immediate aftermath (1994–96).

Even putting aside those emerging economies where growth of the local government bond market over the past decade has been driven either (as in emerging Asia) by the need to recapitalize banking systems severely damaged by crisis or (as in parts of Latin America) by long-running fiscal deficits and exchange rate depreciation (cum exchange rate–linked debt), there are many notable improvements that have favorable implications for control of currency mismatches. So too, albeit to a lesser extent, for local corporate bond markets. A few examples taken from a recent IMF (2002b) report convey the flavor. China's local government bond market has grown from 12 percent of GDP in 1994 to nearly 30 percent in 2001 to become the largest (in absolute terms) in the region (excluding Japan). The Hong Kong bond market has more than doubled (relative to GDP) since 1994. Singapore's government bond market has also doubled (again relative to GDP) over this period, and the yield curve has been extended to 15 years. Hungary has, since 1997, followed a debt issuance strategy aimed at reducing currency risk and rollover risk—with the result that, inter alia, the share of foreign-currency debt in total government debt has been reduced from 41 to 30 percent. Chile has made extensive use of inflation-indexed debt, in concert with a transition to fiscal responsibility and the development of a deep institutional investor base, to support healthy government and corporate bond markets, with maturities on corporate bonds now extending to 20 years or more. Admittedly, emerging economies still have a long way to go in terms of improving the liquidity of their bond markets, and some developing countries are probably too small to develop their own bond markets. Nevertheless, local bond market developments over the past decade should be regarded as positive.

We would be remiss, too, if we did not draw attention to the large buildup in foreign exchange reserves by emerging economies over the past decade, especially since 1995. Relative to GDP, average reserve holdings of emerging economies were twice as high in 2001 as in 1990–94 (IMF 2002a). As noted in Turner (2003), aggregate foreign exchange reserves in

---

4. The OSH apparently discounts all these positive developments since it records Mexico as having an original sin ratio of one (the highest possible number) throughout 1993–2001.

emerging Asia (excluding financial centers Hong Kong and Singapore) now exceed aggregate domestic currency by almost $400 billion (figure 7.1), and in some emerging economies, reserves exceed domestic currency by several multiples (figure 7.2). These increases in reserves not only serve to reduce the aggregate effective currency mismatch but also offer an opportunity to deepen domestic debt markets—because of the domestic liabilities on the central bank's balance sheet as a counterpart to its foreign exchange assets (as discussed in chapter 8).

Fourth, the discussion in the previous chapter shows how many emerging economies have upgraded their supervisory regimes and recognized the importance of their loan customers' mismatches. Even if banking supervisors are not able to catch all foreign exchange exposures of banks (direct as well as indirect), determined efforts to limit exposures to a limited share of bank capital should still reduce losses from currency mismatches to a tolerable level. Supervisors are now more aware of the need to frame regulations and supervisory guidelines in ways that deter banks from using sophisticated derivative instruments to evade the prudential oversight of currency mismatches. In any case, as pointed out by Paul Krugman (2000), there is an inconsistency in arguing—as does the OSH—that today's capital markets are too "imperfect" to hedge emerging-market currency risk but are "perfect" enough to undo any regulations on foreign-exchange exposure.

Finally, one should not underplay the growth potential of financial markets while overplaying the influence of "original" sins. On the first count, recent history is replete with financial markets—ranging from asset-backed securities to credit derivatives—that did not exist for long periods but rapidly became sizable once they reached a critical mass.[5] Also, as shown in table 9.2, though starting from a very low base, the share of cross-border bank loans denominated in local currency has gone up substantially in most emerging-market regions over the past decade. On the second count, while a country's longer-term credit history matters, improved policy performance in the more recent period can lead to much-improved market access and terms of financing. In this connection, Reinhart, Rogoff, and Savastano (2003b) have calculated default/restructuring probabilities for various emerging economies going back to 1824. In their sample, Mexico turns out to be the country that has had the highest historical default probability. Yet Mexico's much-improved economic performance over the past decade or so has now been rewarded by quite low interest rate spreads (roughly 200 basis points over US Treasuries) on its benchmark bonds. Clearly, the market does not focus only on "original" sins; current and recent policy sins—or lack of them—count more.

---

5. The BIS triennial survey indicated that positions in the global credit derivatives market increased from $118 billion in June 1998 to $693 billion in June 2001.

Table 9.2 Share of external debt denominated in local currency
(percent, position at end of period shown)

Country	Cross-border bank loans[a]			International debt securities	
	1990	1995	2002	1995	2002
Latin America[b]	**1.5**	**1.2**	**1.4**	**0.0**	**0.3**
Argentina	1.7	1.2	2.1	0.0	0.7
Brazil	1.4	0.6	1.2	0.0	0.0
Chile	4.4	4.8	1.8	0.0	0.0
Colombia	0.8	0.0	0.1	0.0	0.0
Mexico	1.1	1.0	1.5	0.0	0.0
Peru	0.7	3.0	2.9	0.0	0.0
Venezuela	1.4	2.2	0.9	0.0	0.0
China	0.3	1.0	3.7	0.0	0.0
India	0.9	5.2	7.1	0.0	0.0
Korea	1.8	1.5	3.9	0.0	0.0
Taiwan	1.0	3.0	6.9	0.0	0.0
Other Asia[b]	**1.5**	**2.0**	**3.7**	**0.7**	**2.8**
Indonesia	1.1	1.7	3.5	0.0	0.0
Malaysia	5.2	6.7	1.9	0.0	0.2
Philippines	0.5	3.6	3.1	1.8	0.1
Thailand	0.8	1.2	6.4	1.4	14.2
Central Europe[b]	**11.6**	**7.3**	**15.8**	**0.0**	**0.5**
Czech Republic[c]	17.6	11.7	20.0	0.0	0.0
Hungary	8.1	4.2	12.1	0.0	0.9
Poland	11.9	4.9	15.2	0.0	0.0
Russia[d]	22.2	22.9	1.2	0.0	0.0
Israel	1.1	2.7	1.4	0.0	0.0
Turkey	0.9	1.1	2.2	0.0	0.0
Saudi Arabia	5.8	6.9	5.4	0.0	0.0
South Africa	2.3	6.7	15.6	0.0	9.2
Memorandum:					
Australia	18.1	14.8	52.3	33.9	14.0
Sweden	5.7	22.1	30.1	1.7	3.4

a. BIS reporting banks collect a breakdown of their cross-border claims in US dollar, euro, yen, pound sterling, Swiss franc, and residual currencies. This table uses data on residual currencies as a proxy for loans in local currency of the debtor country. For example, a Spanish bank's claim on Mexico in residual currencies most likely (but not exclusively) represents lending to the country in Mexican pesos. Data for 1990 use total claims in residual currencies as a proxy for loans in local currencies.
b. Sum of the countries shown.
c. Data for 1990 relate to former Czechoslovakia.
d. Data for 1990 relate to former Soviet Union.

Sources: Data have been obtained from the Bank of England, Dealogic, Euroclear, the International Securities Market Association, Thomson Financial Securities, national sources, and the Bank for International Settlements.

To sum up, it is too pessimistic to conclude that, in the absence of an international initiative, emerging economies will be powerless to overcome their own currency mismatch problems within a relevant time frame. There is much that can be done at the national level to develop the supply of local currency–denominated finance and to improve the incentives to hedge against excessive currency risk. As Burger and Warnock (2002) concluded from their examination of the behavior of global investors toward emerging-market securities, a key policy objective should be the development of local bond markets and the concomitant development of derivative instruments, which will not only provide a multiplicity of financing sources if foreign investors shy away from placing funds but will also transfer currency risk to those best able to bear it and allow the decoupling of bond and currency investments. This is why in addition to monetary policy and the currency regime, our action plan pays attention, inter alia, to measures that can help broaden the investor base for bonds, develop more liquid benchmark securities, ensure that bond yields are market-determined, foster a repo market in government bonds, ease restrictions on short selling, promote derivatives markets, move away from currency-linked debt to inflation-indexed debt as an intermediate step toward local currency–denominated fixed-rate debt, and maintain a suitable cushion of international reserves.

Summary

The currency mismatch problem in emerging economies is serious, and a sustained effort to overcome it merits high priority in any reform of the international financial architecture. We believe that a major implication of the original sin hypothesis, namely that absent an international initiative, emerging economies are doomed to borrow abroad in foreign currencies, has—rightly or wrongly—led many to draw misleading policy implications.

The most useful way to define currency mismatching is the sensitivity of net worth (and net income) to changes in the exchange rate. To measure the extent of currency mismatch, attention needs to be paid to both the asset and liability sides of balance sheets, to the response of non-interest flows (like exports) to an exchange rate change, and to the ability of emerging economies to borrow domestically—not just internationally—in the local currency. Our new AECM indicator—which could and should be further refined—suggests that it is possible to construct a measure that incorporates these desirable features.

We see significant differences among emerging economies in their capacity to hedge currency risk. We find that national macroeconomic and exchange rate policies—and the incentives linked to them—matter a great deal for generating and managing currency mismatches, and that significant progress can be made in reducing such mismatches over the medium term. Debt management policies are important. We also find that institutional microeconomic policies—notably developing bond markets and ensuring that official oversight of financial institutions limits currency mismatches (indirect as well as direct)—are also crucial.

Developments over the past decade in several countries suggest that the benefits of better policies are likely to show up first in the development of domestic financial markets. Only when progress is sustained can one expect changes in the currency composition of international borrowing and in cross-border bank lending by international banks.

Although the primary responsibility for controlling currency mismatches resides at the national level (in emerging economies), international financial institutions could help by monitoring currency mismatches in their publications and—where they are excessive—by making reduction of those mismatches over the medium term a condition for IMF loans.

APPENDICES

Appendix A
Measuring Mismatches:
Some Cautionary Notes

As in many areas of economics, there is a significant gap between theory and practice in the measurement of currency mismatches. This appendix outlines some methodological issues that arise in translating theoretical concepts into practical measures. It suggests how certain difficulties could be addressed.

The theoretical ideal is to measure how a change in the exchange rate will affect the present discounted value of an agent's income and expenditure flows over time. How should this present discounted value be measured? In the case of income from financial assets (or expenditure to service liabilities), an obvious approximation is the market value of the financial asset. Hence a first approximation to measuring an agent's vulnerability to currency mismatch would be to take the difference between foreign-currency liabilities and assets as a proportion of some measure of income. Such measures are indeed widely compiled.

The shortcoming is that no account is taken of the denomination of other types of income. In the example cited at the beginning of the book—the apartment in London financed by borrowing dollars—the currency of denomination of rental income (presumably pounds) needs to enter the picture. But calculating the present discounted value of such income flows is necessarily much more approximate (and subject to guesswork) than the value of financial assets—future income flows and their currency of denomination are not known with any degree of precision. One simple (but far from satisfactory) approximation is to assume that exports and imports are denominated in foreign currency and other items of expenditure in local currency. The next section considers some important issues of measurement, and the section following that outlines some statistical lacunae.

Theory and Practice: Some Important Issues

Currency of Denomination of Financial Assets and Liabilities: Importance of Maturity Profiles

Consider the simplest case of a firm whose income is derived only from financial assets and whose only expenditure is the service of debt—that is, a purely financial firm.[1] This is a useful abstraction because it can be applied to any financing structure, even that of a nonfinancial firm with "real" income and earnings. In the case of the financial firm, the structure of the balance sheet will determine the impact of exchange rate changes on income and expenditure flows. If the capital structure is "inverted," borrowing costs will rise when the exchange rate falls. If it is "correlated," borrowing costs may fall. An additional complication is whether the drop in the exchange rate leads to changes in interest rates (e.g., due to changes in domestic interest rates, a widening of credit spreads, and so on). A financial firm attempting to analyze its exposure to exchange rate changes will allow for such secondary effects. Table A.1, which summarizes such effects for the liability side of the balance sheets by looking at common forms of debt, is drawn from a recent book by a market practitioner (Pettis 2001).

In all but one case (fixed-rate, local-currency debt), borrowing costs rise after a depreciation of the exchange rate. A similar tabulation can be made for the asset side of the balance sheet, substituting "earnings" for "costs." The future income and expenditure flows of an entity with identical asset and liability structures would be affected identically by a change in the exchange rate. Only in this limiting case could it be said that the entity has no currency mismatch. Once these restrictive assumptions are relaxed and some differences introduced between the nature of assets and liabilities, the identity of exchange rate impacts on income and expenditure breaks down. Given maturity differences, net income can change in response to an exchange rate change, even if foreign-currency assets and liabilities are equal. For instance, an entity with long-term peso assets but short-term peso liabilities will see its debt-service costs rise but its interest income unchanged after a sharp change in the exchange rate—on the assumption that domestic interest rates rise.

The implication of these considerations is that currency mismatches cannot be fully captured simply by comparing the currency of denomination of assets and liabilities. The maturity structure will also be relevant. Hence an entity that has an identical proportion of assets and liabilities in

---

1. In this case, the asset/liability and income/expenditure definitions of mismatch converge, on the assumption that the value of foreign-currency assets (liabilities) is just the present discounted value of all future foreign-currency income (expenditure).

Table A.1 Impact of an exchange rate change on borrowing costs
(according to different debt structures)

Type of funding	Sharp fall of the exchange rate in a crisis	Widening of credit spreads
Inverted		
Short-term dollar debt	Costs ↑	Refinancing risk can become a major factor
Short-term peso debt	Costs ↑ if domestic interest rates rise in real terms	Refinancing risk for corporations; government can print money
Floating-rate peso debt	Costs ↑	Avoids refinancing risk
Long-term floating dollar debt	Costs ↑	Avoids refinancing risk
Long-term fixed dollar debt	Costs ↑	Avoids refinancing risk
Correlated		
Long-term fixed-rate peso debt	Costs ↓ in real terms	Avoids refinancing risk

Note: The term "peso debt" is used as a short-hand for debt denominated in local currency.

Source: Based partly on table 6.2 in Pettis (2001).

pesos could nevertheless find that its future income and spending streams (and thus its net present value) will be differently affected if maturity structures differ. However, the analysis of such impacts will depend on making assumptions about how other variables change when the exchange rate changes (e.g., do domestic interest rates rise or fall in real terms after an exchange rate collapse? Do credit spreads widen when the exchange rate falls? And so on).

An exchange rate collapse was indeed associated with a sharp subsequent rise in domestic interest rates in most recent crises in emerging markets. If a firm has long-term local-currency assets but short-term liabilities (on which interest rates rise), its net income will fall. For this reason, some analysts prefer to focus on the *liquidity* of foreign-currency assets and liabilities rather than on currency mismatches per se. Borrowers face liquidity risks ("balance sheet vulnerability") if "actual or potential obligations on foreign currency exceed the amount of foreign currency that can be addressed on short notice."[2] By focusing on foreign-currency assets that can be accessed "on short notice," one might exclude, inter alia, from the currency-mismatch calculation foreign currency–denominated loans that are illiquid and foreign exchange reserves that the government has lent to offshore branches of commercial banks. Liquidity considerations also

---

2. Chang and Velasco (1999) call this "international illiquidity."

highlight the (remaining) maturity structure of debt and of put options in debt contracts—not just on its original currency composition.

Currency of Denomination of Noninterest Income Flows

The above analysis was couched in terms of a financial entity where income is derived only from financial assets and whose only expenditure is the service of debt. This focus is useful for comparing financial strategies. However, the analysis changes when borrowers have other income and expenditures because changes in exchange rate will also affect such income and expenditures, and this has obvious bearings on the meaning of currency mismatches.

For instance, a firm that is a net earner of foreign exchange will lose from an exchange rate appreciation. This possible loss can be hedged by creating a foreign exchange exposure on its financial balance sheet. Hence what may appear as a currency mismatch defined in terms of assets and liabilities may actually represent a hedge once account is taken of all the firm's activities. Some recent studies have attempted to analyze firms' decisions on the currency composition of debt in terms of their activities (see, for example, Keloharju and Niskanen 2001 and Martinez and Werner 2001).

Similar considerations apply to countries. Most taxes are denominated in local currency, which, prima facie, suggests that borrowing should be in local currency. However, the taxation of tradable output could change this prescription. For instance, foreign currency–denominated funding for countries with very open economies (high proportion of output tradable) will be more sustainable—indeed more desirable—than similar funding for countries with more closed economies. The implication of this is that any currency mismatch derived from balance sheet statistics should be considered in the context of the currency of denomination of noninterest income flows—a point further explored later.

The analysis is further complicated by the fact that financing strategies may involve deliberately taking (or avoiding) exchange rate positions to hedge not only direct and obvious exchange rate exposures but also exposures to associated risks. For example, a European company selling in the United States faces the risk that its goods would become less competitive if the dollar were to depreciate against the euro. It could hedge this by issuing debt denominated in dollars. Other examples could be constructed to incorporate hedges for changes in other variables (e.g., income, credit spreads) associated with exchange rate changes. The fact that changes in the exchange rate are normally associated with changes in other macroeconomic variables (income, exports, and so on) makes it more difficult to pin down the effect of a depreciation on a firm's income or on a country. It makes it harder to know how far an apparent currency mismatch represents a genuine vulnerability.

Financial Institutions and Indirect Currency Mismatches

Defining a mismatch in terms of the sensitivity of net worth to changes in the exchange rate underlines the fact that a currency mismatch can occur from indirect as well as direct currency exposures. Consider, for example, the banking system's exposure to currency risk when its corporate customers have foreign currency–denominated liabilities but only local-currency earnings and limited foreign-currency assets. In such a situation, a large devaluation would increase the debt burden of such borrowers and make them a worse credit risk. The risk-adjusted present discounted value of loans to such borrowers would decline. While such loan deterioration might be formally classified as credit risk (for banks), there is little doubt that the causal factor is an exchange rate change imposed on mismatched currency positions among bank customers. Note that in this example, devaluation would adversely affect the net worth of the banking sector even if the banking system's direct asset/liability position was perfectly matched—that is, even if the foreign-currency share of bank deposits was identical to the foreign-currency share of bank loans.

Balance Sheet Mismatches as a Proportion of Income

Calculating the ratio of some measure of the balance sheet (e.g., net foreign-currency position) to income has the problem that one is denominated in foreign currency and the other mainly in domestic currency. This means that the ratio will change as the exchange rate changes—even if nothing else (e.g., liabilities, income) changes. This truism has often been overlooked in assessing the vulnerability of borrowing countries. As noted earlier, many crises in emerging markets have been preceded by periods of capital inflow–driven real exchange rate appreciation, which drives up the value of nominal GDP relative to foreign-currency debts. With a grossly overvalued exchange rate, the foreign debt/GDP ratio is misleadingly low. Once the exchange rate collapses after a crisis, it rises sharply. There is no simple solution to this problem. One practical solution is to use some proxy for tradables in GDP (e.g., total exports or imports).

Aggregation

The measures discussed in the book and summarized at the end of this appendix are typically *aggregate* measures of economywide mismatches. Such measures provide a useful diagnostic about how manageable mismatches in the country are likely to be. However, a small economywide mismatch need not imply that serious mismatches at the sectoral level are absent. The example offered by Dixon and Hayes (2000) illustrates why the offsetting of one sector's foreign-currency assets against another sector's foreign-currency liabilities implicit in the aggregation process may not be feasible or desirable in practice. Suppose the corporate sector has a sizable excess of foreign currency–denominated liabilities over its liquid foreign-currency assets, but the public sector has large foreign-currency reserves and little foreign-currency liabilities. The economywide mismatch may therefore be minimal. But this does not mean that the sovereign would be willing to use its net reserves to guarantee the corporate sector's net for-eign-currency liability position—especially if the sovereign were worried about extending unduly the official safety net or maintaining a large enough reserve cushion to counter shocks in the currency markets. A large unexpected devaluation would thus leave the corporate sector in a vulnerable position—the small size of the economywide mismatch notwithstanding. Similarly, the household sector may have a positive net foreign-currency position (based on large holdings of foreign-currency assets abroad) at the same time that the sovereign is facing a large nega-tive foreign-currency position. But if the sovereign is not able to induce households to repatriate some of those foreign-held assets and thereby increase its tax revenue (in foreign-currency terms), the sovereign may face a liquidity crisis despite the absence of an economywide currency mismatch.

Contingent Liabilities

Potential foreign-currency liabilities can wreak as much havoc as actual liabilities. When an emerging economy is defending an explicit exchange rate target, the authorities have to stand ready to convert into foreign exchange (at a fixed price) a whole set of domestic-currency liabilities.[3] When market participants come to the view that serious overvaluation makes devaluation inevitable, the set of potential foreign-currency liabil-ities of the government can expand rapidly, as residents begin to convert a wider set of domestic-currency liabilities (including time deposits and government bonds) into foreign exchange. Moreover, if an attempt were made to clear capital flight by offering foreign currency–denominated deposits in local banks, the stock of foreign-currency liabilities would expand further. In such a situation, the precrisis stock of foreign currency–denominated liabilities would not be a good guide either to the potential

---

3. Similarly, a crisis characterized by a sudden stop in capital inflows to emerging economies would render imprudent a reserve-adequacy guideline based on the assumption that capi-tal inflows would continue at the actual pace of recent years. Indeed, it is with such contin-gencies in mind that some officials have recommended a more conservative reserve man-agement guideline for emerging economies that would permit external debt to be serviced on time even if the borrowing country were cut off from new external borrowing for a year. See Calvo and Goldstein (1996).

foreign currency–denominated liabilities or to the size of the potential currency mismatch.[4] It should be recognized further that the onset of financial distress could cause lenders or borrowers to alter the form and currency composition of lending. For example, foreign lenders may refuse to supply local currency–denominated finance once they sense a heightened risk of devaluation. And recent events in Argentina demonstrated that borrowers in dire circumstances may unilaterally redefine the currency composition of existing financial contracts, if the systemic consequences of a large existing currency mismatch cum devaluation are regarded as too costly.

Some Statistical Lacunae

In theory, the obvious starting point for measuring currency mismatches for a country as a whole is to examine the national balance sheet of assets and liabilities. In practice, however, few countries attempt to produce comprehensive data on their external balance sheet position, distinguishing between foreign currency–denominated assets and domestic currency–denominated assets. Chapter 4 cited the example of Thailand (table 4.2). Such estimates, however, are typically incomplete.

Table A.2 reports on a BIS survey of central banks on data published by most of the major emerging-market countries. This shows that the coverage of government data is fairly comprehensive and regarded as reliable, although in some cases the data on individual state-owned enterprises' balance sheets are not aggregated into an overall figure. In some cases, the treatment of government debt issue with exchange rate–linked coupons or principal is unclear (it should be reported as foreign-currency debt). Another complication is that the currency of denomination of some financial instruments changes in response to a given event (e.g., becoming dollar-denominated if the exchange rate falls by more than x percent).

The data on banks' balance sheets are generally regarded as good. Such data are summarized in table 7.2. These data show that there is nothing irreversible about a high dollar (or foreign currency) denomination of banks' balance sheets: Chile, Indonesia, and Mexico have experienced substantial reductions in the degree of dollarization after crises. There are some major gaps for financial institutions other than banks.

The main sectors for which data are generally unavailable and/or of low quality are the corporate sector, and, even more so, the household sector (in some cases household data are not separately distinguished from the corporate sector). Some countries rely on data collected from foreign lenders (including the BIS) or samples of large companies' annual reports for data on the corporate sector's external debt.

---

4. See discussion of the so-called Greenspan and Guidotti rules in chapter 4.

Table A.2 Survey on data published by major emerging-market economies (percent)

	Central government	Central bank	Other government	State-owned enterprises	Banks	Other financial intermediaries	Companies	Households
External debt								
Domestic currency	83	89	67	50	78	44	67	22
Foreign currency	83	89	67	44	83	39	67	17
Of which: Short-term	67	78	67	28	67	33	50	n.a.
Domestic debt								
Domestic currency	100	78	50	28	72	44	67	17
Foreign currency	83	83	61	39	56	44	39	22
Liquid foreign-currency assets	61	78	61	28	56	39	17	11
Credit lines in foreign currency	50	28	61	6	33	22	11	n.a.

n.a. = not available.

Note: Eighteen economies surveyed. Includes cases where debt is prohibited.

Source: Hawkins and Turner (2000).

One particular lacuna in the statistics on external positions is (unregistered) resident holdings of foreign securities or bank accounts held abroad, which tend to be significant in countries with a history of expropriation or high inflation. In some instances, the same local business entity (typically small firms, including family-owned firms) will have dollar-denominated liabilities onshore and dollar-denominated assets offshore. In such a case, the statistics will overstate the effective degree of currency mismatch to which the firm is exposed. But it is unclear whether the existence of dollar assets held abroad provides any comfort for a local bank that has lent dollars to such a firm. The improved viability of a company due to assets held abroad—often secretly—that cannot be touched inevitably limits the degree of comfort afforded to local bank creditors. In the aftermath of several recent banking crisis in the emerging markets, attempts by local banks or publicly financed asset management corporations to recover such assets from solvent borrowers (i.e., solvent when account is taken of the assets secreted abroad) who have defaulted on local loans have not been encouraging.

Moreover, entities with dollar liabilities will often not be the ones that hold the dollar assets. From the point of view of credit risks as assessed by the bank, the mismatch would be best measured by the net liability positions of debtors—with no account taken of the residents with large creditor positions. From the point of view of the macroeconomic wealth effect of devaluation, however, some account should be taken of resident holdings of foreign-currency assets abroad, even if such assets continue to be held largely offshore.

The gaps and the lack of uniformity in data compiled by major debtor countries can to some extent be compensated by the use of data compiled from creditor sources.[5] The most comprehensive data that explicitly measure currency denomination are probably those on international banking flows, which are drawn from the reports to creditor banks and published by the BIS, and on international bond issuance. One big advantage of such data is that they distinguish flows and stocks according to the currency of denomination. The other advantages are their objectivity (debtors do not attempt to massage the figures) and availability for all countries. These data can be summarized in many different ways: detailed tabulations for all emerging-market countries can be found in tables A.3 and A.4. Such data at least provide a convenient starting point—and hopefully can prompt national authorities to cross-check and improve their own statistics.

---

5. Von Kleist (2002) provides one useful comparison.

Table A.3 Ratio of M2 to foreign exchange reserves, 1990–2002

Region/country	1990	1995	1996	1997	1998	1999	2000	2001	2002
Latin America[a]	**5.5**	**4.1**	**3.8**	**3.9**	**4.2**	**4.3**	**4.4**	**4.3**	**3.4**
Argentina	3.3	3.8	3.5	3.5	3.5	3.4	3.7	5.0	2.5
Brazil	5.9	3.7	3.1	4.2	5.0	4.4	4.5	3.9	3.0
Chile	1.1	1.5	1.7	1.7	2.0	2.1	2.1	2.0	1.9
Colombia	1.5	2.0	2.1	2.4	2.9	2.8	2.4	2.3	2.0
Mexico	10.6	7.5	7.4	6.1	5.7	7.2	7.3	7.0	6.1
Peru	2.4	1.3	1.2	1.5	1.7	2.0	2.0	2.0	2.0
Venezuela	1.6	2.1	1.0	1.2	1.5	1.5	1.6	2.5	1.7
Asia, large economies[a]	**35.2**	**9.7**	**9.1**	**8.4**	**8.3**	**8.4**	**8.3**	**7.5**	**6.6**
China	9.8	9.9	8.7	7.9	8.8	9.5	9.9	8.9	7.9
Hong Kong	6.3	5.3	5.1	3.9	4.5	4.5	4.4	4.1	4.0
India	111.6	8.5	8.8	7.7	7.6	7.3	6.7	6.1	4.9
Korea	14.0	15.0	15.4	15.5	10.2	8.0	5.8	5.7	6.1
Taiwan	3.3	5.4	6.0	5.5	5.6	5.3	5.4	4.6	3.6
Other Asia[a]	**6.6**	**5.4**	**5.0**	**4.2**	**3.6**	**3.4**	**3.0**	**3.1**	**3.1**
Indonesia	6.1	7.2	6.6	4.7	3.2	3.5	2.8	3.0	3.2
Malaysia	3.0	3.2	3.5	3.5	2.9	2.8	3.2	3.2	2.9
Philippines	15.2	6.0	4.7	5.3	4.6	3.6	3.2	3.1	3.4
Singapore	1.5	1.3	1.3	1.2	1.3	1.4	1.2	1.3	1.3
Thailand	4.6	3.7	3.9	3.6	4.6	3.8	3.7	3.7	3.3
Central Europe[a]	**21.4**	**2.5**	**2.7**	**2.7**	**2.6**	**2.4**	**2.6**	**3.1**	**2.9**
Czech Republic	62.9	2.7	3.2	3.6	3.4	3.0	3.0	3.2	2.4
Hungary	13.3	1.5	1.9	2.2	2.2	1.9	1.9	2.4	3.5
Poland	4.1	2.8	2.6	2.4	2.3	2.4	2.6	3.3	3.0
Russia	37.2	3.3	4.6	4.9	2.8	3.1	1.7	1.6	1.5
Israel	5.8	8.0	6.9	4.1	3.7	4.3	4.7	4.7	4.6
Turkey	5.3	3.3	3.0	2.8	3.3	3.2	3.8	3.9	3.0
Saudi Arabia	n.a.	n.a.	5.4	5.4	5.9	5.2	4.7	6.0	6.1
South Africa	51.9	23.9	64.6	14.5	15.7	11.7	10.5	7.6	12.3
Memorandum:									
Australia	9.6	17.9	17.0	12.9	15.8	12.4	12.9	14.0	15.3
Sweden	6.2	4.8	6.5	10.8	8.4	8.1	7.4	7.6	7.9
Switzerland	6.2	8.5	7.4	7.3	7.4	7.3	7.4	7.7	8.2

M2 = broad money liabilities
n.a. = not available

a. Weighted average of countries shown, based on 1995 GDP and PPP exchange rates.

Sources: IMF's *International Financial Statistics* and national sources.

Table A.4   Domestic debt securities outstanding, 1994–2002
(billions of dollars)

	1994	1995	1996	1997	1998	1999	2000	2001	2002
Latin America[a]	**270**	**314**	**395**	**467**	**519**	**447**	**483**	**508**	**386**
Argentina	30	26	29	34	40	43	47	37	18
Brazil	173	231	297	344	391	294	298	312	212
Chile	25	29	32	37	34	33	35	35	35
Colombia	4	5	7	8	10	12	15	18	18
Mexico	37	22	24	38	38	57	74	88	88
Peru	1	1	1	2	2	3	4	4	4
Venezuela	n.a.	n.a.	5	4	4	5	10	14	11
China	66	93	119	162	228	293	355	419	480
India	64	71	81	75	86	102	114	130	156
Korea	185	227	239	130	240	265	269	293	381
Taiwan	68	76	100	101	124	126	123	124	141
Hong Kong	17	24	34	41	40	43	43	44	45
Singapore	20	23	25	24	29	36	43	51	55
Other Asia[a]	**94**	**105**	**118**	**85**	**109**	**121**	**126**	**141**	**152**
Malaysia	54	62	73	57	62	66	75	83	83
Philippines	26	26	28	18	21	22	20	22	22
Thailand	14	16	17	10	24	32	31	36	47
Central Europe[a]	**40**	**49**	**53**	**51**	**67**	**69**	**72**	**90**	**129**
Czech Republic	7	12	12	12	22	25	23	26	43
Hungary	12	12	15	14	16	17	17	20	31
Poland	21	25	26	25	29	27	32	44	55
Russia	3	17	43	65	8	9	8	5	7
Israel	86	94	103	103	99	102	103	101	106
Turkey	16	21	27	30	38	43	55	85	92
South Africa	97	98	79	80	69	69	58	39	53
Total[a]	**1,029**	**1,215**	**1,416**	**1,416**	**1,654**	**1,724**	**1,851**	**2,030**	**2,184**
Memorandum:									
Australia	181	176	198	170	168	206	172	170	207
Sweden	228	271	281	241	250	238	197	160	207

n.a. = not available

a. Sum of the countries shown.

Note: Data are by country of issuer, outstanding year-end positions.

Sources: Central banks, IMF's *International Financial Statistics*, and the Bank for International Settlements.

Appendix B
Evolution of the Original Sin Hypothesis

The original sin hypothesis (OSH) is most closely associated with the work of Barry Eichengreen, Ricardo Hausmann, and Ugo Panizza, in various combinations—that is, Eichengreen and Hausmann (1999, 2003a–c); Eichengreen, Hausmann, and Panizza (2002, 2003a–e); and Hausmann and Panizza (2002, 2003). OSH was first defined as a situation "in which the domestic currency cannot be used to borrow abroad or to borrow long term, even domestically" (Eichengreen and Hausmann 1999, 330).

The first version of the OSH stressed the incompleteness of financial markets as the main culprit of financial fragility; for example, Eichengreen and Hausmann (1999, 330) argued that currency mismatches exist not because banks and firms in emerging economies lack the prudence to hedge their exposures but rather because they are *unable* (emphasis added) to do so (since foreigners are unwilling to take the other side of a hedge contract). The OSH authors regarded the causes of original sin as an open question. They seemed to reject the proposition that original sin was mainly due to a borrower's history of inflation and currency depreciation, since their measure of original sin suggested that it was present in more than a few emerging economies without a recent history of high inflation. They leaned instead toward an explanation that emphasizes incomplete information and sovereign risk; more specifically, they suggested that foreign investors were reluctant to invest in domestic currency–denominated assets (of the borrower) because they could not tell which borrowers would manipulate the currency to minimize debt payments. To explain relatively low levels of original sin in a few nonreserve-currency countries (e.g., Australia), Eichengreen and Hausmann (1999) speculated that because these countries developed their domestic financial markets first (i.e., before relying on external borrowing), they created a political constituency that opposed opportunistic depreciation (thereby easing the concerns of foreign investors).

Whatever its causes, the original interpretation of OSH saw just two ways out of the original sin trap. One was to eliminate the exchange rate by dollarizing (or the euro equivalent). This would dissolve currency mismatches since income streams would then be denominated in the same currency unit as liabilities. But there was a worry that if dollarization proceeded before other risks to financial stability were eliminated, the attendant removal of lender-of-last-resort facilities and the loss of independent monetary policy could prove hazardous. The other way out of original sin would be to embark on an effort to build deep and liquid domestic markets in long-term domestic currency–denominated securities. But this route to redemption was regarded both as taking too long and as being increasingly difficult to achieve in a world of liberalized financial markets and floating exchange rates.

The mark II version of the OSH, as best captured in Eichengreen, Hausmann, and Panizza (2002) included some notable changes. To begin with, the domestic element in OSH was discarded. Original sin was then defined simply as a situation in which "most countries cannot borrow abroad in their own currencies" (Eichengreen, Hausmann, and Panizza 2002, 1). As in the original version of the OSH, original sin was again measured by the shares of cross-border bank loans and international bonds that were denominated in domestic currency. The authors showed that aside from the issuers of the five major currencies (that is, the United States, euro area, Japan, the United Kingdom, and Switzerland), the phenomenon of original sin was both widespread and persistent over time. Outliers (i.e., nonreserve-currency countries with relatively low levels of original sin, such as Poland, New Zealand, South Africa, and the Czech Republic) were regarded as not challenging the basic OSH because over 80 percent of their debt issued in local currency was accounted for by nonresidents, especially the international financial institutions (IFIs) such as the World Bank.

Notably, the mark II version of the OSH made no attempt to distinguish original sin from aggregate currency mismatch; indeed, quite the contrary. In explaining the "pain of original sin," Eichengreen, Hausmann, and Panizza (2002, 10) argued that "countries with original sin that have net foreign debt will have a currency mismatch on their national balance sheets." This tight link between original sin and aggregate currency mismatch allowed them to argue that movements in exchange rates would generate wealth effects that would limit the effectiveness of monetary policy, that central banks would be less willing to let exchange rates move and would be less able to avert liquidity crises, and that dollar-denominated debts and the associated volatility of domestic interest rates would heighten the uncertainty associated with public debt service—thereby lowering credit ratings. In their empirical work, Eichengreen, Hausmann, and Panizza (2002) ran a series of regressions that tested the pain of original sin—usually regressing various outcome variables (e.g., real output volatility, international capital flow volatility, country credit ratings) on various measures of original sin. Underlining the assumed equivalence between original sin and aggregate currency mismatch, the sector headings for these regression results carried labels like "Currency mismatches and exchange rate volatility" (p. 11) and "Currency mismatches and output and capital-flow volatility" (p. 14)—even though the variable that actually appears in these regressions is original sin. Likewise, throughout the text, original sin and aggregate currency mismatch were used interchangeably; for example, in summarizing their empirical findings, Eichengreen, Hausmann, and Panizza (2002, 16) stated: "In sum, we find statistically significant and economically important effects of original sin on exchange rate and GDP volatility and on country credit ratings. Currency mismatches clearly create serious problems for the countries saddled with them, and as we showed in Section 2 above, these problems are pervasive."

The mark II explanation for original sin rested on transactions costs and network externalities. Building on their empirical finding that the only robust determinant of original sin was country size, Eichengreen, Hausmann, and Panizza (2002) argued that in a world of transactions costs, the optimal portfolio would have a finite number of currencies, and that the benefits of further diversification from adding new currencies would fall faster than the costs. Most strikingly, Eichengreen, Hausmann, and Panizza (2002) maintained (again supported by their regression results) that original sin was *not* related to weaknesses of national macroeconomic policies or institutions. This comes across most clearly in the concluding paragraph (p. 42) of their paper:

> The evidence is strong that original sin is not going to go away anytime soon as a result of the standard recipe of macroeconomic prudence and institution building. Neither cross-country nor time-series evidence supports the view that efforts to strengthen policies and institutions will suffice to ameliorate the problem over the horizon relevant for practical policy decisions.

Eichengreen, Hausmann, and Panizza (2002) proposed an *international* initiative to solve the problem because they saw original sin as being generated primarily by international transactions costs and network externalities; the dollarization option has apparently been discarded. They recommended that a basket index of emerging-market currencies be developed, that both the IFIs and the G-10 countries issue debt denominated in the index (so as to transform the structure of the global portfolio in favor of emerging-market currencies), and that swaps be encouraged between the IFIs and G-10 countries on the one hand and the individual countries in the index on the other. Once a liquid market in this index of emerging-market currencies had developed, the IFIs and G-10 countries could scale back their role. Again, the concluding sentence of Eichengreen, Hausmann, and Panizza (2002, 42) highlights the low importance accorded to good domestic policies:

> The *only* practical way for a large group of countries representing over 90 percent of the population and the GDP of the developing world to escape original sin is an international initiative to develop an EM index and a market in claims denominated in it (emphasis added).

The mark III version of the OSH appears in the 2003 papers of Eichengreen and Hausmann (2003), Eichengreen, Hausmann, and Panizza (2003a–e), and Hausmann and Panizza (2003). In some of the papers written between August and November of 2003 (Eichengreen and Hausmann 2003b, 2003c and Eichengreen, Hausmann, and Panizza 2003d, 2003e), the authors respond explicitly to criticisms of their earlier work by Goldstein and Turner (2003), Reinhart, Rogoff, and Savastano (2003b), and Burger and Warnock (2002). As suggested in chapter 1, the mark III version of the OSH modifies significantly the arguments put forward in the two earlier versions of the OSH. Three modifications merit explicit mention.

First, Eichengreen, Hausmann, and Panizza and Hausmann and Panizza jettison the mark II practice of looking only at the "international" dimension of original sin. In a footnote, Eichengreen, Hausmann, and Panizza (2003e) explain that they had focused on the international aspect of original sin because that problem seemed particularly intractable. More significantly, they acknowledge that a growing number of countries are showing an ability to develop domestic bond markets.[1] In recognition of that reality, they define domestic original sin as the "inability to borrow domestically long-term at fixed rates in local currency" (Hausmann and Panizza 2003, 963). Although they do not have data either on domestic bank loans, or on private domestic bonds, or on nontraded, domestic government bonds, they are able to classify (traded) domestic government bonds by maturity, currency, and coupon (fixed and indexed rates).[2] They find that only Argentina, among the 21 emerging economies included in their sample, has as much as half its domestic public debt denominated in foreign currency—thereby supporting our finding in chapter 3 that the foreign-currency composition of domestic bonds is very different from

---

1. This seems a switch in view. In Eichengreen and Hausmann (1999), the authors concluded that building a demand for long-term, domestic currency–denominated securities may be even harder in today's world of liberalized financial markets and floating exchange rates. In Eichengreen, Hausmann, and Panizza (2002), they question what governments in emerging economies can do to promote the development of a large constituency of domestic bondholders and are skeptical about any approach that would require banks, pension funds, and the social security system to hold long-term, domestic currency–denominated, fixed-rate debt.

2. Hausmann and Panizza (2003) note that domestic private debt instruments are important in Singapore, Korea, Taiwan, and Thailand.

that for international bonds. Hausmann and Panizza (2003) also report that for about half the countries in their sample, the sum of domestic-currency, fixed-rate bonds and domestic-currency, inflation-indexed bonds accounts for half or more of domestic public debt. Similarly, in 9 of the 21 countries, long-term, fixed-rate, domestic-currency bonds represented half or more of the total.[3] These figures would seem to support our argument in chapter 3 that domestic bond markets in emerging economies are already quite important.

When Hausmann and Panizza (2003) compute correlations between measures of domestic and international original sin, they find that the correlations are positive but are not strong and are rarely statistically significant. Perhaps more interesting, when they look at countries with original sin ratios of 0.75 or higher, they report that no country with high domestic original sin has low international original sin—a result they themselves interpret as suggesting that convincing one's residents to lend in local currency at long maturities seems to be a necessary condition to convince foreigners to do the same. At the same time, they find that seven countries had low domestic original sin but relatively high international original sin, implying that dominant use of the local currency in domestic financial markets is not a sufficient condition for dominant use internationally. Hausmann and Panizza (2003) discount the possibility that the escape from international sin merely lags the escape from domestic original sin by arguing that the country composition of international original sin is similar between the international bond market of the mid-19th century and that of more recent years.

A second major modification in the mark III version of the OSH concerns the distinction between aggregate currency mismatch and (international) original sin. As argued earlier, we found that all the OSH papers written up until the latter part of August 2003 essentially used the two terms interchangeably and suggested strongly that (international) original sin implied an aggregate currency mismatch for the vast majority of developing countries. In the (latest) mark III version, Eichengreen, Hausmann, and Panizza (2003e) and Eichengreen and Hausmann (2003) reject our interpretation of their earlier work. For the first time, they now state explicitly that the two concepts are *not* the same and argue that those working on original sin are trying to measure something different from currency mismatch. In particular, Eichengreen, Hausmann, and Panizza (2003e, 16) now maintain that one consequence of original sin is the tendency for afflicted countries to accumulate international reserves as a way of protecting themselves from the potentially destabilizing financial consequences; as such, "where an aggregate mismatch is one possible conse-

---

3. Hausmann and Panizza (2003) choose instead to highlight the finding that only 5 of the 21 countries had a share of long-term, fixed-rate, domestic-currency bonds that was 75 percent or higher.

quence of original sin, it is not a necessary one." In addition, instead of asserting (as they did earlier) that an aggregate currency mismatch will occur when there is a net debt to foreigners, they now argue (as in Goldstein and Turner 2003) that an aggregate mismatch exists when there is net debt to foreigners *denominated in foreign currency*;[4] this modification is necessary to reflect the fact (noted in chapter 3) that some significant portion of debt owed to foreigners is not denominated in foreign currency (i.e., net debtor status is based on a country's net international investment position, which is not necessarily equivalent to its net currency mismatch).

While we believe there are many reasons (not just reserve accumulation) why aggregate currency mismatch may differ from (international) original sin, we welcome and agree with the mark III distinction; indeed, this distinction formed much of our earlier criticism of the OSH in Goldstein and Turner (2003).

In addition to clarifying the distinction between aggregate currency mismatch and (international) original sin, the mark III version of the OSH includes some new empirical material on the impact of original sin versus that of aggregate currency mismatch. Because the Goldstein-Turner (2003) measure of aggregate effective currency mismatch (AECM) was available for only 22 emerging economies and because Eichengreen, Hausmann, and Panizza (2003e) wanted a larger sample, they decided to replace our measure with their own mismatch variable that combines information on reserves, international debt, exports, and original sin. As Eichengreen, Hausmann, and Panizza (2003e) acknowledge (in a footnote), their mismatch variable does not capture either net international assets or the currency composition of total debt; as such, it differs nontrivially from our measure, although Eichengreen, Hausmann, and Panizza (2003e) report that the correlation between the two measures (for countries for which both series are available) was reasonably high (0.8). Eichengreen, Hausmann, and Panizza (2003e) conduct a set of regression exercises where both original sin and aggregate currency mismatch are included (simultaneously) as explanatory variables. In brief, they find that original sin is significantly related to exchange rate flexibility whereas mismatch is not, that neither original sin nor mismatch is significantly correlated with the volatility of growth or capital flows, and that both original sin and mismatch are significantly correlated with country credit ratings.

Eichengreen, Hausmann, and Panizza (2003e) regard these results as supporting their view that original sin has important consequences for financial fragility even if it doesn't measure aggregate currency mismatch. We, in contrast, regard these new empirical results as having lim-

---

4. As late as August 2003, Eichengreen, Hausmann, and Panizza (2003c, 15) were still arguing: "Our point is that an aggregate mismatch is unavoidable when a country suffers from original sin and there is a *net* foreign debt" (emphasis added).

ited value in assessing the usefulness of our AECM measure and as lending little support to the OSH. As noted in chapter 3, we see the AECM as a useful shorthand stress test of the impact of currency mismatches on the real economy, contingent on a large exchange rate change taking place. The regressions reported in Eichengreen, Hausmann, and Panizza (2003e) have at best only a weak link with such stress tests. As Eichengreen, Hausmann, and Panizza (2003e) argue themselves, whereas original sin and debt intolerance seek to explain the same phenomenon—namely, the volatility of emerging-market economies and the difficulty that these countries have in servicing and repaying their debts, currency mismatching is concerned instead with the "consequences" of these problems. For these reasons, comparisons of original sin with measures of currency mismatch in volatility regressions don't shed much light on the distinctions between them. In addition, the Eichengreen, Hausmann, and Panizza (2003e) measure of aggregate mismatch leaves out some key components found in our measure (AECM). As for the OSH itself, we read the regression results in Eichengreen, Hausmann, and Panizza (2003e) as suggesting that the effect of original sin on the volatility of real output and of capital flows is quite sensitive to the inclusion of other (currency composition) variables, and that original sin is hardly unique (among currency composition variables) in affecting country credit ratings.

Yet a noteworthy third modification found in the mark III version of the OSH is that the importance of national policies and institutions has been upgraded, while the necessity of an international initiative (to escape from original sin) has been downgraded somewhat.

The earlier versions of the OSH conveyed the impression (at least to us and many others) that national policies and institutions had little impact on (international) original sin and on aggregate currency mismatch relative to international factors. In contrast, the mark III version seems to accord the former at least equal, if not greater, status. Specifically, in Eichengreen, Hausmann, and Panizza (2003e, 5), the authors state that "the intermediate position is that domestic policies and institutions are important for the ability of countries to borrow abroad in their own currencies but so are factors largely beyond the control of the individual country;" they then go on to indicate that this "intermediate position" is a fair summary of their view on the origins of original sin. Similarly, in Eichengreen and Hausmann (2003b, 6), the authors characterize their position as suggesting that original sin, and hence the susceptibility to exchange rate–related balance sheet effects, reflects "not just weaknesses of their own policies and institutions but also something about the structure of the international financial system." And in Eichengreen and Hausmann (2003c, 3), the authors explain that "we have no quibble with arguments for robust institutions that guarantee the rule of law, strengthen property rights, and encourage responsible fiscal, monetary, and financial policies. We would certainly encourage countries to develop long-term fixed rate domestic debt markets in local currency, in nominal terms where possible and in inflation-indexed terms where not." Note that in their most recent empirical work, Eichengreen, Hausmann, and Panizza (2003d) still fail to find any evidence that international original sin is significantly associated with domestic policies and institutions—rendering somewhat mysterious their statement that good policies are necessary but not sufficient for escaping from original sin. But they do find that monetary policy credibility and exchange rate flexibility, alongside other factors, are significantly related to domestic original sin.

Similar recent changes are evident in the discussion of their international initiative (the new EM index). Whereas Eichengreen, Hausmann, and Panizza (2002) described their proposed EM index as "the only practical way" to escape from original sin, Eichengreen and Hausmann argue in their October 2003 paper (2003c, 3) that in addition to better domestic policies and institutions, "an international initiative *may* be required" (emphasis added). In the latter paper, Eichengreen and Hausmann also characterize their proposal as one of several instruments (including GDP- and commodity-linked bonds) aimed at increased international risk sharing and at helping complete incomplete financial markets.

To sum up, the OSH hypothesis has undergone a series of changes since its debut in the 1999 paper of Eichengreen and Hausmann. In the mark I and II versions, the OSH was very bold in its claims about the link between original sin and aggregate currency mismatch, about the importance of international financial markets relative to domestic ones, about the lack of differentiation among emerging economies in their capacity to cope with currency mismatches, about the role of international network externalities and transactions costs relative to domestic policies and institutions in causing original sin, and about the necessity of an international initiative to escape from original sin. In the mark III version of the OSH, these bold claims seem (at least to us) to have been scaled back significantly—moving the OSH closer both to the mainstream view of financial fragility in emerging economies and to the view expressed in this book about the desirability of a (largely) domestic agenda for dealing with the currency mismatch problem.

To be clear, we are not critical of the authors of the OSH for having modified over time their view on original sin and on aggregate currency mismatch in light of further research and critical comment. After all, that is how economic science progresses. Also, much has been learned from the ongoing debate on the OSH, including the contribution that the OSH has made to a better understanding of what determines the currency composition of international bonds and cross-border bank loans. We do not want to be seen as suggesting that domestic policies and institutions are the only thing (rather than the main thing) that matters for the currency mismatch problem, or that emerging economies would not find life easier if more of them could borrow abroad in their own currency, or that it does not take time before the progress in developing a healthy domestic-currency local bond market spills over into international claims, or that some financial innovations would not be helpful in improving emerging economies' ability to pay in the face of large shocks; indeed, on the last point, we have argued that there would be merit in further exploring the use of GDP-indexed bonds. Where we parted company with the mark I and II versions of OSH was on how best to define and measure aggregate currency mismatch, on differentiation among emerging economies in their ability to cope with currency mismatches, and on how much weight to give the "domestic" versus "international" elements of currency mismatch. The mark III version of the OSH reduces but by no means eliminates this disagreement.

References

ABS (Australian Bureau of Statistics). 2001. Measuring Australia's Foreign Currency Exposure. In *Balance of Payments and International Investment Position, Australia* (December quarter). Canberra: Australian Bureau of Statistics.

Aghion, Philippe, Philippe Bacchetta, and Abhijit Banerjee. 2001. A Corporate Balance Sheet Approach to Currency Crises. Harvard University, Department of Economics. Photocopy.

Alba, Pedro, Amar Bhattacharya, Stijn Claessens, Swati Ghosh, and Leonardo Hernandez. 1998. *Volatility and Contagion in a Financially Integrated World: Lessons from East Asia's Recent Experience*. World Bank Policy Research Working Paper 2008 (November). Washington: World Bank.

Allen, Mark, Christopher Rosenberg, Christian Keller, Brad Setser, and Nouriel Roubini. 2002. *A Balance-Sheet Approach to Financial Crisis*. IMF Working Paper 02/210 (December). Washington: International Monetary Fund.

Anderson, P. 1999. Sovereign Debt Management in an Asset-Liability Management Framework. Paper presented at the Second Sovereign Debt Management Forum, World Bank, Washington, November 1–3.

Arteta, Carlos. 2002. *Exchange Rate Regimes and Financial Dollarization: Does Flexibility Reduce Bank Currency Mismatches?* International Finance Discussion Papers 738 (September). Washington: Board of Governors of the Federal Reserve System.

Arteta, Carlos. 2003. *Are Financially Dollarized Countries More Prone to Costly Crises?* International Finance Discussion Papers 763 (March). Washington: Board of Governors of the Federal Reserve System.

Aturupane, Chonira, Nicholas Blancher, Sergei Dodzin, and Christian Mulder. 2004 (forthcoming). Reserve-Related Indicators of External Vulnerability. Washington: International Monetary Fund. Photocopy.

Balino, Tomas, Adam Bennett, and Eduardo Borensztein. 1999. *Monetary Policy in Dollarized Economies*. IMF Occasional Paper 171. Washington: International Monetary Fund.

BIS (Bank for International Settlements). 1997. Financial Fragility in Asia. *67th Annual Report*. Bank for International Settlements, Basel (June).

BIS (Bank for International Settlements). 1998. *68th Annual Report*. Bank for International Settlements, Basel (June).

BIS (Bank for International Settlements). 2002. *Comparison of Creditor and Debtor Data on Short-Term External Debt*. BIS Policy Papers no. 13. Basel: Bank for International Settlements.

Barth, James, Gerard Caprio, and Ross Levine. 2000. *Banking Systems Around the Globe*. World Bank Policy Research Paper 2325 (April). Washington: World Bank.

Basel Committee on Banking Supervision. 1992. *A Framework for Measuring and Managing Liquidity*. Basel: Bank for International Settlements (September).

Basel Committee on Banking Supervision. 1996. *Amendment of the Capital Accord to Incorporate Market Risks*. Basel Committee Publications no. 24 (January, updated April 1998). Basel: Bank for International Settlements

Basel Committee on Banking Supervision. 2000. *Sound Practices for Managing Liquidity in Banking Organisations*. Basel Committee Publications no. 69 (February). Basel: Bank for International Settlements.

Bell, J. 2000. Leading Indicator Model of Banking Crises—A Critical Review. *Financial Stability Review* (December). Bank of England, London.

Benston, George, and George Kaufman. 1988. Risk and Solvency Regulation of Depository Institutions: Past Policies and Current Options. *Monograph Series in Finance and Economics*. New York: Stern School of Business, New York University.

Berg, Andrew, Eduardo Borensztein, Gian Maria Milesi-Ferretti, and Catherine Pattillo. 1999. *Anticipating Balance of Payments Crises: The Role of Early Warning Systems*. IMF Occasional Paper 186. Washington: International Monetary Fund.

Bernanke, Ben, Thomas Laubach, Frederic Mishkin, and Adam Posen. 1999. *Inflation Targeting: Lessons from the International Experience*. Princeton: Princeton University Press.

Bevilaqua, Afonso, and Marcio Garcia. 2000. *Debt Management in Brazil: Evaluation of the Real Plan and Challenges Ahead*. World Bank Policy Research Paper 2402 (July). Washington: World Bank.

Bleakley, Hoyt, and Kevin Cowan. 2002. Corporate Dollar Debt and Devaluations: Much Ado About Nothing? Massachusetts Institute of Technology, Cambridge, MA. Photocopy (February).

Bordo, Michael, Christopher Meissner, and Angela Redish. 2002. How Original Sin Was Overcome: The Evolution of External Debt Denominated in Domestic Currencies in the United States and the British Dominions, 1800–2000. Paper presented at a conference on Currency and Maturity Matchmaking: Redeeming Debt from Original Sin, Inter-American Development Bank, November 21–22, Washington.

Borensztein, Eduardo, and Paolo Mauro. 2002. Reviving the Case for GDP-Indexed Bonds. IMF Policy Discussion Paper no. 02/10. Washington: International Monetary Fund (September).

Broda, Christian, and Eduardo Levy Yeyati. 2003. *Endogenous Deposit Dollarization*. Federal Reserve Bank of New York Staff Report 160. New York: Federal Reserve Bank of New York.

Burger, John, and Francis Warnock. 2002. *Diversification, Original Sin, and International Bond Portfolios*. Washington: International Finance Division, Board of Governors of the Federal Reserve System (December).

Burnside, Craig, Martin Eichenbaum, and Sergio Rebelo. 1999. *Hedging and Financial Fragility in Fixed Exchange Rate Regimes*. NBER Working Paper 7143. Cambridge, MA: National Bureau of Economic Research.

Bussiere, Matthieu, and Christian Mulder. 1999. *External Vulnerability in Emerging Market Economies: How High Liquidity Can Offset Weak Fundamentals and The Effects of Contagion*. IMF Working Paper 99/88 (July). Washington: International Monetary Fund.

Caballero, Ricardo, and Arvind Krishnamurthy. 1998. *Emerging Market Crises: An Asset Markets Prospective*. NBER Working Paper 6843 (December). Cambridge, MA: National Bureau of Economic Research.

Caballero, Ricardo J., and Arvind Krishnamurthy. 2002. A Dual Liquidity Model for Emerging Markets. *American Economic Review* (May): 33–37.

Calvo, Guillermo, and Morris Goldstein. 1996. What Role for the Official Sector? In *Private Capital Flows to Emerging Economies after the Mexican Crisis*, ed., Guillermo Calvo, Morris Goldstein, and Eduard Hochreiter. Washington: Institute for International Economics.

Calvo, Guillermo, and Carmen Reinhart. 2000. *Fear of Floating*. NBER Working Paper 7993 (November). Cambridge, MA: National Bureau of Economic Research.

Calvo, Guillermo, and Carmen Reinhart. 2001. Fixing for Your Life. In *Brookings Trade Forum: 2000*, ed., Susan M. Collins and Dani Rodrik. Washington: Brookings Institution.

Caprio, Gerard, and Patrick Honohan. 2001. *Finance for Growth: Policy Choices in a Volatile World*. Washington and Oxford: World Bank and Oxford University Press.

Cavallo, Michele, Kate Kisselev, Fabrizio Perri, and Nouriel Roubini. 2001. Exchange Rate Overshooting and the Cost of Floating. Paper presented at the NBER IFM Spring Meeting, Princeton (March).

CGFS (Committee on the Global Financial System). 2004. Report of the Working Group on Foreign Direct Investment in the Financial System of Emerging Economies (Christine Cumming, chair). Bank for International Settlements, Basel (April).

Chang, Roberto, and Andres Velasco. 1999. *Liquidity Crises in Emerging Markets: Theory and Policy*. NBER Working Paper 7272. Cambridge, MA: National Bureau of Economic Research.

Chrystal, Alec. 1984. On the Theory of International Money. In *Problems of International Finance: Papers on the Seventh Annual Conference of the International Economics Study Group*, ed., John Black and G. S. Dorrance. New York: Palgrave Macmillan.

Corbo, Vittorio, Oscar Moreno, and Klaus Schmidt-Hebbel. 2001. Assessing Inflation Targeting After a Decade of Experience. Central Bank of Chile, Santiago. Photocopy (March).

Corden, W. Max. 2002. *Too Sensational: On the Choice of Exchange Rate Regimes*. Cambridge, MA: MIT Press.

Cowan, Kevin. 2003. Firm Level Determinants of Dollar Debt. Inter-American Development Bank, Washington. Photocopy (May).

Cuevas, A., and A. Werner. Mexico's Experience with a Flexible Exchange Rate Regime. *International Management* 8, no. 1. Montreal.

De Nicolo, Gianni, Patrick Honohan, and Alan Ize. 2003. *Dollarization of the Banking System: Good or Bad?* World Bank Policy Research Working Paper 3116. Washington: World Bank (August).

Disyatat, Piti. 2001. *Currency Crises and the Real Economy: The Role of Banks*. IMF Working Paper 01/49 (May). Washington: International Monetary Fund.

Dixon, Liz, and Simon Hayes. 2000. Vulnerability Indicators from the National Balance Sheet. Bank of England, London. Photocopy (December).

Edison, Hali. 2000. *Do Indicators of Financial Crises Work? An Evaluation of an Early Warning System*. International Finance Discussion Paper 675 (July). Washington: Board of Governors of the Federal Reserve System.

Eichengreen, Barry, and Ricardo Hausmann. 1999. Exchange Rates and Financial Fragility. In *New Challenges for Monetary Policy*. Proceedings of a symposium sponsored by the Federal Reserve Bank of Kansas City, August 26–28, Jackson Hole, Wyoming. Kansas City: Federal Reserve Bank of Kansas City.

Eichengreen, Barry, and Ricardo Hausmann. 2003a. Original Sin: The Road to Redemption. University of California, Berkeley, and Harvard University. Unpublished paper (June).

Eichengreen, Barry, and Ricardo Hausmann. 2003b. Debt Denomination and Financial Instability in Emerging Market Economies: Editors' Introduction. University of California, Berkeley, and Harvard University. Unpublished paper (September).

Eichengreen, Barry, and Ricardo Hausmann. 2003c. Original Sin: The Road to Redemption. University of California, Berkeley, and Harvard University. Unpublished paper (October).

Eichengreen, Barry, Ricardo Hausmann, and Ugo Panizza. 2002. Original Sin: The Pain, the Mystery, and the Road to Redemption. Paper presented at a conference on Currency and Maturity Matchmaking: Redeeming Debt from Original Sin, Inter-American Development Bank, November 21–22, Washington.

Eichengreen, Barry, Ricardo Hausmann, and Ugo Panizza. 2003a. The Mystery of Original Sin. University of California, Berkeley, Harvard University, and Inter-American Development Bank. Unpublished paper (June).

Eichengreen, Barry, Ricardo Hausmann, and Ugo Panizza. 2003b. The Pain of Original Sin. University of California, Berkeley, Harvard University, and Inter-American Development Bank. Unpublished paper (June).

Eichengreen, Barry, Ricardo Hausmann, and Ugo Panizza. 2003c. The Mystery of Original Sin. University of California, Berkeley, Harvard University, and Inter-American Development Bank. Unpublished paper (August).

Eichengreen, Barry, Ricardo Hausmann, and Ugo Panizza. 2003d. The Pain of Original Sin. University of California, Berkeley, Harvard University, and Inter-American Development Bank. Unpublished paper (August).

Eichengreen, Barry, Ricardo Hausmann, and Ugo Panizza. 2003e. *Currency Mismatches, Debt Intolerance, and Original Sin: Why They Are Not the Same and Why It Matters.* NBER Working Paper 10036. Cambridge, MA: National Bureau of Economic Research.

Financial Stability Forum. 2000. Report of the Working Group on Capital Flows (Mario Draghi, Chair). Basel, April.

Flandreau, Marc, and Nathan Sussman. 2002. Old Sins: Exchange Clauses and European Foreign Lending in the 19th Century. Paper presented at a conference on Currency and Maturity Matchmaking: Redeeming Debt from Original Sin, Inter-American Development Bank, November 21–22, Washington.

Frankel, Jeffrey. 1995. Still the Lingua Franca: The Exaggerated Death of the Dollar. *Foreign Affairs* 74, no. 4: 9–16.

Frenkel, Jacob, and Morris Goldstein. 1999. The International Role of the Deutsch Mark. In *Fifty Years of the Deutsche Mark*, Deutsche Bundesbank. Oxford: Oxford University Press.

Furman, Jason, and Joseph Stiglitz. 1998. *Economic Crises: Evidence and Insights from East Asia.* Brookings Papers on Economic Activity 1998: 2. Washington: Brookings Institution.

Garber, Peter. 1998. *Derivatives in International Capital Flows.* NBER Working Paper 6623 (June). Cambridge, MA: National Bureau of Economic Research.

Gelos, Gaston R., and Shang-Jin Wei. 2002. *Transparency and International Investor Behavior.* IMF Working Paper 02/174. Washington: International Monetary Fund (October).

Goldstein, Morris. 1998. *The Asian Financial Crisis: Causes, Consequences, and Systemic Implications.* POLICY ANALYSES IN INTERNATIONAL ECONOMICS 55. Washington: Institute for International Economics.

Goldstein, Morris. 2002. *Managed Floating Plus.* POLICY ANALYSES IN INTERNATIONAL ECONOMICS 66. Washington: Institute for International Economics.

Goldstein, Morris. 2003. *Debt Sustainability, Brazil, and the IMF.* Institute for International Economics Working Paper 03-1. Washington: Institute for International Economics (February).

Goldstein, Morris, and Philip Turner. 1996. *Banking Crises in Emerging Economies: Origins and Policy Options.* BIS Economic Papers no. 46 (October). Basel: Bank for International Settlements.

Goldstein, Morris, and Philip Turner. 2003. Currency Mismatching in Emerging Economies. Paper presented at an Institute for International Economics seminar, August 14, Washington.

Goldstein, Morris, Graciela Kaminsky, and Carmen Reinhart. 2000. *Assessing Financial Vulnerability: An Early Warning System for Emerging Markets.* Washington: Institute for International Economics.

Gray, Dale. 1999. *Assessment of Corporate Sector Value and Vulnerability: Links to Exchange Rate and Financial Crises.* World Bank Technical Paper 455. Washington: World Bank.

Gray, Dale. 2002. Macro Finance: The Bigger Picture. *Risk Magazine*, June 17–19.

Greenspan, Alan. 2001. Globalization. First Annual Stavros S. Niarchos Lecture at the Institute for International Economics, Washington, October 24.

Guidotti, Pablo. 1999. Remarks at the G-33 seminar in Bonn, April.

Gupta, Poonam, Deepak Mishra, and Ratna Sahay. 2001. Output Responses to Currency Crises. Paper presented at the International Monetary Fund's Annual Research Conference, November 29–30, Washington.

Haggard, Stephen. 2000. *The Political Economy of the Asian Financial Crisis*. Washington: Institute for International Economics.

Haüsler, Gerd, Donald J. Mathieson, and Jorge Roldos. 2003. Trends in Developing-Country Capital Markets Around the World. In *The Future of Domestic Capital Markets in Developing Countries*, ed., Robert E. Litan, Michael Pomerleano, and V. Sundararajan. Washington: Brookings Institution.

Hausmann, Ricardo, Ugo Panizza, and Ernesto Stein. 2000. *Why Do Countries Float the Way They Float?* IADB Working Paper 418 (May). Washington: Inter-American Development Bank.

Hausmann, Ricardo, and Ugo Panizza. 2002. The Mystery of Original Sin: The Case of the Missing Apple. Harvard University and Inter-American Development Bank. Photocopy (July).

Hausmann, Ricardo, and Ugo Panizza. 2003. On the Determinants of Original Sin: An Empirical Investigation. *Journal of International Money and Finance* 22: 957–90.

Hawkins, John. 2003. International Bank Lending: Water Flowing Uphill? In *From Capital Surges to Drought: Seeking Stability for Emerging Economies*, ed., Ricardo Ffrench-Davis and Stephany Griffith-Jones. Basingstoke, UK: United Nations University/Macmillan.

Hawkins, John, and Marc Klau. 2000. *Measuring Potential Vulnerabilities in Emerging Market Economies*. BIS Working Paper no. 91 (October). Basel: Bank for International Settlements.

Hawkins, John, and Philip Turner. 1999. *Bank Restructuring in Practice: An Overview*. In *Bank Restructuring in Practice*. BIS Policy Papers no. 6 (August). Basel: Bank for International Settlements.

Hawkins, John, and Philip Turner. 2000. Managing Foreign Debt and Liquidity Risks in Emerging Economies: An Overview. In *Managing Foreign Debt and Liquidity Risks*. BIS Policy Papers no. 8 (September). Basel: Bank for International Settlements.

Herring, R., and N. Chatusripitak. 2001. *The Case Of The Missing Market: The Bond Market And Why It Matters For Financial Development*. Wharton Financial Institutions Center Working Paper, University of Pennsylvania. (An earlier version appeared as an Asian Development Bank Institute Working Paper 11, July 2000.)

IMF (International Monetary Fund). 2001. *World Economic Outlook*. Washington: International Monetary Fund.

IMF (International Monetary Fund). 2002a. Emerging Local Bond Markets. In *Global Financial Stability Report*. Washington: International Monetary Fund.

IMF (International Monetary Fund). 2002b. The Role of Financial Derivatives in Emerging Markets. In *Global Financial Stability Report*. Washington: International Monetary Fund.

IMF (International Monetary Fund). 2003a. Local Securities and Derivatives Markets in Emerging Markets: Selected Policy Issues. In *Global Financial Stability Report*, March. Washington: International Monetary Fund.

IMF (International Monetary Fund). 2003b. *World Economic Outlook*. Washington: International Monetary Fund.

IMF (International Monetary Fund). 2003c. Financial Stability in Dollarized Economies. International Monetary Fund, Washington. Photocopy (April).

Jeanne, Olivier. 2001. Why Do Emerging Economies Borrow in Foreign Currency? International Monetary Fund, Washington. Photocopy (October).

Jeanne, Olivier, and Jeromin Zettelmeyer. 2002. Original Sin, Balance Sheet Crises, and the Roles of International Lending. Paper presented at the conference on Currency and Maturity Mismatching: Redeeming Debt from Original Sin, Inter-American Development Bank, November 21–22, Washington.

JP Morgan Securities. 1997. The Emerging Local Markets Index Plus (ELMI+). New York: JP Morgan Securities (November).

Kaminsky, Graciela, and Carmen Reinhart. 1999. The Twin Crises: The Causes of Banking and Balance of Payments Problems. *American Economic Review* 89, no. 3: 473–800 (June).

Keloharja, Matti, and Mervi Niskanen. 2001. Why Do Firms Raise Foreign Currency-Denominated Debt? Evidence from Finland. *European Financial Management* 7, no. 4: 481–96.

Khan, Mohsin, and Abdelhak Senhadji. 2000. *Financial Development and Economic Growth: An Overview*. IMF Working Paper 00/209. Washington: International Monetary Fund.

Khan, Mohsin, Abdelhak Senhadji, and Bruce Smith. 2001. *Inflation and Financial Depth*. IMF Working Paper 01/44 (April). Washington: International Monetary Fund.

King, Robert, and Ross Levine. 1993a. Finance, Entrepreneurship, and Growth: Theory and Evidence. *Journal of Monetary Economics* 32, no. 3: 513–42.

King, Robert, and Ross Levine. 1993b. Finance and Growth: Schumpeter Might Be Right. *Quarterly Journal of Economics* 108, no. 3: 717–37.

Krueger, Anne. 2000. Conflicting Demands on the International Monetary Fund. *American Economic Review* 90, no. 2: 38–42.

Krueger, Anne, and Aaron Tornell. 1999. The Role of Bank Restructuring in Recovering from Crises: Mexico, 1995–98. NBER Working Paper 7042 (March). Cambridge, MA: National Bureau of Economic Research.

Krugman, Paul. 1999. Balance Sheets, the Transfer Problem, and Financial Crises. In *International Finance*, ed., Peter Isard, Asif Razia, and Andrew Rose. Kluwer.

Krugman, Paul. 2000. Crises: The Price of Globalization. In *Global Economic Integration: Opportunities and Challenges*. Kansas City: Federal Reserve Bank of Kansas City.

Lamfalussy, Alexandre. 2000. *Financial Crises in Emerging Markets: An Essay on Financial Globalization and Fragility*. London and New Haven: Yale University Press.

La Porta, Rafael, Florencio Lopez-de-Silanes, and Andrei Shleifer. 1998. *Corporate Ownership Around the World*. NBER Working Paper 6625. Cambridge, MA: National Bureau of Economic Research (June).

Lubin, David. 2003. Bank Lending in Emerging Markets: Crossing the Border. In *From Capital Surges to Drought: Seeking Stability for Emerging Economies*, ed., Ricardo Ffrench-Davis and Stephany Griffith-Jones. Basingstoke, UK: United Nations University/Macmillan.

McCauley, Robert. 2003. Unifying Government Bond Markets in East Asia. *BIS Quarterly Review* (December): 89–98.

McCauley, Robert, and Eli Remolona. 2000. Size and Liquidity of Government Bond Markets. *BIS Quarterly Review* (November): 52–58.

Marshall, Jorge. 2000. Managing Foreign Debt and Liquidity Risks in Chile. In *Managing Foreign Debt and Liquidity Risks*, September. Basel: Bank for International Settlements.

Martinez, Lorenza, and Alejandro Werner. 2001. The Exchange Rate Regime and the Currency Composition of Corporate Debt: The Mexican Experience. Paper presented at the National Bureau of Economic Research Inter-American Seminar on Economics, July 20–21, Cambridge, MA.

Merrill Lynch. 2002. *Size and Structure of the World Bond Market*. New York: Merrill Lynch.

Mihaljek, Dubravko, Michela Scatigna, and Agustin Villar. 2002. Recent Trends in Bond Markets. In *The Development of Bond Markets in Emerging Economies*. BIS Policy Papers no. 11. Basel: Bank for International Settlements (June–July).

Mishkin, Frederic. 2000. Inflation Targeting in Emerging-Market Countries. *American Economic Review* 90, no. 2: 105–09 (May).

Mishkin, Frederic, and Klaus Schmidt-Hebbel. 2001. *One Decade of Inflation Targeting in the World: What Do We Know and What Do We Need to Know*. NBER Working Paper 8397. Cambridge, MA: National Bureau of Economic Research.

Mohanty, M. S. 2002. Improving Liquidity in Government Bond Markets: What Can Be Done? In *The Development of Bond Markets in Emerging Economies*. BIS Policy Papers no. 11. Basel: Bank for International Settlements (June–July).

Mohanty M. S., and Michela Scatigna. 2003. Countercyclical Policy and Central Banks. In *Fiscal Issues and Central Banking in Emerging Economies*. BIS Policy Papers no. 20 (October). Basel: Bank for International Settlements.

Mulder, Christian, Robert Perrelli, and Manuel Rocha. 2002. *The Role of Corporate, Legal, and Macroeconomic Balance Sheet Indicators in Crisis Detection and Prevention*. IMF Working Paper 02/59. Washington: International Monetary Fund.

Mussa, Michael, and Morris Goldstein. 1993. The Integration of World Capital Markets. In *Changing Capital Markets: Implications for Monetary Policy*: 245–314. Kansas City: Federal Reserve Bank of Kansas City.

Mussa, Michael, Paul Masson, Alexander Swoboda, Esteban Jadresic, Paolo Mauro, and Andy Berg. 2000. *Exchange-Rate Regimes in an Increasingly Integrated World Economy*. IMF Occasional Paper 193. Washington: International Monetary Fund.

Neumann, Uwe, and Philip Turner. 2002. *Regulation and Banking in Emerging Markets: External Versus Internal Guidelines*. Bank for International Settlements, Basel. Photocopy.

Obstfeld, Maurice. 1993. International Capital Mobility in the 1990s. Paper presented at the conference celebrating the 50th anniversary of the *Essays in International Finance*, Princeton University. Photocopy (April).

O'Dogherty, Pascual, and Moisés J. Schwartz. 2001. Prudential Regulation of Foreign Exchange: The Mexican Experience. In *Marrying the Macro- and Micro-Prudential Dimensions of Financial Stability*. BIS Policy Papers no. 1. Basel: Bank for International Settlements (March).

Packer, Frank. 2003. Mind the Gap: Domestic Versus Foreign Currency Sovereign Ratings. *BIS Quarterly Review* (September). Basel: Bank for International Settlements.

Pettis, Michael. 2001. *The Volatility Machine*. Oxford: Oxford University Press.

Prasad, Eswar, Kenneth Rogoff, Shang-Jin Wei, and M. Ayhan Kose. 2003. *Effects of Financial Globalization on Developing Countries: Some Empirical Evidence*. Washington: International Monetary Fund (March).

Reddy, Y. V. 1997. Exchange Rate Management Dilemmas. Inaugural address at the 12th National Assembly of the Foreign Exchange Association of India, Goa, August 15. Reprinted in 1999 in *Monetary And Financial Sector Reforms in India: A Central Banker's Perspective by Y. V. Reddy*. New Delhi: UBS Publishers.

Reddy, Y. V. 2002. Issues and challenges in the development of the debt market in India. In *The Development of Bond Markets in Emerging Economies*. BIS Policy Papers no. 11. Basel: Bank for International Settlements (June–July).

Reinhart, Carmen, Kenneth Rogoff, and Miguel Savastano. 2003a. *Addicted to Dollars*. NBER Working Paper 10015. Cambridge, MA: National Bureau of Economic Research.

Reinhart, Carmen, Kenneth Rogoff, and Miguel Savastano. 2003b. *Debt Intolerance*. Brookings Papers on Economic Activity 1: 1–62. Washington: Brookings Institution.

Reisen, Helmut. 2000. *Pensions, Savings, and Capital Flows: From Aging to Emerging Markets*. Cheltenham, UK: Edward Elgar.

Reserve Bank of India. 2003. *Mid-Term Review of Monetary and Credit Policy for the Year 2003–04*. Mumbai: Reserve Bank of India.

Rodriguez, Pedro. 2002. On the Impact of Devaluations on Investment: The Role of Currency Mismatches. University of Maryland. Photocopy (February).

Rodrik, Dani, and Andres Velasco. 1999. Short-Term Capital Flows. *Annual World Bank Conference on Development Economics*: 59–90. Washington: World Bank.

Sachs, Jeffrey, A. Tornell, and A. Velasco. 1996. *Financial Crises in Emerging Markets: The Lessons from 1995*. Brookings Papers on Economic Activity 1. Washington: Brookings Institution.

Salomon Smith Barney. 2001. *Local Markets Handbook*. New York: Salomon Smith Barney (November 14).

Savastano, Miguel. 1996. *Dollarization in Latin America: Recent Evidence and Some Policy Issues*. IMF Working Paper 96/4 (January). Washington: International Monetary Fund.

Schaechter, Andrea, Mark Stone, and Mark Zelmer. 2000. *Adopting Inflation Targeting:*

Practical Issues for Emerging-Market Countries. IMF Occasional Paper 202. Washington: International Monetary Fund.

Sidaoui, José. 2002. The Role of the Central Bank in Developing Debt Markets in Mexico. In *The Development of Bond Markets in Emerging Economies.* BIS Policy Papers no. 11. Basel: Bank for International Settlements (June–July).

Sokoler, Meir. 2002. The Importance of a Well-Developed Bond Market—An Israeli Perspective. In *The Development of Bond Markets in Emerging Economies.* BIS Policy Papers no. 11. Basel: Bank for International Settlements (June–July).

Stebbing, Peter. 1997. Debt Management Practices in Australia: Some Recent History. Paper presented at the IMF/Bank of Korea seminar on Fiscal and Monetary Policies and Public Debt Management in Asian Transition Economies, Seoul, November.

Stone, Mark. 2000. *The Corporate-Sector Dynamics of Systemic Financial Crises.* IMF Working Paper 00/114. Washington: International Monetary Fund.

Truman, Edwin. 2003. *Inflation Targeting in the World Economy.* Washington: Institute for International Economics.

Turner, Philip. 2002. Bond Markets in Emerging Economies: An Overview of Policy Issues. In *The Development of Bond Markets in Emerging Economies.* BIS Policy Papers no. 11. Basel: Bank for International Settlements (June–July).

Turner, Philip. 2003. *Bond Market Development: What Are the Policy Issues?* In *The Future of Domestic Capital Markets in Developing Countries,* ed., Robert E. Litan, Michael Pomerleano, and V. Sundararajan. Washington: Brookings Institution.

Von Kleist, Karsten. 2002. *Comparison of Creditor and Debtor Data on Short-Term External Debt.* Basel: Bank for International Settlements.

Wijnholds, Onno de Beaufort, and Arend Kapteyn. 2001. *Reserve Adequacy in Emerging Market Economies.* IMF Working Paper 01/43 (September). Washington: International Monetary Fund.

Williamson, John. 2000. *Exchange Rate Regimes for Emerging Markets: Reviving the Intermediate Option.* POLICY ANALYSES IN INTERNATIONAL ECONOMICS 60. Washington: Institute for International Economics.

Wooldridge, Philip, Dietrich Domanski, and Anna Cobau. 2003. Changing Links between Mature and Emerging Financial Markets. *BIS Quarterly Review* (September). Basel: Bank for International Settlements.

Worrell, DeLisle, and Hyginus Leon. 2001. *Price Volatility and Financial Instability.* IMF Working Paper 01/60 (May). Washington: International Monetary Fund.

World Bank and IMF (International Monetary Fund). 2001. *Developing Government Bond Markets: A Handbook.* Washington: World Bank and International Monetary Fund.

Index

AECM. *See* Aggregate effectiveness currency mismatch

Africa. *See also* Emerging economies
  foreign banks' claims, local/international, 28*t*
  measures of original sin by country subgroupings, simple averages, 22*t*

Aggregate effectiveness currency mismatch (AECM), 2, 4. *See also* Currency mismatch
  AECM definition, 44–45
  in general, 37–42
  modifications of, 51-56
  modified AECM estimates, 50*t*
  net foreign-currency assets, 45*t*
  new measure of, 42–51
  original AECM estimates, 48*t*
  original sin and, 6–7

Argentina. *See also* Latin America
  banking crisis, 46, 103
  borrowing by domestic banks from international banks, 13*t*
  domestic bank credit to private sector, 17*t*
  domestic debt securities outstanding, 61*t*
  emerging-market financing, 32
  export openness, 23*t*
  foreign-currency share of total debt, 47, 47*t*, 51

foreign exchange turnover, 58*t*
guidelines or regulations for currency mismatches in banks, 91*t*, 93
modified AECM estimates, 50*t*, 51
net foreign-currency assets, 45*t*
original AECM estimates, 48*t*, 49
original sin ratios, 55*t*
outstanding government debt by type (original maturity), 73*t*
rules on fund managers' holdings of foreign-currency assets, 99*t*
share of external debt denominated in local currency, 118*t*
short-term external debt as percentage of foreign exchange reserves, 115
top 10 countries in bond trading volume, 60*t*

ASEAN. *See* Association of Southeast Asian Nations

Asia. *See also* Asia Pacific; Asian financial crisis; *specific Asian countries*
  AECMs, 53
  bank credit relative to GDP, 16
  bond market development, 26*t*
  borrowing by domestic banks from international banks, 13*t*
  currency denomination of bank balance sheets, 94*t*
  domestic bank credit to private sector, 17*t*
  domestic bond market, 26–27

153

Asia (*continued*)
   domestic debt securities outstanding,
      61t
   emerging-market debt, 32
   emerging-market financing, all sectors,
      31t
   export openness, 23t
   foreign assets and reserves, 24, 46
   foreign banks' claims,
      local/international, 28t
   foreign-currency share of total debt, 47t,
      80
   modified AECM estimates, 50t
   net foreign-currency assets, 45t
   original AECM estimates, 48t
   original sin ratios, 55t
   share of external debt denominated in
      local currency, 118t
   total debt as percent of GDP, 52t
   type of domestic debt at issuance, 65t
Asia Pacific
   foreign banks' claims,
      local/international, 28t
   measures of original sin by country
      subgroupings, simple averages,
      22t
Asian financial crisis
   currency mismatch affecting, 11, 13–14,
      16, 18
   factors affecting, 46, 67, 71, 74–75, 78,
      103, 114
Association of Southeast Asian Nations
      (ASEAN), 11. *See also* Asian
      financial crisis
Australian Bureau of Statistics, 40
Australia
   Asian financial crisis response, 16
   domestic bank credit to private sector,
      17t
   foreign-currency exposure by financial
      sector, 39t, 40–41
   foreign exchange turnover, 58t, 59
   original sin, 70–71
   share of external debt denominated in
      local currency, 118t

Bailouts, 83
Balance sheet
   currency denomination of bank balance
      sheets, 94t
   debt, 71–73
   foreign currency balance sheet of
      partially dollarized economy, 38f
Bank failure, 16–18, 102. *See also* Banks

Bank for International Settlements, 26, 42
Bank of Australia, Asian financial crisis
      response, 16
Bank of Thailand, 41
Banks. *See also* Financial institutions
   aggregate mismatches in banking
      system, 97–98
   borrowing by domestic banks from
      international banks, 13t
   credit risk and mismatch, 87–88
   currency denomination of bank balance
      sheets, 94t
   domestic bank credit to private sector,
      17t
   foreign bank presence in emerging
      market, 27
   foreign banks' claims,
      local/international, 28t
   foreign-exchange exposure, 11
   foreign-owned, barrier to entry, 5, 29
   guidelines or regulations for currency
      mismatches in banks, 91t–92t
   market share of foreign-owned banks in
      emerging markets, 28f
   monitoring and oversight
      recommendations, 3–4
   "outsourcing", 107
   regulation in borrowing countries
      foreign-currency denominated
         securities limits, 83–84, 96–97
      foreign exchange limits, 89–94
      in general, 89
      liquidity risks, 94–96
      reserve requirements, 96
   regulation in major lending centers,
      85–88
Basel Accord, 88
Bolivia. *See also* Latin America
   loans in nontradables sector, 68
Bonds. *See also* Debt
   bond market development, 26t
   domestic market, 4–5, 25–34, 59, 60, 79,
      85–86
      accounting rules that deter trading,
         79–80
      Asia, 26–27
      factors affecting, 113–14
      fragmented issuance by official
         borrowers, 80–82
      liquidity, 59–60
      narrow investor base/captive
         market, 82
      official attempts to stabilize market,
         82

original sin and, 6–7, 30–33
domestic debt securities outstanding,
    61*t*
GDP-indexed, 110
top 10 countries in bond trading
    volume, 60*t*
Brazil. *See also* Latin America
AECM, 53
bank credit relative to GDP, 16
banking crisis, 46, 103
borrowing by domestic banks from
    international banks, 13*t*
commitment to exchange rate, 16
domestic bank credit to private sector,
    17*t*
domestic debt securities outstanding,
    61*t*
export openness, 23*t*
foreign assets and reserves, 24, 30, 33,
    47
foreign-currency share of total debt, 47*t*,
    72
foreign exchange turnover, 58*t*, 59
hedging, 62
modified AECM estimates, 50*t*, 51
net foreign assets of monetary
    authorities, 81*f*
net foreign-currency assets, 45*t*
original AECM estimates, 48*t*, 49
original sin ratios, 55*t*
outstanding government debt by type
    (original maturity), 73*t*
public-sector debt service, 12
share of external debt denominated in
    local currency, 118*t*
short-term external debt as percentage
    of foreign exchange reserves,
    115
top 10 countries in bond trading
    volume, 60*t*
total debt as percent of GDP, 52*t*

Canada
bond market development, 26*t*, 27
original sin, 70–71
Caribbean. *See also* Latin America
America, foreign bank presence, 27
foreign banks' claims,
    local/international, 28*t*
measures of original sin by country
    subgroupings, simple averages,
    22*t*
Central Bank of Chile, 78
Central Europe. *See also specific countries*

borrowing by domestic banks from
    international banks, 13*t*
domestic bank credit to private sector,
    17*t*
domestic debt securities outstanding,
    61*t*
emerging-market financing, all sectors,
    31*t*, 32
export openness, 23*t*
foreign banks' claims,
    local/international, 28*t*
foreign-currency share of total debt, 47*t*
foreign exchange turnover, 58*t*
hedging, 62
measures of original sin by country
    subgroupings, simple averages,
    22*t*
modified AECM estimates, 50*t*
net foreign-currency assets, 45*t*
original AECM estimates, 48*t*
original sin ratios, 55*t*
short-term external debt as percentage
    of foreign exchange reserves, 115*t*
total debt as percent of GDP, 52*t*
type of domestic debt at issuance, 65*t*
Chile, 82. *See also* Latin America
borrowing by domestic banks from
    international banks, 13*t*
Central Bank of Chile, 78
currency denomination of bank balance
    sheets, 94*t*
domestic bank credit to private sector,
    17*t*
domestic debt securities outstanding,
    61*t*
emerging-market financing, 32
export openness, 23*t*
foreign assets and reserves, 24
foreign bank presence, 27
foreign-currency share of total debt, 47*t*
foreign exchange turnover, 58*t*
guidelines or regulations for currency
    mismatches in banks, 91*t*, 93–94
hedging, 62
modified AECM estimates, 50*t*
net foreign-currency assets, 45*t*
original AECM estimates, 48*t*
pension fund assets, 101*t*
rules on fund managers' holdings of
    foreign-currency assets, 99*t*
share of external debt denominated in
    local currency, 118*t*
short-term external debt as percentage
    of foreign exchange reserves, 115

Chile (*continued*)
  total debt as percent of GDP, 52*t*
China, 116. *See also* Asia
  borrowing by domestic banks from
    international banks, 13*t*
  domestic bank credit to private sector,
    17*t*
  domestic debt securities outstanding,
    61*t*
  export openness, 23*t*
  foreign-currency share of total debt, 47*t*
  guidelines or regulations for currency
    mismatches in banks, 91*t*
  modified AECM estimates, 50*t*, 51
  net foreign assets of monetary
    authorities, 81*f*
  net foreign-currency assets, 45*t*, 46
  original AECM estimates, 48*t*, 49
  original sin ratios, 55*t*
  outstanding government debt by type
    (original maturity), 73*t*
  rules on fund managers' holdings of
    foreign-currency assets,
    99*t*
  share of external debt denominated in
    local currency, 118*t*
  short-term external debt as percentage
    of foreign exchange reserves, 115
  total debt as percent of GDP, 52*t*
Colombia. *See also* Latin America
  borrowing by domestic banks from
    international banks, 13*t*
  currency denomination of bank balance
    sheets, 94*t*
  domestic bank credit to private sector,
    17*t*
  domestic debt securities outstanding,
    61*t*
  emerging-market financing, 32
  export openness, 23*t*
  foreign-currency share of total debt,
    47*t*
  foreign exchange turnover, 58*t*, 59
  guidelines or regulations for currency
    mismatches in banks, 91*t*
  modified AECM estimates, 50*t*
  net foreign-currency assets, 45*t*
  original AECM estimates, 48*t*
  original sin ratios, 55*t*
  outstanding government debt by type
    (original maturity), 73*t*
  pension fund assets, 101*t*
  rules on fund managers' holdings of
    foreign-currency assets, 99*t*

share of external debt denominated in
    local currency, 118*t*
  short-term external debt as percentage
    of foreign exchange reserves, 115
  total debt as percent of GDP, 52*t*
Corporations, rules for nonfinancial,
    102–03
Costa Rica. *See also* Latin America
  loans in nontradables sector, 68
Credit rating, 88
Credit risk. *See also* Currency risk
  compared with market risk, 86
  currency mismatch and, 87–88
Currency mismatch. *See also* Aggregate
    effectiveness currency mismatch;
    Currency mismatch measurement;
    Original sin hypothesis
  aggregate effectiveness currency
    mismatch, 2
  credit risk and, 87–88
  definition, 1, 37
  guidelines or regulations for currency
    mismatches in banks, 91*t*–92*t*
  international solutions, 105–11
  national weaknesses affecting, 3
  proxies for currency mismatches before
    the Asian crisis, 12*t*
  reducing
    domestic agenda, 113–20
    "least cost resolution", 4, 79
    new basket index of emerging-
      market currencies, 6, 105–06
    "prompt corrective action", 4, 79
    "socialized" mismatch, 16
    "stock" aspect of, 1
Currency mismatch measurement. *See also*
    Aggregate effectiveness currency
    mismatch
  in general, 21
  original sin and, 21–35
Currency regime, monetary policy and,
    63, 67–69
Currency risk. *See also* Credit risk
  capital charge, 27
  currency regime and, 63, 67–68, 74–75
  emerging economy, 25
  hedging, 33–34, 59, 60–62, 67, 83, 117
Currency swap, 33–34
Czech Republic, 105. *See also* Central
    Europe
  borrowing by domestic banks from
    international banks, 13*t*
  derivatives market, 34
  domestic bank credit to private sector, 17*t*

domestic debt securities outstanding, 61*t*
emerging-market financing, 32
export openness, 23*t*
foreign assets and reserves, 24
foreign bank presence, 27
foreign-currency share of total debt, 47*t*
foreign exchange turnover, 58*t*
guidelines or regulations for currency mismatches in banks, 92*t*
hedging, 62
modified AECM estimates, 50*t*
net foreign-currency assets, 45*t*
original AECM estimates, 48*t*
original sin ratios, 55*t*
outstanding government debt by type (original maturity), 73*t*
rules on fund managers' holdings of foreign-currency assets, 99*t*
share of external debt denominated in local currency, 118*t*
short-term external debt as percentage of foreign exchange reserves, 115
total debt as percent of GDP, 52*t*

Debt, 63. *See also* Bonds; Debt management; Derivatives; Monetary policy
balance sheet perspective, 71–73
borrowing by domestic banks from international banks, 13*t*
"debt intolerance", 70
domestic bank credit to private sector, 17*t*
domestic debt securities outstanding, 61*t*
foreign currency–denominated and domestic, 2, 25–26, 45–47, 71–73, 78–79, 97
foreign-currency share of total debt, 47*t*
loans in nontradables sector, 68
public debt ratio, 69–71
share of external debt denominated in local currency, 118*t*
short-term external debt as percentage of foreign exchange reserves, 115
total debt as percent of GDP, 52*t*
type of domestic debt at issuance, 65*t*
Debt management, 71–73. *See also* Monetary policy
Default, 88
Derivatives, 33–34, 68–69, 90
Developed countries, measures of original sin by country subgroupings, simple averages, 22*t*

Developing countries. *See also* Emerging economies
measures of original sin by country subgroupings, simple averages, 22*t*
Dollarization
discussed, 19–20
domestic dollarization, 64–65, 70
foreign currency balance sheet of partially dollarized economy, 38*f*
role in financial crisis, 15, 96–97

Economic growth, factors affecting, 29–30
Ecuador. *See also* Latin America
foreign assets and reserves, 24
ELMI. *See* Emerging Local Markets Index
Emerging economies. *See also* Developing countries; Original sin hypothesis
bond markets, 27
credit rating, 87–88
currency risk, 25
differentiation in, 57
with debt to reserve ratios of less than one, 37
Emerging Local Markets Index, 108–09
emerging-market financing, all sectors, 31*t*
exchange rates, 69
export openness, 23*t*
"fear of floating", 18–19
foreign banks' claims, local/international, 28*t*
foreign exchange turnover, 58*t*
inflation targeting, 18–19
market share of foreign-owned banks in emerging markets, 28*f*
net foreign assets of monetary authorities in selected emerging-market countries, 81*f*
original sin ratios, 55*t*
recommendations for monetary policy of, 4
Emerging Local Markets Index (ELMI), 108–09
Exchange rate. *See also* Foreign exchange
fixed vs. floating rate, 3
floating rate, 18, 67–69
"fear of floating", 18-19
leverage affecting, 51-52
relation to currency mismatch, 1, 2, 66–67
relation to financial crisis, 1, 15, 72–73
Export openness, 23*t*

Federal Deposit Insurance Corporation
Improvement Act (FDICIA), 4, 79
Financial centers, measures of original sin
by country subgroupings, simple
averages, 22*t*
Financial crisis. *See also specific country or
regional crisis*
emerging economies with debt to
reserve ratios of less than one, 37
role of currency mismatch in, 2, 11–19,
56
short-term debt affecting, 12, 95
Financial institutions. *See also* Banks;
Institutional incentives
net foreign assets less currency held
outside banks, 81*f*
net foreign assets of monetary
authorities in selected emerging-
market countries, 81*f*
oversight of, 82–85
regulation of, 98–102
mutual funds/unit trusts, 98
Fiscal policy
debt levels and, 69–71
Foreign exchange. *See also* Exchange rate
Guidotti Rule, 74-75
limits on liabilities, 90–94
limits on positions, 89–90
reserves, 74–75
short-term external debt as percentage
of foreign exchange reserves, 115
swap, 33
turnover, 58*t*
Forwards, 33–34, 90

G-7
efforts for currency mismatch
identification, 2
"home bias", 98
legislation for liabilities abroad, 85
G-10, recommendations for reducing
currency mismatch, 6
GDP. *See* Gross domestic product
Germany. *See also* Europe
currency denomination of bank balance
sheets, 94*t*
Globalization, 30
Gross domestic product (GDP)
factors affecting, 15–16, 105–06
Guidotti Rule, 74–75

Hedging, domestic bond market, 4–5
"Home bias", 98
Hong Kong, 116. *See also* Asia

derivatives market, 34
domestic bank credit to private sector,
17*t*
domestic debt securities outstanding,
61*t*
emerging-market financing, 32
foreign assets and reserves, 24, 80
foreign exchange turnover, 58*t*, 59
guidelines or regulations for currency
mismatches in banks, 91*t*
hedging, 62
rules on fund managers' holdings of
foreign-currency assets, 99*t*
top 10 countries in bond trading
volume, 60*t*
Hungary, 116. *See also* Central Europe
borrowing by domestic banks from
international banks, 13*t*
currency denomination of bank balance
sheets, 94*t*
derivatives market, 34
domestic bank credit to private sector,
17*t*
domestic debt securities outstanding,
61*t*
emerging-market financing, 32
export openness, 23*t*
foreign bank presence, 27
foreign-currency share of total debt, 47*t*
foreign exchange turnover, 58*t*
guidelines or regulations for currency
mismatches in banks, 92*t*
hedging, 62
modified AECM estimates, 50*t*
net foreign-currency assets, 45*t*
original AECM estimates, 48*t*
original sin ratios, 55*t*
outstanding government debt by type
(original maturity), 73*t*
pension fund assets, 101*t*
rules on fund managers' holdings of
foreign-currency assets, 99*t*
share of external debt denominated in
local currency, 118*t*
short-term external debt as percentage
of foreign exchange reserves, 115
top 10 countries in bond trading
volume, 60*t*
total debt as percent of GDP, 52*t*

IMF. *See* International Monetary Fund
India. *See also* Asia
borrowing by domestic banks from
international banks, 13*t*

domestic bank credit to private sector,
17*t*, 72
domestic debt securities outstanding,
61*t*
emerging-market financing, 32
export openness, 23*t*
foreign-currency share of total debt, 47*t*,
72
foreign exchange turnover, 58*t*
guidelines or regulations for currency
mismatches in banks, 91*t*, 93
modified AECM estimates, 50*t*, 51
net foreign assets of monetary
authorities, 81*f*
net foreign-currency assets, 45*t*
original AECM estimates, 48*t*, 49
original sin ratios, 55*t*
outstanding government debt by type
(original maturity), 73*t*
Reserve Bank of India, 93
rules on fund managers' holdings of
foreign-currency assets, 99*t*
share of external debt denominated in
local currency, 118*t*
short-term external debt as percentage
of foreign exchange reserves, 115
total debt as percent of GDP, 52*t*
Indonesia, 78. *See also* Asia
bank crisis, 46
borrowing by domestic banks from
international banks, 13*t*
currency denomination of bank balance
sheets, 94*t*
domestic bank credit to private sector,
17*t*
domestic debt securities outstanding,
61*t*
exchange rates, 67
export openness, 23*t*
foreign-currency share of total debt, 47,
47*t*, 51
foreign exchange turnover, 58*t*
guidelines or regulations for currency
mismatches in banks, 91*t*
Indonesian Debt Restructuring Agency,
78
institutional foreign exchange exposure,
11
modified AECM estimates, 50*t*
net foreign-currency assets, 45*t*
original AECM estimates, 48*t*
original sin ratios, 55*t*
outstanding government debt by type
(original maturity), 73*t*

pension fund assets, 101*t*
proxies for currency mismatches before
the Asian crisis, 12*t*
rules on fund managers' holdings of
foreign-currency assets, 99*t*
share of external debt denominated in
local currency, 118*t*
short-term external debt as percentage
of foreign exchange reserves, 115
total debt as percent of GDP, 52*t*
Inflation, 3, 106. *See also* Inflation targeting
monetary policy and, 63, 64–67
Inflation targeting, 3. *See also* Exchange
rate
emerging economy, 18–19, 66
Institutional incentives. *See also* Financial
institutions
for bond market development, 79–82
in general, 77–79
International financial institutions (IFIs),
recommendations for reducing
currency mismatch, 6
International Monetary Fund (IMF), 42
Balance of Payments Yearbook, 24
efforts for currency mismatch
identification, 2, 4
proposals discouraging currency
mismatch, 18
special drawing right, 108
Israel. *See also* Middle East
borrowing by domestic banks from
international banks, 13*t*
currency denomination of bank balance
sheets, 94*t*
domestic bank credit to private sector,
17*t*
domestic debt securities outstanding,
61*t*
export openness, 23*t*
foreign-currency share of total debt, 47*t*
foreign exchange turnover, 58*t*
guidelines or regulations for currency
mismatches in banks, 92*t*
modified AECM estimates, 50*t*
net foreign-currency assets, 45*t*
original AECM estimates, 48*t*
original sin ratios, 55*t*
outstanding government debt by type
(original maturity), 73*t*
pension fund assets, 101*t*
rules on fund managers' holdings of
foreign-currency assets, 99*t*
share of external debt denominated in
local currency, 118*t*

Israel (*continued*)
  short-term external debt as percentage
    of foreign exchange reserves, 115
  total debt as percent of GDP, 52*t*

Japan, 16, 116. *See also* Asia
  bond market development, 26*t*
  currency denomination of bank balance
    sheets, 94*t*

Korea, 16, 78. *See also* Asia
  bank foreign exchange exposure, 11
  borrowing by domestic banks from
    international banks, 13*t*
  currency denomination of bank balance
    sheets, 94*t*
  domestic bank credit to private sector,
    17*t*
  domestic debt securities outstanding, 61*t*
  emerging-market financing, 32
  exchange rates, 67, 68, 69
  export openness, 23*t*
  foreign assets and reserves, 24
  foreign-currency share of total debt, 47,
    47*t*
  foreign exchange turnover, 58*t*, 59
  guidelines or regulations for currency
    mismatches in banks, 91*t*
  hedging, 62
  modified AECM estimates, 50*t*, 51
  net foreign assets of monetary
    authorities, 81*f*
  net foreign-currency assets, 45*t*
  original AECM estimates, 48*t*, 49
  original sin ratios, 55*t*
  outstanding government debt by type
    (original maturity), 73*t*
  pension fund assets, 101*t*
  proxies for currency mismatches before
    the Asian crisis, 12*t*
  rules on fund managers' holdings of
    foreign-currency assets, 99*t*
  share of external debt denominated in
    local currency, 118*t*
  short-term external debt as percentage
    of foreign exchange reserves, 115
  total debt as percent of GDP, 52*t*

Latin America. *See also specific countries*
  AECM, 53, 114
  bank credit relative to GDP, 16
  bond market development, 26*t*, 27
  borrowing by domestic banks from
    international banks, 13*t*

currency denomination of bank balance
    sheets, 94*t*
  domestic bank credit to private sector,
    17*t*
  domestic debt securities outstanding,
    61*t*
  emerging-market financing, all sectors,
    31*t*, 32
  export openness, 23*t*
  foreign assets and reserves, 46
  foreign bank presence, 27
  foreign banks' claims,
    local/international, 28*t*
  foreign-currency share of total debt, 47*t*
  foreign exchange turnover, 58*t*, 59
  guidelines or regulations for currency
    mismatches in banks, 91*t*
  loans in nontradables sector, 68
  measures of original sin by country
    subgroupings, simple averages,
    22*t*
  modified AECM estimates, 50*t*
  net foreign-currency assets, 45*t*
  original AECM estimates, 48*t*
  original sin ratios, 55*t*
  proxies for currency mismatches before
    the Asian crisis, 12*t*
  share of external debt denominated in
    local currency, 118*t*
  short-term external debt as percentage
    of foreign exchange reserves, 115
  total debt as percent of GDP, 52*t*
  type of domestic debt at issuance, 65*t*
Liquidity risk, 94–96
  "maturity ladder", 95

Malaysia, 78, 102. *See also* Asia
  borrowing by domestic banks from
    international banks, 13*t*
  domestic bank credit to private sector,
    17*t*
  domestic debt securities outstanding,
    61*t*
  emerging-market financing, 32
  exchange rates, 67
  export openness, 23*t*
  foreign assets and reserves, 24
  foreign-currency share of total debt, 47*t*
  foreign exchange turnover, 58*t*, 59
  modified AECM estimates, 50*t*, 51
  net foreign assets of monetary
    authorities, 81*f*
  net foreign-currency assets, 45*t*
  original AECM estimates, 48*t*, 49

original sin ratios, 55*t*

outstanding government debt by type (original maturity), 73*t*

proxies for currency mismatches before the Asian crisis, 12*t*

share of external debt denominated in local currency, 118*t*

short-term external debt as percentage of foreign exchange reserves, 115

total debt as percent of GDP, 52*t*

Market risk. *See also* Currency risk
compared with credit risk, 86

Mexican peso crisis 1994–95, factors affecting, 12–14, 14*f*, 46, 90

Mexico, 102, 116. *See also* Latin America
borrowing by domestic banks from international banks, 13*t*
currency denomination of bank balance sheets, 94*t*
currency mismatch and financial crisis, 24, 47, 114
derivatives market, 34
domestic bank credit to private sector, 17*t*
domestic debt securities outstanding, 61*t*
emerging-market financing, 32
exchange rates, 68, 69
export openness, 23*t*
FICORCA, 78
foreign-currency share of total debt, 47*t*
foreign exchange turnover, 58*t*, 59
guidelines or regulations for currency mismatches in banks, 91*t*, 93–94
hedging, 62
net foreign assets of monetary authorities, 81*f*
net foreign-currency assets, 45*t*
original AECM estimates, 48*t*, 49
original sin ratios, 55*t*
outstanding government debt by type (original maturity), 73*t*
risk coverage trust fund, 78
rules on fund managers' holdings of foreign-currency assets, 99*t*
share of external debt denominated in local currency, 118*t*
short-term external debt as percentage of foreign exchange reserves, 115
top 10 countries in bond trading volume, 60*t*
total debt as percent of GDP, 52*t*

Middle East. *See also specific countries*
foreign banks' claims, local/international, 28*t*

measures of original sin by country subgroupings, simple averages, 22*t*

Monetary policy
currency mismatch and, 2, 4, 16–18
currency regime, 67–69
debt management, 71–73
foreign exchange reserves, 74–75
in general, 63
inflation and, 64–67
relation to original sin, 5–6, 7

Mutual funds, 98. *See also* Financial institutions
pension fund assets, 101*t*
rules on fund managers' holdings of foreign-currency assets, 99*t*

Net international investment position (NIIP), 54

New Zealand, 105. *See also* Asia; Australia
balance sheet perspective, 71
original sin, 70–71

NIIP. *See* Net international investment position

Norway, 78. *See also* Europe

Original sin hypothesis (OSH). *See also* Emerging economy
domestic bond markets, 30–31, 32
factors affecting, 5–8, 106–07
as measure of currency mismatch, 21–35, 63, 68, 113
measures of original sin by country subgroupings, simple averages, 22*t*
ratios, 54–55

Original sin ratios, 55*t*

OSH. *See* Original sin hypothesis

Paraguay. *See also* Latin America
loans in nontradables sector, 68

Pension funds. *See* Mutual funds *and specific countries*

Peru. *See also* Latin America
borrowing by domestic banks from international banks, 13*t*
currency denomination of bank balance sheets, 94*t*
domestic bank credit to private sector, 17*t*
domestic debt securities outstanding, 61*t*
export openness, 23*t*

Peru (*continued*)

foreign-currency share of total debt, 47t, 51

foreign exchange turnover, 58t, 59

guidelines or regulations for currency mismatches in banks, 91t

loans in nontradables sector, 68

modified AECM estimates, 50t, 51

net foreign-currency assets, 45t

original AECM estimates, 48t, 49

original sin ratios, 55t

outstanding government debt by type (original maturity), 73t

rules on fund managers' holdings of foreign-currency assets, 99t

share of external debt denominated in local currency, 118t

short-term external debt as percentage of foreign exchange reserves, 115

pension fund assets, 101t

total debt as percent of GDP, 52t

Philippines. *See also* Asia

bank foreign exchange exposure, 11

borrowing by domestic banks from international banks, 13t

domestic bank credit to private sector, 17t

domestic debt securities outstanding, 61t

emerging-market financing, 32

exchange rates, 67

export openness, 23t

foreign assets and reserves, 24

foreign-currency share of total debt, 47t

foreign exchange turnover, 58t, 59

guidelines or regulations for currency mismatches in banks, 92t

modified AECM estimates, 50t

net foreign assets of monetary authorities, 81f

net foreign-currency assets, 45t

original AECM estimates, 48t, 49

original sin ratios, 55t

outstanding government debt by type (original maturity), 73t

share of external debt denominated in local currency, 118t

short-term external debt as percentage of foreign exchange reserves, 115

total debt as percent of GDP, 52t

Poland, 105. *See also* Central Europe

borrowing by domestic banks from international banks, 13t

derivatives market, 34

domestic bank credit to private sector, 17t

domestic debt securities outstanding, 61t

emerging-market financing, 32

exchange rates, 69

export openness, 23t

foreign assets and reserves, 24

foreign bank presence, 27

foreign-currency share of total debt, 47t

foreign exchange turnover, 58t

guidelines or regulations for currency mismatches in banks, 92t

hedging, 62

modified AECM estimates, 50t

net foreign assets of monetary authorities, 81f

net foreign-currency assets, 45t

original AECM estimates, 48t

original sin ratios, 55t

outstanding government debt by type (original maturity), 73t

pension fund assets, 101t

rules on fund managers' holdings of foreign-currency assets, 99t

share of external debt denominated in local currency, 118t

short-term external debt as percentage of foreign exchange reserves, 115

top 10 countries in bond trading volume, 2001, 60t

total debt as percent of GDP, 52t

Real estate investment, 25. *See also* Debt

Recession, 17–18

Reserve Bank of Australia, 40

Reserve Bank of India, 93

Russia, 78. *See also* Europe

AECM, 53

borrowing by domestic banks from international banks, 13t

currency denomination of bank balance sheets, 94t

domestic bank credit to private sector, 17t

domestic debt securities outstanding, 61t

export openness, 23t

foreign assets, 46

foreign-currency share of total debt, 47, 47t

foreign exchange turnover, 58t

guidelines or regulations for currency mismatches in banks, 92t

hedging, 62
modified AECM estimates, , 50*t*, 51, 114
net foreign-currency assets, 45*t*
original AECM estimates, 48*t*
original sin ratios, 55*t*
outstanding government debt by type
    (original maturity), 73*t*
share of external debt denominated in
    local currency, 118*t*
short-term external debt as percentage
    of foreign exchange reserves, 115
top 10 countries in bond trading
    volume, 60*t*
total debt as percent of GDP, 52*t*

Saudi Arabia. *See also* Middle East
currency denomination of bank balance
    sheets, 94*t*
domestic bank credit to private sector,
    17*t*
foreign exchange turnover, 58*t*, 59
guidelines or regulations for currency
    mismatches in banks, 92*t*
pension fund assets, 101*t*
share of external debt denominated in
    local currency, 118*t*
short-term external debt as percentage
    of foreign exchange reserves, 115

Singapore. *See also* Asia
derivatives market, 34
domestic bank credit to private sector,
    17*t*
domestic debt securities outstanding,
    61*t*
emerging-market financing, 32
exchange rates, 69
foreign assets and reserves, 24, 80
foreign exchange turnover, 58*t*, 59
guidelines or regulations for currency
    mismatches in banks, 92*t*
rules on fund managers' holdings of
    foreign-currency assets, 99*t*
top 10 countries in bond trading
    volume, 60*t*
South Africa, 105
borrowing by domestic banks from
    international banks, 13*t*
derivatives market, 34
domestic bank credit to private sector,
    17*t*
domestic debt securities outstanding,
    61*t*
exchange rates, 69

export openness, 23*t*
foreign-currency share of total debt, 47*t*
foreign exchange turnover, 58*t*, 59
guidelines or regulations for currency
    mismatches in banks, 92*t*
hedging, 62
modified AECM estimates, 50*t*, 51, 114
net foreign-currency assets, 45*t*
original AECM estimates, 48*t*
original sin, 70–71
original sin ratios, 55*t*
outstanding government debt by type
    (original maturity), 73*t*
rules on fund managers' holdings of
    foreign-currency assets, 99*t*
share of external debt denominated in
    local currency, 118*t*
short-term external debt as percentage
    of foreign exchange reserves, 115
top 10 countries in bond trading
    volume, 60*t*
total debt as percent of GDP, 52*t*
Sweden, 78. *See also* Europe
domestic bank credit to private sector,
    17*t*
foreign exchange turnover, 58*t*, 59
share of external debt denominated in
    local currency, 118*t*
Switzerland, 105. *See also* Europe
domestic bank credit to private sector,
    17*t*
foreign exchange turnover, 58*t*, 59

Taiwan. *See also* Asia
borrowing by domestic banks from
    international banks, 13*t*
domestic bank credit to private sector,
    17*t*
domestic debt securities outstanding,
    61*t*
export openness, 23*t*
foreign-currency share of total debt, 47*t*
foreign exchange turnover, 58*t*
hedging, 62
modified AECM estimates, 50*t*
net foreign-currency assets, 45*t*, 46
original AECM estimates, 48*t*, 49
original sin ratios, 55*t*
share of external debt denominated in
    local currency, 118*t*
short-term external debt as percentage
    of foreign exchange reserves, 115
top 10 countries in bond trading
    volume, 60*t*

total debt as percent of GDP, 52t
Taxes, 83, 97
Thailand, 78. *See also* Asia
  bank crisis, 46, 53
  bank foreign exchange exposure, 11
  borrowing by domestic banks from
    international banks, 13t
  domestic bank credit to private sector,
    17t
  domestic debt securities outstanding,
    61t
  emerging-market financing, 32
  export openness, 23t
  foreign-currency share of total debt, 47,
    47t
  foreign exchange turnover, 58t
  guidelines or regulations for currency
    mismatches in banks, 92t
  intersectoral asset and liability position,
    December 1996, 40t, 41
  modified AECM estimates, 50t, 51
  net foreign assets of monetary
    authorities, 81f
  net foreign-currency assets, 45t
  original AECM estimates, 48t
  original sin ratios, 55t
  outstanding government debt by type
    (original maturity), 73t
  proxies for currency mismatches before
    the Asian crisis, 12t
  rules on fund managers' holdings of
    foreign-currency assets, 99t
  share of external debt denominated in
    local currency, 118t
  short-term external debt as percentage
    of foreign exchange reserves, 115
  total debt as percent of GDP, 52t
Transaction costs, 107
Turkey
  AECM, 53
  banking crisis, 46
  borrowing by domestic banks from
    international banks, 13t
  domestic bank credit to private sector,
    17t
  domestic debt securities outstanding,
    61t
  export openness, 23t
  foreign-currency share of total debt, 47,
    47t, 51
  foreign exchange turnover, 58t, 59
  hedging, 62

modified AECM estimates, 50t, 51, 114
net foreign-currency assets, 45t
original AECM estimates, 48t, 49
original sin ratios, 55t
outstanding government debt by type
  (original maturity), 73t
share of external debt denominated in
  local currency, 118t
short-term external debt as percentage
  of foreign exchange reserves, 115
top 10 countries in bond trading
  volume, 60t
total debt as percent of GDP, 52t

United Kingdom, 105.
  bond market development, 26t, 27
  currency denomination of bank balance
    sheets, 94t
United States
  bond market development, 26t
  currency denomination of bank balance
    sheets, 94t
  original sin, 70–71

Venezuela. *See also* Latin America
  borrowing by domestic banks from
    international banks, 13t
  currency denomination of bank balance
    sheets, 94t
  domestic bank credit to private sector,
    17t
  domestic debt securities outstanding,
    61t
  export openness, 23t
  foreign-currency share of total debt,
    47t
  guidelines or regulations for currency
    mismatches in banks, 91t
  modified AECM estimates, 50t, 51
  net foreign-currency assets, 45t
  original AECM estimates, 48t, 49
  original sin ratios, 55t
  rules on fund managers' holdings of
    foreign-currency assets, 99t
  share of external debt denominated in
    local currency, 118t
  short-term external debt as percentage
    of foreign exchange reserves, 115
  top 10 countries in bond trading
    volume, 60t
  total debt as percent of GDP, 52t
Vietnam, 94. *See also* Asia

Other Publications from the Institute for International Economics

* = out of print

POLICY ANALYSES IN
INTERNATIONAL ECONOMICS Series

1 The Lending Policies of the International
   Monetary Fund*   John Williamson
   August 1982   ISBN 0-88132-000-5
2 "Reciprocity": A New Approach to World
   Trade Policy?*   William R. Cline
   September 1982   ISBN 0-88132-001-3
3 Trade Policy in the 1980s*
   C. Fred Bergsten and William R. Cline
   November 1982   ISBN 0-88132-002-1
4 International Debt and the Stability of the
   World Economy*   William R. Cline
   September 1983   ISBN 0-88132-010-2
5 The Exchange Rate System,* Second Edition
   John Williamson
   Sept. 1983, rev. June 1985 ISBN 0-88132-034-X
6 Economic Sanctions in Support of Foreign
   Policy Goals*
   Gary Clyde Hufbauer and Jeffrey J. Schott
   October 1983   ISBN 0-88132-014-5
7 A New SDR Allocation?*   John Williamson
   March 1984   ISBN 0-88132-028-5
8 An International Standard for Monetary
   Stabilization*   Ronald L. McKinnon
   March 1984   ISBN 0-88132-018-8
9 The Yen/Dollar Agreement: Liberalizing
   Japanese Capital Markets*   Jeffrey A. Frankel
   December 1984   ISBN 0-88132-035-8
10 Bank Lending to Developing Countries: The
   Policy Alternatives*   C. Fred Bergsten,
   William R. Cline, and John Williamson
   April 1985   ISBN 0-88132-032-3
11 Trading for Growth: The Next Round of
   Trade Negotiations*
   Gary Clyde Hufbauer and Jeffrey J. Schott
   September 1985   ISBN 0-88132-033-1
12 Financial Intermediation Beyond the Debt
   Crisis*   Donald R. Lessard, John Williamson
   September 1985   ISBN 0-88132-021-8
13 The United States-Japan Economic Problem*
   C. Fred Bergsten and William R. Cline
   October 1985, 2d ed. January 1987
                              ISBN 0-88132-060-9
14 Deficits and the Dollar: The World Economy
   at Risk*   Stephen Marris
   December 1985, 2d ed. November 1987
                              ISBN 0-88132-067-6
15 Trade Policy for Troubled Industries*
   Gary Clyde Hufbauer and Howard R. Rosen
   March 1986   ISBN 0-88132-020-X
16 The United States and Canada: The Quest for
   Free Trade*   Paul Wonnacott, with an
   appendix by John Williamson
   March 1987   ISBN 0-88132-056-0
17 Adjusting to Success: Balance of Payments
   Policy in the East Asian NICs*
   Bela Balassa and John Williamson
   June 1987, rev. April 1990   ISBN 0-88132-101-X
18 Mobilizing Bank Lending to Debtor
   Countries*   William R. Cline
   June 1987   ISBN 0-88132-062-5
19 Auction Quotas and United States Trade
   Policy*   C. Fred Bergsten, Kimberly Ann
   Elliott, Jeffrey J. Schott, and Wendy E. Takacs
   September 1987   ISBN 0-88132-050-1
20 Agriculture and the GATT: Rewriting the
   Rules*   Dale E. Hathaway
   September 1987   ISBN 0-88132-052-8
21 Anti-Protection: Changing Forces in United
   States Trade Politics*
   I. M. Destler and John S. Odell
   September 1987   ISBN 0-88132-043-9
22 Targets and Indicators: A Blueprint for the
   International Coordination of Economic
   Policy
   John Williamson and Marcus H. Miller
   September 1987   ISBN 0-88132-051-X
23 Capital Flight: The Problem and Policy
   Responses*   Donald R. Lessard and
   John Williamson
   December 1987   ISBN 0-88132-059-5
24 United States-Canada Free Trade: An
   Evaluation of the Agreement*
   Jeffrey J. Schott
   April 1988   ISBN 0-88132-072-2
25 Voluntary Approaches to Debt Relief*
   John Williamson
   Sept.1988, rev. May 1989 ISBN 0-88132-098-6
26 American Trade Adjustment: The Global
   Impact*   William R. Cline
   March 1989   ISBN 0-88132-095-1
27 More Free Trade Areas?*
   Jeffrey J. Schott
   May 1989   ISBN 0-88132-085-4
28 The Progress of Policy Reform in Latin
   America*   John Williamson
   January 1990   ISBN 0-88132-100-1
29 The Global Trade Negotiations: What Can Be
   Achieved?*   Jeffrey J. Schott
   September 1990   ISBN 0-88132-137-0
30 Economic Policy Coordination: Requiem or
   Prologue?*   Wendy Dobson
   April 1991   ISBN 0-88132-102-8

31 The Economic Opening of Eastern Europe*
John Williamson
May 1991 ISBN 0-88132-186-9

32 Eastern Europe and the Soviet Union in the World Economy*
Susan M. Collins and Dani Rodrik
May 1991 ISBN 0-88132-157-5

33 African Economic Reform: The External Dimension* Carol Lancaster
June 1991 ISBN 0-88132-096-X

34 Has the Adjustment Process Worked?*
Paul R. Krugman
October 1991 ISBN 0-88132-116-8

35 From Soviet disUnion to Eastern Economic Community?*
Oleh Havrylyshyn and John Williamson
October 1991 ISBN 0-88132-192-3

36 Global Warming The Economic Stakes*
William R. Cline
May 1992 ISBN 0-88132-172-9

37 Trade and Payments After Soviet Disintegration* John Williamson
June 1992 ISBN 0-88132-173-7

38 Trade and Migration: NAFTA and Agriculture* Philip L. Martin
October 1993 ISBN 0-88132-201-6

39 The Exchange Rate System and the IMF: A Modest Agenda Morris Goldstein
June 1995 ISBN 0-88132-219-9

40 What Role for Currency Boards?
John Williamson
September 1995 ISBN 0-88132-222-9

41 Predicting External Imbalances for the United States and Japan*William R. Cline
September 1995 ISBN 0-88132-220-2

42 Standards and APEC: An Action Agenda*
John S. Wilson
October 1995 ISBN 0-88132-223-7

43 Fundamental Tax Reform and Border Tax Adjustments* Gary Clyde Hufbauer
January 1996 ISBN 0-88132-225-3

44 Global Telecom Talks: A Trillion Dollar Deal*
Ben A. Petrazzini
June 1996 ISBN 0-88132-230-X

45 WTO 2000: Setting the Course for World Trade Jeffrey J. Schott
September 1996 ISBN 0-88132-234-2

46 The National Economic Council: A Work in Progress * I. M. Destler
November 1996 ISBN 0-88132-239-3

47 The Case for an International Banking Standard Morris Goldstein
April 1997 ISBN 0-88132-244-X

48 Transatlantic Trade: A Strategic Agenda*
Ellen L. Frost
May 1997 ISBN 0-88132-228-8

49 Cooperating with Europe's Monetary Union
C. Randall Henning
May 1997 ISBN 0-88132-245-8

50 Renewing Fast Track Legislation* I. M.Destler
September 1997 ISBN 0-88132-252-0

51 Competition Policies for the Global Economy
Edward M. Graham and J. David Richardson
November 1997 ISBN 0-88132 -249-0

52 Improving Trade Policy Reviews in the World Trade Organization Donald Keesing
April 1998 ISBN 0-88132-251-2

53 Agricultural Trade Policy: Completing the Reform Timothy Josling
April 1998 ISBN 0-88132-256-3

54 Real Exchange Rates for the Year 2000
Simon Wren Lewis and Rebecca Driver
April 1998 ISBN 0-88132-253-9

55 The Asian Financial Crisis: Causes, Cures, and Systemic Implications Morris Goldstein
June 1998 ISBN 0-88132-261-X

56 Global Economic Effects of the Asian Currency Devaluations
Marcus Noland, LiGang Liu, Sherman Robinson, and Zhi Wang
July 1998 ISBN 0-88132-260-1

57 The Exchange Stabilization Fund: Slush Money or War Chest? C. Randall Henning
May 1999 ISBN 0-88132-271-7

58 The New Politics of American Trade: Trade, Labor, and the Environment
I. M. Destler and Peter J. Balint
October 1999 ISBN 0-88132-269-5

59 Congressional Trade Votes: From NAFTA Approval to Fast Track Defeat
Robert E. Baldwin and Christopher S. Magee
February 2000 ISBN 0-88132-267-9

60 Exchange Rate Regimes for Emerging Markets: Reviving the Intermediate Option
John Williamson
September 2000 ISBN 0-88132-293-8

61 NAFTA and the Environment: Seven Years Later Gary Clyde Hufbauer, Daniel Esty, Diana Orejas, Luis Rubio, and Jeffrey J. Schott
October 2000 ISBN 0-88132-299-7

62 Free Trade between Korea and the United States? Inbom Choi and Jeffrey J. Schott
April 2001 ISBN 0-88132-311-X

63 New Regional Trading Arrangements in the Asia Pacific?
Robert Scollay and John P. Gilbert
May 2001 ISBN 0-88132-302-0

64 Parental Supervision: The New Paradigm for Foreign Direct Investment and Development
Theodore H. Moran
August 2001 ISBN 0-88132-313-6

65 The Benefits of Price Convergence:
    Speculative Calculations
    Gary Clyde Hufbauer, Erika Wada,
    and Tony Warren
    December 2001   ISBN 0-88132-333-0
66 **Managed Floating Plus**
    Morris Goldstein
    March 2002   ISBN 0-88132-336-5
67 **Argentina and the Fund: From Triumph
    to Tragedy**
    Michael Mussa
    July 2002   ISBN 0-88132-339-X
68 **East Asian Financial Cooperation**
    C. Randall Henning
    September 2002   ISBN 0-88132-338-1
69 **Reforming OPIC for the 21st Century**
    Theodore H. Moran
    May 2003   ISBN 0-88132-342-X
70 **Awakening Monster: The Alien Tort
    Statute of 1789**
    Gary C. Hufbauer and Nicholas Mitrokostas
    July 2003   ISBN 0-88132-366-7
71 **Korea after Kim Jong-il**
    Marcus Noland
    January 2004   ISBN 0-88132-373-X

BOOKS

IMF Conditionality* John Williamson, editor
1983   ISBN 0-88132-006-4
Trade Policy in the 1980s* William R. Cline, editor
1983   ISBN 0-88132-031-5
Subsidies in International Trade*
Gary Clyde Hufbauer and Joanna Shelton Erb
1984   ISBN 0-88132-004-8
**International Debt: Systemic Risk and Policy
Response*** William R. Cline
1984   ISBN 0-88132-015-3
**Trade Protection in the United States: 31 Case
Studies*** Gary Clyde Hufbauer, Diane E. Berliner,
and Kimberly Ann Elliott
1986   ISBN 0-88132-040-4
**Toward Renewed Economic Growth in Latin
America*** Bela Balassa, Gerardo M. Bueno, Pedro-
Pablo Kuczynski, and Mario Henrique Simonsen
1986   ISBN 0-88132-045-5
Capital Flight and Third World Debt*
Donald R. Lessard and John Williamson, editors
1987   ISBN 0-88132-053-6
**The Canada-United States Free Trade Agreement:
The Global Impact***
Jeffrey J. Schott and Murray G. Smith, editors
1988   ISBN 0-88132-073-0
World Agricultural Trade: Building a Consensus*
William M. Miner and Dale E. Hathaway, editors
1988   ISBN 0-88132-071-3
Japan in the World Economy*
Bela Balassa and Marcus Noland
1988   ISBN 0-88132-041-2

**America in the World Economy: A Strategy for
the 1990s*** C. Fred Bergsten
1988   ISBN 0-88132-089-7
**Managing the Dollar: From the Plaza to the
Louvre*** Yoichi Funabashi
1988, 2nd ed. 1989   ISBN 0-88132-097-8
**United States External Adjustment and the World
Economy*** William R. Cline
May 1989   ISBN 0-88132-048-X
Free Trade Areas and U.S. Trade Policy*
Jeffrey J. Schott, editor
May 1989   ISBN 0-88132-094-3
**Dollar Politics: Exchange Rate Policymaking in
the United States***
I.M. Destler and C. Randall Henning
September 1989   ISBN 0-88132-079-X
**Latin American Adjustment: How Much Has
Happened?*** John Williamson, editor
April 1990   ISBN 0-88132-125-7
**The Future of World Trade in Textiles and
Apparel*** William R. Cline
1987, 2d ed. June 199   ISBN 0-88132-110-9
**Completing the Uruguay Round: A Results-
Oriented Approach to the GATT Trade
Negotiations*** Jeffrey J. Schott, editor
September 1990   ISBN 0-88132-130-3
Economic Sanctions Reconsidered (2 volumes)
Economic Sanctions Reconsidered:
Supplemental Case Histories
Gary Clyde Hufbauer, Jeffrey J. Schott, and
Kimberly Ann Elliott
1985, 2d ed. Dec. 1990   ISBN cloth 0-88132-115-X
                             ISBN paper 0-88132-105-2
**Economic Sanctions Reconsidered: History and
Current Policy**
Gary Clyde Hufbauer, Jeffrey J. Schott, and
Kimberly Ann Elliott
December 1990   ISBN cloth 0-88132-140-0
                    ISBN paper 0-88132-136-2
**Pacific Basin Developing Countries: Prospects for
the Future*** Marcus Noland
January 1991   ISBN cloth 0-88132-141-9
                   ISBN paper 0-88132-081-1
Currency Convertibility in Eastern Europe*
John Williamson, editor
October 1991   ISBN 0-88132-128-1
**International Adjustment and Financing: The
Lessons of 1985-1991*** C. Fred Bergsten, editor
January 1992   ISBN 0-88132-112-5
**North American Free Trade: Issues and
Recommendations***
Gary Clyde Hufbauer and Jeffrey J. Schott
April 1992   ISBN 0-88132-120-6
Narrowing the U.S. Current Account Deficit*
Allen J. Lenz
June 1992   ISBN 0-88132-103-6
The Economics of Global Warming
William R. Cline/*June 1992*   ISBN 0-88132-132-X

U.S. Taxation of International Income: Blueprint for Reform*   Gary Clyde Hufbauer, assisted by Joanna M. van Rooij
October 1992   ISBN 0-88132-134-6

Who's Bashing Whom? Trade Conflict in High-Technology Industries   Laura D'Andrea Tyson
November 1992   ISBN 0-88132-106-0

Korea in the World Economy*   Il SaKong
January 1993   ISBN 0-88132-183-4

Pacific Dynamism and the International Economic System*
C. Fred Bergsten and Marcus Noland, editors
May 1993   ISBN 0-88132-196-6

Economic Consequences of Soviet Disintegration*
John Williamson, editor
May 1993   ISBN 0-88132-190-7

Reconcilable Differences? United States-Japan Economic Conflict*
C. Fred Bergsten and Marcus Noland
June 1993   ISBN 0-88132-129-X

Does Foreign Exchange Intervention Work?
Kathryn M. Dominguez and Jeffrey A. Frankel
September 1993   ISBN 0-88132-104-4

Sizing Up U.S. Export Disincentives*
J. David Richardson
September 1993   ISBN 0-88132-107-9

NAFTA: An Assessment
Gary Clyde Hufbauer and Jeffrey J. Schott/ *rev. ed.*
October 1993   ISBN 0-88132-199-0

Adjusting to Volatile Energy Prices
Philip K. Verleger, Jr.
November 1993   ISBN 0-88132-069-2

The Political Economy of Policy Reform
John Williamson, editor
January 1994   ISBN 0-88132-195-8

Measuring the Costs of Protection in the United States
Gary Clyde Hufbauer and Kimberly Ann Elliott
January 1994   ISBN 0-88132-108-7

The Dynamics of Korean Economic Development*   Cho Soon
March 1994   ISBN 0-88132-162-1

Reviving the European Union*
C. Randall Henning, Eduard Hochreiter, and Gary Clyde Hufbauer, editors
April 1994   ISBN 0-88132-208-3

China in the World Economy   Nicholas R. Lardy
April 1994   ISBN 0-88132-200-8

Greening the GATT: Trade, Environment, and the Future   Daniel C. Esty
July 1994   ISBN 0-88132-205-9

Western Hemisphere Economic Integration*
Gary Clyde Hufbauer and Jeffrey J. Schott
July 1994   ISBN 0-88132-159-1

Currencies and Politics in the United States, Germany, and Japan
C. Randall Henning
September 1994   ISBN 0-88132-127-3

Estimating Equilibrium Exchange Rates
John Williamson, editor
September 1994   ISBN 0-88132-076-5

Managing the World Economy: Fifty Years After Bretton Woods   Peter B. Kenen, editor
September 1994   ISBN 0-88132-212-1

Reciprocity and Retaliation in U.S. Trade Policy
Thomas O. Bayard and Kimberly Ann Elliott
September 1994   ISBN 0-88132-084-6

The Uruguay Round: An Assessment*
Jeffrey J. Schott, assisted by Johanna W. Buurman
November 1994   ISBN 0-88132-206-7

Measuring the Costs of Protection in Japan*
Yoko Sazanami, Shujiro Urata, and Hiroki Kawai
January 1995   ISBN 0-88132-211-3

Foreign Direct Investment in the United States, 3d ed., Edward M. Graham and Paul R. Krugman
January 1995   ISBN 0-88132-204-0

The Political Economy of Korea-United States Cooperation*
C. Fred Bergsten and Il SaKong, editors
February 1995   ISBN 0-88132-213-X

International Debt Reexamined*   William R. Cline
February 1995   ISBN 0-88132-083-8

American Trade Politics, 3d ed., I.M. Destler
April 1995   ISBN 0-88132-215-6

Managing Official Export Credits: The Quest for a Global Regime*   John E. Ray
July 1995   ISBN 0-88132-207-5

Asia Pacific Fusion: Japan's Role in APEC*
Yoichi Funabashi
October 1995   ISBN 0-88132-224-5

Korea-United States Cooperation in the New World Order*
C. Fred Bergsten and Il SaKong, editors
February 1996   ISBN 0-88132-226-1

Why Exports Really Matter!*   ISBN 0-88132-221-0
Why Exports Matter More!*   ISBN 0-88132-229-6
J. David Richardson and Karin Rindal
July 1995; February 1996

Global Corporations and National Governments
Edward M. Graham
May 1996   ISBN 0-88132-111-7

Global Economic Leadership and the Group of Seven   C. Fred Bergsten and C. Randall Henning
May 1996   ISBN 0-88132-218-0

The Trading System After the Uruguay Round*
John Whalley and Colleen Hamilton
July 1996   ISBN 0-88132-131-1

Private Capital Flows to Emerging Markets After the Mexican Crisis*   Guillermo A. Calvo, Morris Goldstein, and Eduard Hochreiter
September 1996   ISBN 0-88132-232-6

The Crawling Band as an Exchange Rate Regime: Lessons from Chile, Colombia, and Israel
John Williamson
September 1996   ISBN 0-88132-231-8

Flying High: Liberalizing Civil Aviation in the Asia Pacific*
Gary Clyde Hufbauer and Christopher Findlay
November 1996   ISBN 0-88132-227-X

Measuring the Costs of Visible Protection in Korea*   Namdoo Kim
November 1996   ISBN 0-88132-236-9

The World Trading System: Challenges Ahead
Jeffrey J. Schott
December 1996   ISBN 0-88132-235-0

Has Globalization Gone Too Far?   Dani Rodrik
March 1997   ISBN cloth 0-88132-243-1

Korea-United States Economic Relationship*
C. Fred Bergsten and Il SaKong, editors
March 1997   ISBN 0-88132-240-7

Summitry in the Americas: A Progress Report
Richard E. Feinberg
April 1997   ISBN 0-88132-242-3

Corruption and the Global Economy
Kimberly Ann Elliott
June 1997   ISBN 0-88132-233-4

Regional Trading Blocs in the World Economic System   Jeffrey A. Frankel
October 1997   ISBN 0-88132-202-4

Sustaining the Asia Pacific Miracle: Environmental Protection and Economic Integration Andre Dua and Daniel C. Esty
October 1997   ISBN 0-88132-250-4

Trade and Income Distribution   William R. Cline
November 1997   ISBN 0-88132-216-4

Global Competition Policy
Edward M. Graham and J. David Richardson
December 1997   ISBN 0-88132-166-4

Unfinished Business: Telecommunications after the Uruguay Round
Gary Clyde Hufbauer and Erika Wada
December 1997   ISBN 0-88132-257-1

Financial Services Liberalization in the WTO
Wendy Dobson and Pierre Jacquet
June 1998   ISBN 0-88132-254-7

Restoring Japan's Economic Growth
Adam S. Posen
September 1998   ISBN 0-88132-262-8

Measuring the Costs of Protection in China
Zhang Shuguang, Zhang Yansheng, and Wan Zhongxin
November 1998   ISBN 0-88132-247-4

Foreign Direct Investment and Development: The New Policy Agenda for Developing Countries and Economies in Transition
Theodore H. Moran
December 1998   ISBN 0-88132-258-X

Behind the Open Door: Foreign Enterprises in the Chinese Marketplace
Daniel H. Rosen
January 1999   ISBN 0-88132-263-6

Toward A New International Financial Architecture: A Practical Post-Asia Agenda
Barry Eichengreen
February 1999   ISBN 0-88132-270-9

Is the U.S. Trade Deficit Sustainable?
Catherine L. Mann
September 1999   ISBN 0-88132-265-2

Safeguarding Prosperity in a Global Financial System: The Future International Financial Architecture, Independent Task Force Report Sponsored by the Council on Foreign Relations
Morris Goldstein, Project Director
October 1999   ISBN 0-88132-287-3

Avoiding the Apocalypse: The Future of the Two Koreas   Marcus Noland
June 2000   ISBN 0-88132-278-4

Assessing Financial Vulnerability: An Early Warning System for Emerging Markets
Morris Goldstein, Graciela Kaminsky, and Carmen Reinhart
June 2000   ISBN 0-88132-237-7

Global Electronic Commerce: A Policy Primer
Catherine L. Mann, Sue E. Eckert, and Sarah Cleeland Knight
July 2000   ISBN 0-88132-274-1

The WTO after Seattle   Jeffrey J. Schott, editor
July 2000   ISBN 0-88132-290-3

Intellectual Property Rights in the Global Economy   Keith E. Maskus
August 2000   ISBN 0-88132-282-2

The Political Economy of the Asian Financial Crisis   Stephan Haggard
August 2000   ISBN 0-88132-283-0

Transforming Foreign Aid: United States Assistance in the 21st Century   Carol Lancaster
August 2000   ISBN 0-88132-291-1

Fighting the Wrong Enemy: Antiglobal Activists and Multinational Enterprises Edward M.Graham
September 2000   ISBN 0-88132-272-5

Globalization and the Perceptions of American Workers
Kenneth F. Scheve and Matthew J. Slaughter
March 2001   ISBN 0-88132-295-4

World Capital Markets: Challenge to the G-10
Wendy Dobson and Gary C. Hufbauer, assisted by Hyun Koo Cho
May 2001   ISBN 0-88132-301-2

Prospects for Free Trade in the Americas
Jeffrey J. Schott
August 2001   ISBN 0-88132-275-X

Toward a North American Community: Lessons from the Old World for the New
Robert A. Pastor
August 2001   ISBN 0-88132-328-4

Measuring the Costs of Protection in Europe: European Commercial Policy in the 2000s
Patrick A. Messerlin
September 2001   ISBN 0-88132-273-3

Job Loss from Imports: Measuring the Costs
Lori G. Kletzer
September 2001   ISBN 0-88132-296-2
No More Bashing: Building a New Japan–United
States Economic Relationship   C. Fred Bergsten,
Takatoshi Ito, and Marcus Noland
October 2001   ISBN 0-88132-286-5
Why Global Commitment Really Matters!
Howard Lewis III and J. David Richardson
October 2001   ISBN 0-88132-298-9
Leadership Selection in the Major Multilaterals
Miles Kahler
November 2001   ISBN 0-88132-335-7
The International Financial Architecture:
What's New? What's Missing?   Peter Kenen
November 2001   ISBN 0-88132-297-0
Delivering on Debt Relief: From IMF Gold to
a New Aid Architecture
John Williamson and Nancy Birdsall,
with Brian Deese
April 2002   ISBN 0-88132-331-4
Imagine There's No Country: Poverty, Inequality,
and Growth in the Era of Globalization
Surjit S. Bhalla
September 2002   ISBN 0-88132-348-9
Reforming Korea's Industrial Conglomerates
Edward M. Graham
January 2003   ISBN 0-88132-337-3
Industrial Policy in an Era of Globalization:
Lessons from Asia
Marcus Noland and Howard Pack
March 2003   ISBN 0-88132-350-0
Reintegrating India with the World Economy
T.N. Srinivasan and Suresh D. Tendulkar
March 2003   ISBN 0-88132-280-6
After the Washington Consensus:
Restarting Growth and Reform in
Latin America   Pedro-Pablo Kuczynski
and John Williamson, editors
March 2003   ISBN 0-88132-347-0
The Decline of US Labor Unions and
the Role of Trade   Robert E. Baldwin
June 2003   ISBN 0-88132-341-1
Can Labor Standards Improve under
Globalization?
Kimberly Ann Elliott and Richard B. Freeman
June 2003   ISBN 0-88132-332-2
Crimes and Punishments? Retaliation
under the WTO
Robert Z. Lawrence
October 2003   ISBN 0-88132-359-4
Inflation Targeting in the World Economy
Edwin M. Truman
October 2003   ISBN 0-88132-345-4
Foreign Direct Investment and Tax
Competition   John H. Mutti
November 2003   ISBN 0-88132-352-7

Has Globalization Gone Far Enough? The Costs
of Fragmented Markets
Scott Bradford and Robert Z. Lawrence
February 2004   ISBN 0-88132-349-7
Food Regulation and Trade: Toward a Safe
and Open Global System
Tim Josling, Donna Roberts, and David Orden
March 2004   ISBN 0-88132-346-2
Controlling Currency Mismatches in
Emerging Markets
Morris Goldstein and Philip Turner
April 2004   ISBN 0-88132-360-8

SPECIAL REPORTS

1   Promoting World Recovery: A Statement on
     Global Economic Strategy*
     by Twenty-six Economists from Fourteen Countries
     December 1982   ISBN 0-88132-013-7
2   Prospects for Adjustment in Argentina,
     Brazil, and Mexico: Responding to the Debt Crisis*
     John Williamson, editor
     June 1983   ISBN 088132-016-1
3   Inflation and Indexation: Argentina, Brazil,
     and Israel*   John Williamson, editor
     March 1985   ISBN 0-88132-037-4
4   Global Economic Imbalances*
     C. Fred Bergsten, editor
     March 1986   ISBN 0-88132-042-0
5   African Debt and Financing*
     Carol Lancaster and John Williamson, editors
     May 1986   ISBN 0-88132-044-7
6   Resolving the Global Economic Crisis: After
     Wall Street*
     by Thirty-three Economists from Thirteen
     Countries
     December 1987   ISBN 0-88132-070-6
7   World Economic Problems*
     Kimberly Ann Elliott and John Williamson,
     editors
     April 1988   ISBN 0-88132-055-2
     Reforming World Agricultural Trade*
     by Twenty-nine Professionals from Seventeen
     Countries
     1988   ISBN 0-88132-088-9
8   Economic Relations Between the United
     States and Korea: Conflict or Cooperation?*
     Thomas O. Bayard and Soogil Young, editors
     January 1989   ISBN 0-88132-068-4
9   Whither APEC? The Progress to Date and
     Agenda for the Future*
     C. Fred Bergsten, editor
     October 1997   ISBN 0-88132-248-2
10   Economic Integration of the Korean
     Peninsula
     Marcus Noland, editor
     January 1998   ISBN 0-88132-255-5

11 Restarting Fast Track*
    Jeffrey J. Schott, editor
    April 1998   ISBN 0-88132-259-8
12 Launching New Global Trade Talks:
    An Action Agenda   Jeffrey J. Schott, editor
    September 1998   ISBN 0-88132-266-0
13 Japan's Financial Crisis and Its Parallels to
    US Experience
    Ryoichi Mikitani and Adam S. Posen, eds.
    September 2000   ISBN 0-88132-289-X
14 The Ex-Im Bank in the 21st Century: A New
    Approach   Gary Clyde Hufbauer and
    Rita M. Rodriguez, editors
    January 2001   ISBN 0-88132-300-4
15 The Korean Diaspora in the World
    Economy
    C. Fred Bergsten and Inbom Choi, eds.
    January 2003   ISBN 0-88132-358-6
16 Dollar Overvaluation and the World
    Economy
    C. Fred Bergsten and John Williamson, eds.
    February 2003   ISBN 0-88132-351-9

WORKS IN PROGRESS

Transforming the European Economy
Martin Neil Baily and Jacob Kirkegaard
New Regional Arrangements and
the World Economy
C. Fred Bergsten
The Globalization Backlash in Europe and
the United States
C. Fred Bergsten, Pierre Jacquet, and Karl Kaiser
Dollar Adjustment: How Far? Against What?
C. Fred Bergsten and John Williamson, editors
Trade Policy and Global Poverty
William R. Cline
China's Entry into the World Economy
Richard N. Cooper
American Trade Politics, 4th ed.
I.M. Destler
The ILO in the World Economy
Kimberly Ann Elliott
Reforming Economic Sanctions
Kimberly Ann Elliott, Gary C. Hufbauer,
and Jeffrey J. Schott
Cooperation Between the IMF and
the World Bank
Michael Fabricius
Future of Chinese Exchange Rates
Morris Goldstein and Nicholas R. Lardy

NAFTA: A Ten-Year Appraisal
Gary C. Hufbauer and Jeffrey J. Schott
New Agricultural Negotiations in
the WTO
Tim Josling and Dale Hathaway
Workers at Risk: Job Loss from Apparel,
Textiles, Footwear, and Furniture
Lori G. Kletzer
Responses to Globalization: US Textile
and Apparel Workers and Firms
Lori Kletzer, James Levinsohn, and
J. David Richardson
The Strategic Implications of China-Taiwan
Economic Relations
Nicholas R. Lardy
Making the Rules: Case Studies on
US Trade Negotiation
Robert Z. Lawrence, Charan Devereaux,
and Michael Watkins
US-Egypt Free Trade Agreement
Robert Z. Lawrence and Ahmed Galal
High Technology and the Globalization
of America
Catherine L. Mann
International Financial Architecture
Michael Mussa
Germany and the World Economy
Adam S. Posen
The Euro at Five: Ready for a Global Role?
Adam S. Posen, editor
Automatic Stabilizers for the Eurozone
Adam S. Posen
Chasing Dirty Money: Progress on
Anti-Money Laundering
Peter Reuter and Edwin M. Truman
Global Forces, American Faces:
US Economic Globalization at the
Grass Roots
J. David Richardson
US-Taiwan FTA Prospects
Daniel H. Rosen and Nicholas R. Lardy
Bail-in or Bailout? Responding to Financial
Crises in Emerging Economies
Nouriel Roubini and Brad Setser
Free Trade Agreements: US Strategies
and Priorities
Jeffrey J. Schott, editor
The Role of Private Capital in Financing
Development
John Williamson

DISTRIBUTORS OUTSIDE THE UNITED STATES

Australia, New Zealand,
and Papua New Guinea
D.A. Information Services
648 Whitehorse Road
Mitcham, Victoria 3132, Australia
tel: 61-3-9210-7777
fax: 61-3-9210-7788
email: service@adadirect.com.au
http://www.dadirect.com.au

United Kingdom and Europe
(including Russia and Turkey)
The Eurospan Group
3 Henrietta Street, Covent Garden
London WC2E 8LU England
tel: 44-20-7240-0856
fax: 44-20-7379-0609
http://www.eurospan.co.uk

Japan and the Republic of Korea
United Publishers Services, Ltd.
KenkyuSha Bldg.
9, Kanda Surugadai 2-Chome
Chiyoda-Ku, Tokyo 101 Japan
tel: 81-3-3291-4541
fax: 81-3-3292-8610
email: saito@ups.co.jp
For trade accounts only.
Individuals will find IIE books in
leading Tokyo bookstores.

Thailand
Asia Books
5 Sukhumvit Rd. Soi 61
Bangkok 10110 Thailand
tel: 662-714-07402 Ext: 221, 222, 223
fax: 662-391-2277
email: purchase@asiabooks.co.th
http://www.asiabooksonline.com

Canada
Renouf Bookstore
5369 Canotek Road, Unit 1
Ottawa, Ontario KIJ 9J3, Canada
tel: 613-745-2665
fax: 613-745-7660
http://www.renoufbooks.com

India, Bangladesh, Nepal, and Sri Lanka
Viva Books Pvt.
Mr. Vinod Vasishtha
4325/3, Ansari Rd.
Daryaganj, New Delhi-110002
India
tel: 91-11-327-9280
fax: 91-11-326-7224
email: vinod.viva@gndel.globalnet.
ems.vsnl.net.in

Southeast Asia (Brunei, Cambodia,
China, Malaysia, Hong Kong, Indonesia,
Laos, Myanmar, the Philippines, Singapore,
Taiwan, and Vietnam)
Hemisphere Publication Services
1 Kallang Pudding Rd. #0403
Golden Wheel Building
Singapore 349316
tel: 65-741-5166
fax: 65-742-9356

Visit our Web site at:
www.iie.com
E-mail orders to:
orders@iie.com